138278

PN
4797
T43
1983

Teel

Into the newsroom

**CHABOT
COLLEGE
HAYWARD CAMPUS
LEARNING RESOURCE CENTER**

25555 Hesperian Boulevard
Hayward, CA   94545

LEONARD RAY TEEL has been a professional journalist since 1964, working full-time for five newspapers: the *Miami Herald,* the *Fort Lauderdale News,* the *Washington Evening Star,* the *Atlanta Journal-Constitution,* and the *Lancaster* (Pa.) *New Era.* On the *Atlanta Journal,* he won feature writing awards from both The Associated Press and United Press International. Teel is co-author of the oral biography *Erma,* published in 1981 by Random House.

RON TAYLOR, a reporter for the *Atlanta Journal-Constitution,* has won numerous awards for feature writing, spot news, enterprise reporting, reporting on social and mental health issues, and for the best reporting in the Southeast.

Both Teel and Taylor have lectured at Georgia State University and have advised journalism students and beginning reporters. They have co-written various articles.

An Introduction to Journalism

Into the Newsroom

Leonard Ray Teel
Ron Taylor

A SPECTRUM BOOK

Prentice-Hall, Inc.,
Englewood Cliffs, New Jersey 07632

Library of Congress Cataloging in Publication Data

Teel, Leonard Ray.
  Into the newsroom.

  "A Spectrum Book."
  Includes index.
  1. Journalism—Vocational guidance.   I. Taylor,
Ron (date).   II. Title.
PN4797.T43 1983   070′.023   82-21586
ISBN 0-13-477133-8
ISBN 0-13-477125-7 (pbk.)

For Katherine W. Teel

This book is available at a special discount when ordered in
bulk quantities. Contact Prentice-Hall, Inc., General Publishing
Division, Special Sales, Englewood Cliffs, N.J. 07632.

Editorial/production supervision
and interior design: Eric Newman
Cover design: Hal Siegel
Manufacturing buyer: Christine Johnston

10 9 8 7 6 5 4 3 2 1

ISBN 0-13-477133-8

ISBN 0-13-477125-7 {PBK.}

PRENTICE-HALL INTERNATIONAL, INC., *London*
PRENTICE-HALL OF AUSTRALIA PTY. LIMITED, *Sydney*
PRENTICE-HALL CANADA INC., *Toronto*
PRENTICE-HALL OF INDIA PRIVATE LIMITED, *New Delhi*
PRENTICE-HALL OF JAPAN, INC., *Tokyo*
PRENTICE-HALL OF SOUTHEAST ASIA PTE. LTD., *Singapore*
WHITEHALL BOOKS LIMITED, *Wellington, New Zealand*
EDITORA PRENTICE-HALL DO BRASIL LTDA., *Rio de Janeiro*

Contents

Foreword   ix

Preface   xi

1
In the Beginning   1
College studies; college newspaper experience; internships; professional contacts; turning the internship into a job; where to start: a daily or a weekly, features or news; how to avoid those first errors; starting salaries.

2
Working Conditions   11
Legends; power of the press; bylines; being the first to know; the people you meet; access to power; journalist to novelist; salaries; time and the working day.

3
Everyday Problems and Who Solves Them   26
General assignment; the beat; special assignments; travel; deadlines; protecting scoops.

4
Ideas and Assignments   45
Where story ideas come from; how ideas become assignments; the newspaper "budget" of stories; picking the best ideas.

5

Sources and Resources 50

Considering the source and the motives; how to use sources; developing sources; resources and research; using computer libraries.

6

Covering Government 58

The ubiquitous government; making the rounds; the different levels of government: city, county, state, federal; file keeping; directories; executive officers, councils, and boards; public safety; courts; fair trial *vs.* free press; bureaucrats; legislators.

7

Allied Arts 69

Importance of illustrations; working with photographers; charts and graphs; maps.

8

Interviewing and Note Taking 84

Arranging interviews; outmaneuvering evasive interviewees; planning; conducting the interview; how to listen and get answers; developing a personal shorthand; tape recorders: advantages and disadvantages; when *not* to take notes.

9

Ethics 95

Objectivity *vs.* subjectivity; fairness; fact *vs.* truth; libel; bribes; sensationalism; invasion of privacy; advocacy journalism; sources; lies; jokes; obscenity; when not to print; consequences.

10

Journalistic Writing 113

Lingering tradition; the constants; tight writing, short paragraphs; the news story; writing backwards; the five Ws and a few Cs; writing the lead; obituaries; second-day lead; the peculiar language of newspapers; the feature story; the interpretive story; the investigative story; editorials; feature columns; reviews and criticisms; sports writing.

11

Writing with Style: the Forms 132

What style is; general writing tips with disclaimers; the inverted pyramid; the carafe; the narrative; the diamond; the goose egg.

12

Writing with Style: How to Do It   143

Looking out over history; ordinary people; making people feel;
setting scenes; simplifying; weaving the story; writing the
trivial; experimenting; using the language; final warnings.

13

Editing   167

Which editors do what; what editors look for in your stories;
style books; headlines.

14

The First Edition and the Follow-up   174

Deadlines and editions; catching mistakes; making and
remaking the pages; living with continuing stories; the
anniversary story.

15

Upward and Onward   181

The information business; specialized reporting; column
writing; syndication; writing books; freelancing; public
relations; teaching; striking the happy medium.

Index   189

Foreword

They don't issue licenses to practice journalism in this country and there aren't many rules. The main one is to be fair.

The more you know and the smarter you are, the better your chances of getting at the truth and writing it in an intelligible way. But some people who'd pretty much pass for logheads have done very well in the business. Energy and hard work count for a lot. Regardless of all the fancy electronic equipment that has come into use, journalism is still a cottage industry based on one person's finding out what is going on and telling others. It is a grand place for individuals with fire in their souls. You can't be pigeonholed unless you allow yourself to be. Say you're having trouble getting assignments? Just go out and find a good story. Few editors can resist one.

You don't have to be a nice person to be a good journalist. There are plenty of rascals in the field who do a fine job of informing the world at large but make life miserable for their colleagues. Newcomers would be well advised to watch their backs.

Journalism is not a likely way to get rich. Certainly newspaper and magazine work is not. Nobody told me that. But money wasn't the issue. I went into journalism more than twenty years ago figuring it was a way to maybe help make the world a better place to live and that in the course of this good work I'd find adventure and excitement.

A lot of my friends started with the same idea.

Most of us have not helped bring down a corrupt president or gotten a wrongfully convicted man out of jail. But some of us have gotten laws changed or influenced decisions on national and foreign affairs or nudged corporations into recalling faulty products. Many of us have written stories that have helped save an historic building or brought in a fistful of checks for a needy family.

Newspaper stories can make a difference in people's lives. And that's why I like to write them. They aren't always earth-shaking. In fact, usually they're not. Sometimes they merely make a reader smile and feel good. But even that is not such a small thing.

The really twenty-four-carat, wonderful thing about journalism, for me, is that while you're going about being useful, you can have a glorious time. You can have a million roles. You can be a police officer, a fire fighter, a lawyer, a diplomat, a soldier. And when you've finished your story, you can go on to be something else. You get paid to go to some of the most dramatic events—the coronation of a queen, the inauguration of a president, or, more likely at first, the swearing-in of a mayor. Of course, there are ghastly missions, too, like covering plane crashes and murders. Some reporters spend their whole careers in one town; others explore the globe.

The best newspaper reporters can write about anything. They can write hard and crisp and they can write as soft as the morning dew. The authors of this book are reporters of that sort. They do the job well and they do a good job of telling you how to do it. Their text is different from anything I used in college. It doesn't just talk about the techniques of journalism—it shows you how they actually put them to use. They take you along with them on stories and they let you hang around with them in the newsroom, getting to know how editors operate, what they expect from reporters. I wish I'd had their book when I was starting. It would have saved me a lot of time.

JOSEPH B. TREASTER
Reporter, the *New York Times*

Preface

From the beginning, this book was meant to follow one principle, that of explaining the basics of journalism as practiced in the newsroom. And with this in mind, this book is more informal than many traditional textbooks in the field. We have tried to answer the questions most frequently asked us in class by students, and to offer information that we wish we had known before we entered the profession.

Time and time again we have encountered students about to embark on careers in this profession who understood well the complexities of our trade but who knew too little about the actual practice of journalism. We have attempted here to bridge the gap between the theoretical and the practical by pulling the student into the working newsroom and teaching the fundamentals as we know them to be applied.

The refinements of style and technique are constantly changing. Even as we are writing this book, new theories of journalistic writing are developing. The old "inverted pyramid" is more diamond-shaped these days, and some writers are standing the pyramid back on its base, insisting on the narrative form. But before creating a symphony, one needs a working familiarity with the instruments of the orchestra. We deal with the instruments here, playing on them a tune or two of our own to help you see the possibilities.

We start at the beginning with the question we get most often from students: "How do I get a job?" Then we tell the students what will be expected of them—how to wade through resource materials, how to come up with story ideas, how to take notes, how to write news stories and features. We talk about government beats and how to collar ornery officials for interviews. We even tell how to deal with the orneriest people they will encounter—the editors—and explain why editors do what they have to do.

The authors of this book have worked together as colleagues since 1969. The following chapters were undertaken on the basis of areas of interest. Mr. Teel is basically responsible for Chapters 1 through 7; Mr. Taylor for Chapters 8 through 15. But, except for slight differences in style, the content of the book as a whole can be considered the complete product of both authors.

Acknowledgments

We wish to acknowledge the following:

Sherman Johnson, a lawyer who thought briefly about a career change to journalism and initiated the conversation with Leonard Ray Teel that was the seed from which this undertaking grew.

Guy Robinson, who, as a result of that conversation, proposed the Leonard Ray Teel Close-Cover-Before-Striking–Void-Where-Prohibited Matchbook School of Journalism.

Katherine Teel, for suggesting something more serious, for proposing this collaboration, and for serving as our editor, adviser, critic, researcher, cook, nurse, and taskmaster until this project was finished.

George Greiff, professor of journalism, Georgia State University, for his guidance and suggestions and for his example in having students work closely with local reporters and editors.

Karen Harris, for giving us the student's view, then verifying our advice by landing a job and doing well at it.

Roy Peter Clark and the Modern Media Institute of St. Petersburg, Florida, for teaching us a new way to look at newspaper writing.

Fellow reporters, editors, friends, and relatives who saw some of the early versions and liked them.

All the elves responsible for putting this book together, the ones who came to us in the middle of the night or on their days off to help with the editing, proofreading, and research. Among them, Kathryn Andree, Janis Brennan, Midge Yearley, Phyllis Cahoon, Betsy Hilbert, Joe Benton, and Bryan Bishop.

And all the other people along the way: the journalism instructors who taught us the practical side of the profession, the editors who taught us to do right, the good reporters who taught us by their examples.

All I know is just what I read in the papers.
Will Rogers

It takes two to speak the truth—one to speak,
and another to hear.
Henry David Thoreau, from "A Week
on the Concord and Merrimack Rivers," 1849

Obviously, a man's judgment cannot be better than the
information on which he has based it.
Arthur H. Sulzberger, address to New York State
Publishers Association, August 30, 1948

1

In the Beginning

Now, more than ever, college is where careers in American journalism are born. Almost extinct is the cub reporter who starts in the profession straight from writing on the high school biweekly about the honor roll and the shame of the chewing gum under the chairs. It is not a profession into which a person with a flair for writing can simply leap, any more than someone with a flair for first aid can just step into practicing medicine. In this era of rapidly changing information technology, there is a new seriousness and competitiveness in journalism, and training in a variety of skills helps the cub reporter cope. A beginner without college training will certainly be at a disadvantage in the market for a job in daily and even weekly journalism.

Enrollments in college journalism courses are increasing steadily, and today's journalists are the best trained in the history of the profession. The path from college to the profession is a long journey that happily can be divided into manageable steps.

You must study. Then you must practice what you've learned in some journalistic laboratory. Finally, there is the question of how to build a bridge from the insulated world of school to the newsroom, where you will discover, as one student put it, "what it's really like." At each stage there will be many opportunities, some of which you will miss and some of which you will seize. There will be tests at every stage. Expect to make some mistakes and plan to learn from them. The journalist who doesn't repent errors is on the way to succeeding. Don't be afraid to ask yourself along the way, "Is this really something I want to do?"

The earliest decision in college, and the most fundamental for your career, is the choice of your area of specialized studies. Don't be surprised if you discover yourself drawn to more than one academic major. Of course, there is the obvious possibility of majoring in journalism. Be aware, however, that professional journalists disagree on whether this is a wise use of your academic years. Many editors contend that the student coming into journalism needs to have a liberal arts background and requires perhaps only foundation courses in the journalistic skills of basic news writing, feature writing, and copy editing. It is better, these editors argue, to major in some field such as history, English, a foreign language, or political science—these prepare a student for understanding human nature and the world. A student who wants to develop a career in business writing might major in economics or finance. The award-winning science and health writer Charlie Seabrook majored in biology. The author and journalist Chet Fuller, Jr., concentrated on the humanities. We know of a student who concentrated on European history and minored in journalism. His journalism courses amounted to only 12½ percent of his credits over four years, including beginning reporting, advanced reporting, copy editing, law of the press, and history of journalism. This de-emphasis of concentrated journalism study was endorsed by the American Council on Education for Journalism, which recommended that no more than 25 percent of a student's credit hours be in journalism or journalism-related courses.

Whatever you decide depends largely upon what interests you. Keep in mind always, however, that you are likely to write best what you understand best. One successful journalist, Ernest Hemingway, tested himself with this question: "What did I know about truly and care for the most?"

Whatever academic courses you choose, you do need experience writing on deadline for publication. There is truth to the saying that you can learn best by doing. Some journalism professors have designed their reporting classes so that stories have inflexible due dates, and this gives the illusion of a deadline. But there is nothing quite as convincing as writing on deadline for an actual publication, and nothing so satisfying as seeing your work in print beneath your byline. There are two obvious laboratories for beginning journalists. One is a campus newspaper; another is a community newspaper.

Student newspapers traditionally have been a natural bridge from the classroom lessons to practical experience. They are published for the students, and almost always the editors are students who need a great deal of volunteer help for each edition. The freshman or sophomore who begins as a reporter may progress by the junior year to news editor, managing editor, or editor-in-chief. Along the way, you can practice every fundamental classroom lesson in writing, editing, and editorial judgment.

Community newspapers in cities or in suburban areas often cooperate with journalism schools. At the University of Georgia, students could write for the *Athens Daily News* and *Athens Banner-Herald.* At Shaw University in North Carolina, the journalist Angela B. Terrell worked out an arrangement for her students to write for the local newspaper. And at the University of Florida, Professor Hugh Cunningham's students periodically took over both the writing and the editing of the *Gainesville Sun,* a daily.

Your first efforts, whether for the community or college newspaper, will likely be marred by mistakes. Don't be alarmed. Pick yourself up, repair the damage, and go on to the next story, making a note not to repeat the error. This is one of the most important advantages of laboratory journalism: You can make mistakes—and everybody makes them—under the generally protective shield of student license. These early errors—from simple misspelling to more serious misstatement of fact and quotation—are committed in an environment where you are not likely to lose your job.

Perhaps no mistake in journalism is so serious as libel, yet even an occasional libel is usually forgiven on a university newspaper. One student editor at the University of Miami stumbled into libeling the university's unpopular new executive vice president. The editor was scolded by the faculty adviser and required to publish a front-page retraction; but he nevertheless stayed on as editor and the next time was wiser and more cautious.

By contrast, the consequences in the professional world would have been quite serious. Newspapers dread reporters who could cause them lawsuits. It is not uncommon for a newspaper to fire an otherwise talented reporter over the publication of sloppy and erroneous information. Another penalty for mistakes in journalism is banishment to an undesirable job that has fewer responsibilities and risks; one young reporter for a southern newspaper, for instance, wrote a front-page story that a man had been convicted, when in fact his case had ended in a mistrial. In her case it was an honest mistake, but she was reassigned soon afterwards to cover a county that was predominantly pasture.

One other obvious advantage of practicing your journalism in college is that you will learn the importance of typing. Perfect typing is not required, but editors generally respect a reporter who can type reasonably fast. This is particularly true when you are working on deadline and your editor is standing at your back waiting for you to finish. The movie *Superman* was actually not far from the truth when editor Perry White told Lois Lane that Clark Kent had been given her reporting beat partly because ". . . he's the fastest typist I've ever seen." If you took basic typing in high school, you probably have all the skill you need, and practice will make you faster. If you still fumble with the hunt-and-peck system, consider taking at least a beginner's course so that you can use all your fingers and thumbs on the keyboards. Although many newsrooms have eased out typewriters in favor of computers, the keyboards are still generally designed with the letters and numbers in the same places. One Emory University English student who was hired for a summer reporting job quickly started practicing her typing after her first conversation with her city editor. She wrote to a family friend:

> I apologize for the messiness of this letter, but I have a new policy of never writing when I can type. This is mainly because I'm kind of a sorry typist—slow, mistake-riddled, etc.—and Mr. Bob Johnson, the person I'm going to be working for at the *Journal,* said, "Now, honey, learn to type fast, 'cause if I hire a bunch of interns who can't type this summer, they'll fire me." So I'm learning to type fast.

We need to pause and beware of a monster that lies in the path of the student seeking practical experience. While you are paying so much attention to the very satisfying pursuit of publishing stories beneath your byline, you may lose your balance and fall into the academic abyss. In the long run, not many employers will cheer the student who, although publishing beginner stories about campus and community life, meanwhile flunks history, English, and perhaps even law of the press. Like John Bunyan's pilgrim in *Pilgrim's Progress,* you must pick your way past life's dangers, and beware of losing your way.

One veteran journalism professor dreads seeing students "sacrificing" academic performance, and so he discourages students from working on the campus newspaper. One student editor whose newspaper was terribly understaffed, particularly at exam times, found that he had to work nearly all night once a week in order to get the weekly newspaper into print. In his urban sociology class the following mornings, he would be nodding constantly, his falling pen making scribbled lines instead of readable notes. He managed to survive that course with a D, and his other grades pulled up his average. But he believed the lessons of editorship to be worth the time and loss in the course. The problem is one of balancing—classroom and laboratory—and each student must decide how much time can be "sacrificed" from academic studies.

We ought to consider one other aspect of writing for publication during college, and that is cash. There are few students who don't need financial assistance, and even a student in journalism can get some by publishing. There are at least three ways to earn money: (1) an editing stipend, (2) a scholarship or an assistantship, and (3) a newspaper internship.

Many college newspaper editors are rewarded with fixed stipends, compensation for service. Stipends generally are not given to reporters; in most cases, you must work for the newspaper in an unpaid position for a year or more before you become a candidate for a stipend-paying editorship. Of course, this compensation is not great, and it could be lower than the federal minimum wage. Also, the stipend is computed according to level of responsibility, not for hours worked, so the editor receives the highest amount.

Scholarships can be won either before you begin college or during your college years. Consult your local professional association of journalists to find out if it has any yearly grants. The Miami chapter of Sigma Delta Chi, for instance, annually awarded a four-year scholarship to the University of Miami for a promising area high school student. The student had to maintain a B average in academic work and major or minor in journalism.

At some colleges, there are assistantships that pay the tuition of outstanding students who in return work about twenty hours a week for the journalism department. After you have been in college for a year or two, you can apply for financial assistance based on your academic record; in applying for aid to continue in the field of journalism, a portfolio of published stories from the student newspaper can be quite impressive. At Georgia State University, one student won such a scholarship after she had been writing and editing for the student newspaper for about a year. She also was chosen news editor and received a stipend. With a scholarship and the stipend, she had enough income to quit her job as a supermarket checkout cashier and devote more time to journalism.

The third common source of income is the student internship on a local newspaper. Such a paying position usually is not offered to a student until the junior or senior year in college, and it is important for other reasons, which we will discuss later. But the money is certainly helpful. For example, one student secured three consecutive internships during his senior year and used the money to pay the increased expenses involved in making the transition from college to the working world. Another senior, to her delight, was rewarded with an internship on an afternoon newspaper, which paid her $175 a week, a fortune compared with what she had been earning on the campus newspaper staff.

The internship is the third significant phase in the maturation of the college journalist—after academic studies and laboratory publications. The internship is a natural passage from the protected environment of college to the reality of the modern newsroom, where journalism is a serious business and your stories reach a wide and credulous audience.

Securing an internship, therefore, ought to be one of the most important goals of your junior year in college. Ideally, an internship does the most good when it comes at the end of your junior year or during your senior year, when you are about to graduate and are ready, or almost ready, to accept a job if one is offered.

To gain an internship, you will need to organize your accomplishments and introduce yourself. You will need at least three categories of evidence supporting your candidacy: (1) a summary of your academic training and grades, (2) a portfolio of your published work, along with any awards and/or editorships you secured, and (3) a list of people who are willing to vouch for you as references.

Summarizing your academic experience may seem a simple matter, but there ought to be a *pattern* to your presentation. Present not only your grades, but the overall *direction* of your studies, why you chose the courses you elected, generally what you have learned. Name some of the professors and writers who influenced you; it makes good sense to show respect for the people who taught you.

The portfolio also seems to be a simple matter, yet there is also an opportunity here to show that you can organize materials to prove a point. Avoid presenting a conglomeration of clippings jammed indiscriminately into a folder. Resist the temptation to bring in everything you have ever published. Select the best, possibly the best six or eight pieces. Take care that what you present represents a cross-section of your abilities to write news and features. Consult an office supply store about how best to present them. You might consider binding xeroxed sheets in a notebook. This might be especially helpful if you are applying to more than one newspaper. Another thing to remember is that your clippings may not be returned.

The third matter—references from the people you know who are willing to speak on your behalf—very often can decide your success. This is particularly true when several students are applying for the same position and all have high academic averages, publishing experience, and a file of published stories. Obviously, if you have already impressed one of the reporters or editors of the newspaper on which you want an internship, you will benefit if that person writes you a letter of recommendation. Don't be shy about asking for such letters from "contacts"—people you have met and kept in touch with. Keeping in touch with such contacts by letter or by telephone is part of the lively art of interpersonal relationships, and the more successful you are at cultivating such relationships, the more advantages you will have in making new contacts during your internship.

The successful reporter, like the candidates for an internship, thrives according to the ability to contact new people and keep up such relationships. To some students, such adventuresomeness or friendliness comes naturally; others have to concentrate and practice saying hello. But you will discover in journalism that the people who are willing to tell you things and help you solve mysteries are the greatest resources of the successful reporter.

Stepping into the newsroom fresh from the campus, one young woman was impressed after a few weeks with how very different it was from what she expected from her reading. Editors and reporters seemed to ignore her. "The books just don't tell you what it's really like when you get here," she said. "I felt unwelcome in the newsroom. Most people were not friendly and did not introduce themselves. This added to the overall anxiety of being a beginner thrown in with professionals."

With luck and alertness, you have already learned the most important preparatory lessons in college. You have made mistakes and learned from them, and you have developed a dependable habit of doublechecking facts and spellings so that you will catch yourself and not make errors. There is no certain way to prepare totally for specific assignments, but you can rely on your general readiness, just as a third baseman is generally alert to field any baseball hit nearby.

You must always keep aware that the internship is a trial by ordeal. It is a serious time of testing, and the editors who chose you from the list of applicants will test you from the first hour of the first day. Expect them to form quick, first impressions of your talents, reliability, and character. The internship may continue for three months, but the first day sometimes determines how the editors will regard you during the entire period. One Harvard University student got off to a bad start on the first day with the city editor who wanted his interns to be able to type; on top of the typing deficiency, he had a personality clash with the editor. The result was that he was shunted aside for the entire summer and got some meaningful work only because a veteran reporter allowed him to tag along on some assignments.

First impressions, therefore, are unusually important. It is essential to be punctual, to come to work even a little early, to dress conservatively, and to listen carefully when you are spoken to. In fact, one of the handiest techniques is to take notes during your first meetings with the supervising editors. This accomplishes two purposes: They feel that you are taking them seriously, and afterwards you can review what they said when perhaps you were too nervous for everything to sink in. Our giving these cautions is not meant to cause anxiety but simply to awaken you to the significant difference between the campus and the newsroom.

One obvious difference from most classrooms is the equipment, particularly the computerized word processors. Beginning in the 1970s, newspapers began installing computer systems of varying design and sophistication. Systems do vary greatly from newspaper to newspaper, largely because they are often exchanged as technology advances. The computer terminal, complete with expanded keyboard for coding stories in computer language, has replaced the typewriter in a great many daily newspapers. So extensive has the computer revolution been that you will find word processors even on weekly newspapers such as the *Gadsden County Times* in Quincy, Florida.

With computer systems being improved and exchanged, there is no certain way to become familiar with a particular newspaper's computer operation except through on-the-job training. This, therefore, becomes one of the first necessities after you arrive for your internship. If the newspaper has no training staff, you must ask some journalist to give you a fundamental explanation of the keyboard and its functions.

"No one had time to teach me how to use the VDTs [Video Display Terminals]," recalled one bright young journalism intern. "For the most part, I taught myself—trial and error style—and I asked a lot of questions when problems presented themselves. The VDTs were a source of fear, frustration, and intimidation for many weeks."

The student who succeeds in the newsroom, the one who listens well, learns quickly, writes better as the internship proceeds, makes no major errors, spells correctly, and can type on whatever keyboards are available may impress the editors enough to be hired after graduation. That is the ultimate goal of the internship, the reward for the ordeal by fire. If you pass the tests, you may earn your first professional job.

From the first day of your internship, it is helpful to keep some sort of diary or notebook. In it you can jot down your impressions, questions, experiences, advice from editors and reporters, and the names of new contacts, as well as their telephone numbers at work and at home. This sort of notebook helps you sort through the events of each day as they occur, and it gives you something to look back upon in the weeks to come.

It is a helpful device to think of your internship as proceeding in phases, like the phases of the moon. The importance of this is that you have reserved at least one phase near the end in which to show off your best talents and skills, after you have learned the peculiar realities of the newsroom. Saving one phase for personal excellence is important if you want to make a final effort to try for a full-time job.

One intern on a daily newspaper in Pennsylvania had spent nearly his whole summer feeling that he had done nothing outstanding. Among his routine assignments had been an interview with an exchange student from Germany and the daily listing of marriages and divorces. But in the last two weeks, he broke out of the doldrums, created his own journalistic adventure, and impressed the editor. On his own time, he drove to the scene of a Pennsylvania coal mine disaster where three miners were trapped underground and their families were waiting anxiously around the mouth of the mine. His newspaper had not sent a reporter, but instead had printed Associated Press reports. At the scene he took pictures and wrote a story, which he submitted to his editors when he got back. Since he had done it all on his own time, on his own initiative, they were impressed. He was offered a full-time job as soon as he graduated. The major advantage of doing the story on his own time was that the editors could not very well prevent him from going, as they might easily have done if he had asked permission to go on company time.

Be aware that very often the editors will not recognize your abilities to handle major stories. Expect to be passed over when the best stories are assigned. Keep in mind that you are unproven and that the editors naturally presume that a story can be written more effectively by a full-time staffer. To illustrate this problem of working with editors, let us quote from the journal of a student intern who learned the system:

> It seemed that section editors often were too busy to be bothered with me. So, I learned quickly that assignments were not going to fall into my lap—I had to ask for them or come up with my own story ideas. However, I kept a good and understanding attitude toward my editors and did not act "put out" that I was not the subject of more attention. Another student who interned about the same time lost favor in the eyes of the management, I believe, because she complained openly that her editors were not keeping her busy.

Some newspapers shift students from one department to another every few weeks. In this way, one young woman on the *Atlanta Journal* worked two weeks in the features (Lifestyle) section, three weeks in the newsroom, and another two weeks in sports. She had the opportunity to try different types of writing, and the editors could evaluate what she did best.

Other newspapers keep students in the same position for the entire internship. One student at the *Miami Herald*, for instance, spent an entire spring on the copy desk, where he read and edited stories and wrote headlines. While there was not the glamour of publishing stories with his byline, the work was steady rather than sporadic, and he learned to be fast and accurate. Headline writing trained him to be brief, to sum up an entire story in a half dozen or so words. One of the copy editors taught him that headlines can be witty: For a story about Italian schoolchildren who were failing tests in reading, the editor wrote, WHY GIOVANNI CAN'T READ.

Another *Miami Herald* intern was placed for his entire stay on the police beat when the regular reporter was off. It was often routine work, with few good stories; but he did have one opportunity to work with the Pulitzer Prize–winning reporter Gene Miller. And toward the end of his internship he impressed the editors when he succeeded in the almost hopeless assignment of finding and interviewing the family of a migrant worker just charged with the murders of children in the migrant community. In his story, the family members expressed their total shock, explaining that for some of the children the suspect had been a caring babysitter. The student ultimately was hired by the paper.

Thus, your first job in journalism can be simply the next logical step in a series of steps from college to experimental journalism to internship. Whether your first job is on a small-circulation daily or weekly or a large metropolitan paper of 200,000 circulation or more depends largely on decisions and successes along the way. Each measure of acquired experience and each example of published material counts for something as you advance.

But there is one other important factor that often determines an editor's hiring decision, particularly on large newspapers. One managing editor used to say simply to graduating students, "Get some experience on another paper and then come back." Translated, he really meant, "Work out the bugs in your work on some smaller paper where mistakes don't matter as much. After you have developed a stable style, I can consider you." Editors of large newspapers tend to regard the graduate as still somewhat green and prone to make a few errors prior to stabilizing. If you are going to make some mistakes, the editor of the big daily newspaper wants you to make them on someone else's newspaper. The *Miami Herald,* for instance, hired the intern who had interviewed the child killer's family—but hired him only after he had worked for about a year for a small-circulation daily paper. In that year, the green graduate did make one memorable mistake on the small paper. He published a military news release about a local serviceman's being transferred to a helicopter unit in Vietnam; unfortunately, the news release was stale by the time the reporter published the information, and the soldier had been dead for two months, killed along with his helicopter unit. A telephone call to the Army base could have saved the serviceman's family the renewed grief from seeing his name in the newspaper. The editor demanded to know how that happened, and the reporter explained that he had fallen behind in writing up the news releases. In peacetime it had been no problem; but the year was 1964, just after the Gulf of Tonkin incident, and one could no longer assume that a serviceman was alive three months after a news release notified the hometown paper that he had been transferred to the new war zone.

If you want to move to a larger newspaper, you need to learn your lessons as fast as possible and keep alert for opportunities in your state and elsewhere. One reporter, for instance, moved within the space of three years from the *Fort Lauderdale News* to the *Atlanta Journal* to the *Evening Star* in Washington, D.C. With these advances, his weekly starting salary increased by 31 percent from the *News* to the *Journal* and by another 20 percent from the *Journal* to the *Star.*

Now that we have shown you the process of getting through the front door of a newspaper, we will devote several chapters to telling you what is beyond the door and how to get along there.

2

Working Conditions

> Seldom, it is true, do I gather my grandchildren about my knees and tell them tall tales out of my colorful years as a leg man, but I often sit in the cane-seated rocker on the back porch, thinking of the old days and cackling with that glee known only to aging journalists.
>
> James Thurber, "Memoirs of a Drudge"

Rare is the journalist who does not think of the profession with some glee. True, there are certain conditions of employment that rankle, among them the legendary low salary and the tendency of editors to forget what a glorious story you wrote last week. But these clouds are frequently offset by silver linings that have become legends in themselves: the power of the press, the glory of bylines, and the thrill of being among the first to know.

Journalism continues to be regarded as a glamorous line of work. Many people are convinced that journalists have their cake and eat it too, that they spend their days doing interesting things and getting paid for it. A good number of the thousands of students in journalism classes certainly have high expectations; otherwise they would be somewhere else, such as business school. If all goes according to legend, these students believe they will eventually be paid to interview famous and fascinating people. They expect to be granted privileged access to councils of power. They will perhaps crusade against blatant injustice. They may even learn enough about life and writing to become celebrated and rich as writers of novels.

None of these expectations can be judged as wholly true or false for everyone. It is our purpose to examine to what extent the popular legends can be verified by the hard test of experience. In the process, we will present other working conditions, often overlooked, that play important roles in the reporter's profession.

Power of the Press

The classicists who wrote the United States Constitution understood precisely how power can be abused. They therefore built into the government a unique and complex system of checks and balances: The Congress watches the president; the Supreme Court scrutinizes them both; and the press exposes all their discoverable secrets.

To make sure that the press could not be suppressed, the Constitutionalists guaranteed freedom of the press. They provided a sanctuary for journalism and thus built for it a seat of power in American society. (It was the English historian and politician Thomas Babington Macaulay who first noted that the gallery in Parliament where the reporters sit had become a "fourth estate of the realm.") "The basis of our government being the opinion of the people," wrote Thomas Jefferson in 1787, "the very first object should be to keep that right; and were it left to me to decide whether we should have a government without newspapers, or newspapers without a government, I should not hesitate a moment to prefer the latter."

Journalism has, of course, survived and become powerful. This is fortunate in light of the fact that government has become a giant next to which the citizens can easily feel powerless. Sometimes it seems that only journalists, working as they do *outside* government, can sound an effective challenge to corrupt and/or secretive politicians and bureaucrats.

There is sufficient evidence of the power of the press to galvanize public opinion from coast-to-coast. The *New York Times* courageously published "The Pentagon Papers," giving the people a detailed accounting of how its government had conducted the disastrous war in Vietnam. "The Pentagon Papers" caused people to think twice about blindly trusting the government. So did the *Washington Post*'s numerous stories that gradually exposed the Watergate scandal. The Watergate stories by Bob Woodward and Carl Bernstein spurred other newspapers and television networks to follow the connections between a band of Cuban burglars and the president of the United States. More than any single event in modern press history, the Watergate exposés, dramatized by Woodward and Bernstein's book and the movie, *All the President's Men*, reaffirmed the power of the press. Watergate created a mystique of glamour that influenced a whole generation of Americans, among them thousands of young people looking for an exciting profession.

The power of the press is usually far less dramatic and obvious. Away from Washington, at the local newspapers across the land, reporters nevertheless feel that they have a responsibility to look beneath the surface of events. Two reporters exposed the self-enriching process by which a county commissioner raised the value of his own land by the routing of public roads. Day after day, journalists exercise power by what they ignore or by what they choose to publicize. Frequently the magic act does not seem to work. One reporter wrote a special report on car safety seats for small children. He thought the examples of injured children would help win passage of a state law requiring such seats; legislators had bottled up the proposal in a committee. After the story was published, the bill got free of the committees but was openly voted down.

There are many opportunities for crusading against injustice that do not focus on politicians. There is unfairness in every aspect of life, particularly in the working of our economic system. The elderly living on fixed incomes are frequently victims of the economy. One series of stories featured a woman in her seventies who had rented the same rundown house for thirty years; she was fighting eviction by a landlord with a reputation for treating his tenants as shabbily as he maintained his properties. Another story featured a con artist who took money from people in return for a promise to market their inventions; when he went bankrupt, authorities discovered a roomful of dolls and prototype inventions that he had evidently never even tried to market.

There are numerous cases where other very limited but satisfying successes are scored. Hundreds of examples of this occur every Christmas when the public is made aware of some desperate family, one among many in need. Such was the reporter's tale of a mother and her three daughters, all partially blind, who had almost nothing for Christmas. A neighbor told one of the newspaper editors, and he sent the reporter. Readers sent money. Another such story was about an old woman, also blind, who had been beaten by burglars; readers in her neighborhood responded in part by installing burglar bars on her windows.

The beginning reporter is more likely to be writing about such burglars than about the burglars of the Watergate variety. The reason is simple: Newspaper editors guard the power of the press as closely as the bank guards its valuables, and usually the most trusted employees are given the most sensitive assignments.

As with the exercise of any power, there is the possibility of abuse. Abuse of power by journalists is a frequent complaint by politicians. It has been a theme for motion pictures, as in *Absence of Malice*, which was written by Kurt Luedtke, a former reporter and editor at the *Detroit Free Press*. More frequently, however, journalists are accused of abuse by sensationalism, deliberately pumping up stories to sell newspapers. It is a round-about debate, since journalists must admit they are in business to sell newspapers.

Bylines

Journalists publish more frequently than any other writers, but few readers would know their work if it were published without bylines. The byline is such an important part of journalism that reporters consider it one of their fringe benefits. There was a time not long ago when some editors printed bylines only sparingly. At the *New Era* in Lancaster, Pennsylvania, the city editor withheld the byline unless the reporter had shown exceptional enterprise. One beginning reporter managed to win his first byline when he documented the great number of false alarms, together with the waste of money and life; at least one fireman had fallen and died while answering a false alarm.

The modern practice is to identify the author of every story except for the very shortest items. The byline, therefore, is an expected reward. The reporter receives automatic credit. Bylines erase anonymity. Readers know whom to call if they want to complain or, on the positive side, if they have clues for a follow-up story.

In modern journalism, editors insist that you use your own name in your byline. Gone is the era when you could publish under such attributions as "By A Gentleman Over Head and Ears in Love" (London, 1781). As late as 1914, pen names were still used in London, and the British naval journalist Arnold Henry White wrote about World War I under the pseudonym "Vanoc." In the United States, Samuel Clemens explained his choice of "Mark Twain": "I was a fresh, new journalist, and needed a *nom de guerre* [fighting name]." The same pen name had been used earlier by a Captain Isaiah Sellers in the *New Orleans Picayune*.

Having narrowed your choices to your real name, you have only to decide how you want it to appear. One United Press International foreign correspondent, who achieved such successes as an exclusive interview with Benito Mussolini, insisted on using his entire name even though it was quite long: Edwin Ware Hullinger. Later, when he was a professor at the University of Miami, Hullinger urged his students to give serious consideration to the byline as an expression of style.

The First to Know

The communications revolution of the twentieth century drastically altered our perception of the world. Sophisticated electronic technology has speeded news around the globe so that not a day closes in the western hemisphere when we don't know the major public events that occurred on the other side of the world. Tom Wicker, *New York Times* columnist, likened electronic communications to our central nervous system. News, racing along the wires, makes us react: We jump in fright, we go open-mouthed in awe, we run and hide, or we thrill with the drama and excitement. If you are one who feels the thrill, rather than one who hides, journalism offers you the added advantage of being among the first to know.

The newsroom is the center of this nervous system. Into it comes information in various forms: news tips from informants, messages from reporters, stories being dictated, dispatches from correspondents around the world, often transmitted by electronic impulses directly into computer terminals. Often the news is so gripping that reporters themselves hover over the machines to read the latest developments. It was that way on the afternoon and evening of November 22, 1963, when President John Kennedy had been shot and police had arrested the obscure Lee Harvey Oswald; stories were already being transmitted about Oswald. On such occasions, time seems suspended and the future seems to depend on the next development. News of local importance, while lacking the international urgency, can have as much impact on your community.

In short, journalists find themselves at the cutting edge of history. They are chroniclers of the times, recording events as they pulse through this nervous system. Journalists frequently become news junkies, finding that they cannot get enough of the news.

Interesting People

Not all of us are going to be foreign correspondents and interview the likes of Mussolini. Some of the interesting people you meet are not the least bit famous. Katherine Williams, a reporter for the small *Gwinnett Daily News* in Lawrenceville, Georgia, cackles as James Thurber might about the peculiar gardener who used to come to the office with his giant vegetables; once she had to interview him about a turnip that was the size of a melon. Eccentrics also seek out the newspaper as the logical outlet for their revelations. When he was city editor of the *Atlanta Journal*, Bob Johnson turned down a chance for an exclusive interview with God.

Any journalist eventually meets celebrities. The photographer Charles Pugh tells how he took exclusive flash closeups of Senator Edward Kennedy when they wound up in an elevator together; another time, Pugh shot a series of portraits of the poet Carl Sandburg. The fact is that celebrities, whether bold or unassuming, need publicity to advance their careers, whether in politics or poetry, whether they need your vote or your dollar.

Such personalities visit nearly every major community at one time or another.

Of course, you will also meet the interesting local people who move and shake your own community. Some local people may, in fact, become famous beyond the city limits. You will have had the opportunity of watching the maturation of leaders and personalities. Such was the case in Atlanta during the 1960s when the Rev. Dr. Martin Luther King, Jr., a local preacher, became a figure of worldwide importance. Of course, very few reporters then realized that King was to become the most legendary figure in the city's history. Similarly, few reporters thought that Georgia Gov. Jimmy Carter would one day be President.

Among the interesting people you will meet are your fellow journalists. Unlike bankers, newspaper reporters are highly individualistic. If you are fortunate, you will find a staff that includes some seasoned veterans who can help you with your writing and your career. Howard Van Smith, who had won the Pulitzer Prize for his epic stories about the travels and hardships of migrant farm workers, was one such helpful veteran; toward the conclusion of his career, on the staff of the *Fort Lauderdale News*, Smith went out of his way to help talented beginners with career decisions, and on occasion paved the way for a reporter to be interviewed for jobs in Washington and New York. Another Pulitzer winner, Gene Miller of the *Miami Herald*, was expert at demonstrating to rookies how to personalize routine news by riveting the reader's attention on the human struggle; a routine auto death story became more interesting because Miller insisted on asking for a detailed list of what the victims left behind in their car: some undelivered Christmas cards and a bottle of cheap wine. More often than not, experienced veterans are willing to help the beginner who is polite and not pushy. And they give the most interesting advice. Van Smith once told a young journalist, during his first day on the job, that he needed to get out of there, find a better newspaper. The former *Chicago Tribune* reporter William Moore once gave out his secret formula for keeping his job during the Great Depression of the 1930s: "Write animal stories," Moore said. "People love them."

Access to Power

One of the most intriguing aspects of journalism is that you seem to have access to the power structure. Actually, it is only in rare instances and only after years of experience that you ever know what really happens in government decision making. The exercise of political power is not unlike the performance of a magic show: The deed is done, but you seldom figure out *how*.

Government by secrecy has been raised to an art even in democratic nations. Historians have laid much of the blame for World War I upon secret diplomatic and military agreements. Only in the late twentieth century, and only in America, did governments begin to pass anti-secrecy laws. The first were known as "government in the sunshine" acts. The U.S. Congress passed the classic Freedom of Information Act in the mid-1970s. But it was so revolutionary that the Congress also passed a protective Privacy Act. The Freedom of Information Act speeded up the process of government disclosure of matters such as closed FBI investigations. That had been considered none of the public's business. During the Watergate scandals, the press brought home the point that government, in the name of confidentiality, has been able to work against the public interest.

Watergate also educated journalists. Modern reporters tend to be less gullible than those of a generation ago. You don't necessarily believe something to be true because the mayor or the governor or even the president says it is so. This, in turn, has altered the relationship between the reporter and the public official. There are exceptions, of course, especially when you have a long-established relationship, but generally the era of unqualified trust is gone. Consequently, when a journalist reports that a certain law was passed by the legislature or the city council, he or she generally assumes that some of the reasons for passing the law are hidden from view, as in the magician's act. It is a healthy exercise to ask yourself which special interest group benefits most from new laws. And, in some cases, it is useful to wonder if money is changing hands and, if so, who is paying whom.

Journalist to Novelist

One of the mystiques about working in journalism is the illusion that it will lead to an even more glamorous career as a novelist. The connection is legendary. In the nineteenth century, Charles Dickens was a successful reporter covering Parliament for London's *Morning Chronicle*. In the twentieth century, Ernest Hemingway started his career on the *Kansas City Star* before becoming a European correspondent for the *Toronto Star*. Years later he was asked whether he could recommend newspaper work for the young writer. "On the [Kansas City] *Star*," he said, "you were forced to learn to write a simple declarative sentence. This is useful to anyone. Newspaper work will not harm a young writer and could help him if he gets out of it in time." Less encouraging, however, was the advice given by an insightful writing teacher of Hemingway's generation, Dorothea Brande. "There is not much to be said for the recommendation, so often heard," she said, "to serve an apprenticeship to journalism if you intend to write fiction. But a journalist's career does teach two lessons which every writer needs to learn—that it is possible to write for long periods without fatigue, and that if one pushes on past the first weariness, one finds a reservoir of unsuspected energy—one reaches the famous 'second wind.'"

Journalism can teach much more than how to develop clarity of style and how to work long hours. The profession clearly engages the writer with his or her own time, with contemporary events and passions. This outside experience is of lasting value if we assume that the themes of literature are drawn from observation of human nature.

Salaries

The subject of salaries paid to journalists is provocative as well as legendary. A journalism professor wrote in the margin of an essay on low salaries, "Why perpetuate these myths? Journalists are well paid." He objected to giving circulation to President John Kennedy's remark that reporters were "the last of the talented poor." The professor also objected in the same essay to a story about a fifteen-year-old ninth-grader who had interviewed reporters and formed a distorted notion of their earnings. In her term paper she concluded that a reporter has a "hard, tiring and low-paid job—$40 a week for an 80-hour work week." In the margin of her paper her teacher wrote, "This is not truth. I hope you mean it tongue in cheek."

Indeed, the girl was about forty years behind the times. By 1947 a beginning reporter for the *Albuquerque Tribune* was paid well over that— 79½¢ per hour ($35 for a 44-hour week). By the early 1950s, the salary had gone beyond the $50-a-week mark but was still unimpressive to one journalist's wife; she referred to his job as "Charlie's hobby." By 1964, there was noted improvement: One beginner on the Lancaster *New Era* drew $92 a week.

By the last quarter of this century, newspaper publishers were still paying substantially the same wages, although paychecks seemed much higher because of inflated dollars. (The 1980 dollar was worth 36¢ by 1960 standards.) Some newspaper editors wooed good writers with large salaries, but for the most part publishers sought to get more for less. One trend dominated most business transactions between newspaper and reporter: It was a buyer's market. Or was it? Certain big-city newspapers were experiencing a decline in circulation, and writers with talent and energy contended that exceptional writing could compete for the audience's divided attention and that the investment could turn the circulation figures around.

It was with this contradiction in points of view that publishers arrived at their wages. Most generous was the *New York Times;* it offered $556 a week to rookie reporters who had been trained and oriented to become *Times* staffers.

In contrast was the newspaper tucked away in Pennsylvania: the *Valley Independent* in Monessen. Its staff was organized by The Newspaper Guild, as were reporters on the *Times*. But the cost of living is cheaper in Monessen, so the *Valley Independent* was paying $165 a week.

As difficult as it is to compare Monessen with Broadway, it is difficult to account for why other salaries vary so much. In 1980 the Newspaper Guild surveyed the starting salaries for 153 newspapers besides the *Times* and the *Valley Independent*. Only twenty-three publishers paid more than $300 a week; the great majority paid $200 to $300 a week. The *Valley Independent* and twenty or so other small newspapers paid less than $200 a week.

While The Newspaper Guild was polling newspapers, the American Council for Education in Journalism polled accredited schools of journalism and found nothing encouraging. Among their graduates hired by newspapers, the mean salary, halfway between extremes, was $185 a week, or just $20 more than in Monessen. More recently, fifty-nine newspapers responded in 1981 to a survey made with the cooperation of The Newspaper Fund. The average starting weekly salary in these newsrooms was $205. As expected, the smaller papers paid less. The papers with more than 100,000 circulation averaged no higher than $238 a week.

What do all the surveys mean? One professor, Melvin Mencher of Columbia University's respected School of Journalism, concluded that reporters just out of college seemed to be among the worst-paid of all graduates. It seemed that it was far more profitable to study general business, economics, accounting, mathematics, electrical engineering—or computer science. Writing in the *Columbia Journalism Review*, Mencher concluded that there must be some other allure than the money. He decided that reporters are romantics who feel a calling to journalism and consider themselves lucky not to have to do the work of their better-paid classmates who went into advertising and public relations. Wrote Mencher, "Journalists contribute to their inferior wages. They seem not to want it any other way."

Whether journalism is a life's calling is open to debate. One veteran of almost twenty years says that his two big reasons for being in journalism are fun and impact. "If I had to have a third one, it'd be *challenge*," he said, "but that's part of the fun. It's a lot of fun but it's no place to get rich."

Experienced reporters certainly do not get rich from yearly raises. During the 1970s, raises seldom matched the yearly inflation of the cost of living. One reporter received annual raises that varied from $12.50 to $30.00 a week. During ten years his salary doubled, but inflation neutralized his raises. He began the ten years at $200 a week and ended at $418 a week. His next raise added another $25 a week; after taxes, that was reduced to $16 a week, or a 4 percent annual raise. The annual inflation rate was more than twice that.

That reporter's history more or less typifies the salary problem. The 1981 Newspaper Fund survey documented that after five years the journalist can expect an average salary of $332.69 a week. At major newspapers, with more than 100,000 circulation, the average was $445.11. The smaller papers of less than 25,000 circulation paid the five-year veteran an average of $284.70.

Some reporters try to add to their salaries by working overtime. However, newspapers frequently discourage overtime pay and instead ask reporters to take time off when they reach their maximum hours. Even when overtime is paid, as on newspapers with Guild contracts, the reporter experiences the frustration of diminishing returns when the government deducts taxes on the excess earnings.

A close examination of an actual paycheck stub (from 1980) shows how a journalist who earned $418 a week wound up taking home only $292.84 a week. Instead of making $21,736 a year, he actually took home only $15,227.68. What happened to the missing $6,500?

Look for the deductions. There are six on this paycheck. Three are for taxes: federal and state income taxes and the federal Social Security tax. The newspaper also deducts the reporter's share of group health and life insurance premiums. Two deductions are made by the employees' credit union, a $20 payment on a loan and a $15 deposit to savings. Aside from the savings, all the other deductions total 26 percent of the reporter's check. In fact, the three taxes together take 19 percent.

The reporter's indebtedness to the company employees' credit union is not uncommon. This $20-a-week deduction was for payment on a $1,000 personal loan taken out for dental expenses not covered by the medical insurance.

The credit union is a low-interest financial and social service. By being able to borrow quick cash, usually within a week or two, this reporter frequently is able to manipulate his budget during emergencies. The credit union gives the reporter a check with few questions asked: What do you want the money for? How much per week do you want to repay through payroll deductions?

With credit unions, it is no longer necessary for a reporter to take strictly financial problems to his editor. Indeed, it can be embarrassing to a young reporter to discuss a money crisis with the managing editor. One day in the mid-1960s, a reporter with two years' experience went to the managing editor of the *Miami Herald* for a $150 advance on his salary, to make ends meet for the month. The managing editor was George Beebe, a tall man who slanted forward as he stalked around the newsroom. He wore a large watch chain, which glinted as he moved about. Six years earlier, Beebe had been one of three senior journalists who chose this young reporter for a college scholarship.

Beebe sized up the young journalist and frowned. It was probably not the first reporter who couldn't make his paycheck stretch. Beebe decided to give the reporter twenty minutes instead of only a few. In that time, the managing editor taught some tips for handling money closely. Beebe told him that a young couple ought not buy the large bottle of ketchup because it tied up your money. Just buy, he said, the ketchup you will need for the week. The penny-wise practice could be applied as well to mustard and mayonnaise. The lesson was valuable, but the reporter left empty-handed. Giving an advance was considered an unwise company practice. Thus the credit union represents a more effective way of obtaining the money you need, as well as a more dignified alternative to thinly disguised begging.

Despite relatively low salaries, many journalists do make a career that is both constructive and rewarding. Writers who succeed are usually those who develop an original style or new approach, or both, and become distinct voices at least in the community, and sometimes in the region or the nation. "These are journalists," wrote Michael J. Kirkhorn in *The Quill*, "who contribute to our education and fortify our convictions." Some of these become columnists.

The pay scale that rewards editors with higher salaries naturally tempts even a good reporter to take an offer of an editorship. Still other writers work on the side, freelancing to magazines or writing books.

The search for a higher salary leads some journalists straight out the newspaper door. They are lured to television news, where they are often paid handsomely for talking more and writing less. Other reporters locate jobs in teaching, in government, or in public relations. Indeed, public relations firms frequently pay impressive starting salaries to former reporters with contacts and a knowledge of how to get stories published in newspapers.

Time and the Working Day

Daily-newspaper publishers run the presses every day. Theoretically, there are no days off in journalism, just as there are no closings at hospitals and police departments. So, like hospital workers and police officers, journalists work assorted shifts. In between shifts, the reporter and editor are always, like a doctor, subject to being called at home for emergencies.

One of the most demanding shifts is early morning duty for an afternoon paper. During the 1970s, afternoon newspapers began publishing earlier in the day. A first edition that came off the presses around 10 A.M. could be trucked to market farther from the downtown area and could sell to more people on the streets and shopping centers. It would be competitive in some respects with television's noon news. To publish around 10 A.M.,

newspapers moved the first-edition copy deadline to 7 A.M. The first reporter had to be on duty close to 5 A.M.

The early shift is easily one of the most demanding in newspaper
work, and one of the most peculiar. Beginning at 5 A.M. or 6 A.M., the
reporter frequently winds up working right through the routine quitting
time. Indeed, it is not uncommon to work for twelve hours, from 6 A.M. to 6
P.M., going on to write for tomorrow's newspaper after finishing with today's. On such days, the reporter experiences a time disorientation not
unlike jet lag.

This is understandable. Most of the editors and reporters on the day
shift come to work around 8 A.M. Through the day, the editors who make
assignments can forget how long the early reporter has been there. The
reporter's own biological clock is out of synchronization with those of the
staff. Lunchtime, for instance, comes early, not at noon but between 10 and
11 A.M. Later, when most of the regular shift reporters have gone out to
lunch, the early reporter is often the only one available to write a story for
the day's last edition. Frequently, the early reporter also gets an assignment
late in the morning, a timely story to be written for the next day's paper. If
the editor passes out this new assignment around 11 A.M., the early reporter, no matter how hungry, often decides to do the story and skip lunch.
Despite all these demands, the early reporter is still expected to be back
early the next day. Being the only staff writer on duty before dawn, it is
extremely important not to be late. With such demands, it is not unusual
that the person chosen as the early reporter is often one who is young,
seldom sick, resourceful, efficient, fast, and resilient enough to work from
before dawn toward dusk. Given all this, the morning-shift reporter seldom
complains about boredom.

A helpful practice for the reporter who benefits from analyzing the
day's work is to make notes about the various assignments in a personal
diary, journal, or day log. Such logs are kept routinely each day by copy
editors to record what stories they handled and when they moved the stories
to the next editor or to the composing room. A log, kept faithfully, can
show you how much work you did and how long it took; speed (with
accuracy) counts a great deal in journalism, and your log can help you
improve efficiency. The log can be as simple as you like: You may list such
basic information as what time you began and finished an assignment,
whom you contacted, together with telephone numbers for later reference.

Drawing upon a day log of mine (Teel/early shift), I can reconstruct
one of those memorable, busy days as the leadoff morning reporter. The
next few pages, then, is an account of that day during which, for the first
edition, before dawn, I woke up the police chief and luckily reached the
night-shift supervisor in a hospital before she went home to sleep. Before the
next edition's deadline, I had made a dozen long-distance calls and put

together the story of a college romance that had ended in tragedy. For the final edition I raced across the street and back with enough names and witnesses' quotes to publish a half dozen paragraphs about a slab of masonry that had fallen from a building upon an unsuspecting pedestrian. All four stories were written before 1:30 P.M. before I could take a lunch break. Actually, when you're doing interesting or demanding work on deadline, you have little time to think about what you're *not* doing. Each of these four stories underscores the performance under pressure so typical of deadline journalism.

• *The Sleeping Chief.* I had heard about the police story on the radio newscast as I drove to work at 5 A.M. The story was also in the morning newspaper. The chief had fired a police major. The major publicly accused the chief of firing him for political reasons. I had to get the chief's reply. The early city editor spun the phone number file and handed me the chief's number. Out of courtesy or cowardice, I decided to wait until 6 A.M. to call him. He sounded as if I had awakened him. I was quick to apologize, but I went right ahead and told him about the story that was going around and asked him if there was any truth in it. He said simply that he was the chief of police and that firing the major for insubordination was one of his responsibilities. That was all he would say, but it was enough. The brief, one-minute conversation allowed me to: (1) confirm that the major was fired, (2) quote the chief on his reason: insubordination, and (3) give his denial that the reason was political. I had enough to write, but first I had to make a couple of calls for interviews on a second story.

• *The Christmas Child.* This was another story I had heard on the car radio. A seven-year-old boy had been missing for a day and had turned up unharmed at a hospital; he had told the staff that he left his mother's home the day before to find his father for Christmas.

This was a case where I needed to ask the radio reporter for help. Nobody else knew the name of the hospital. The news announcer at the radio station cooperated. I decided to call the hospital before writing the police chief story. Otherwise I was sure I would miss the hospital night shift workers who had seen the boy and knew the circumstances. Luckily, I found the night administrator before she went home. She not only gave me the details about the boy; she also told me the telephone number of the boy's mother. Lucky again, I had a wonderful talk with the mother. She said the seven-year-old wanderer had just gone to sleep. She didn't want to wake him, although I would have been happy to quote him even if he had uttered only a sleepy grunt.

After I wrote the police chief story in thirty minutes, I got back to the Christmas boy and finished that piece in fifteen minutes, right at the 7 o'clock deadline.

• *The Ill-fated Romance.* After a coffee break, I was working again. The city editor asked me if I could check out a campus shooting almost 200 miles away. Within an hour I had reached several people.

A long-distance operator quickly gave me the police telephone number in the city. The police verified that the shooting had taken place, that the students involved were living in a certain off-campus housing project, that a nineteen-year-old coed was in the hospital, and that one person, a young man, was dead. The manager of the off-campus student housing, a witness to the bloody aftermath, told me what he had seen and what he learned afterward.

The hospital staff confirmed that the girl was living. The funeral home in charge of the young man's burial, to be held that afternoon, gave me the name of the rabbi who was scheduled to officiate. The rabbi supplied valuable insights about the young student. He was the last person at the end of the chain of sources, and when I thanked him and hung up, I had been talking to one person after another for thirty minutes. I had thirty more in which to make sense of all the information.

My story began:

> The college romance of Eddie Effel and Ellen York led him Monday to her apartment near the Georgia Southern campus in Statesboro, where he shot her and her new boyfriend and used one of his bullets to kill himself.

• *The Passing Victim.* I was on my way to a late lunch when the managing editor gave me this assignment in front of the building. He was coming back from lunch, had just seen some commotion across the street, and wanted me to cover it, whatever it was.

It was thirty minutes before the deadline of the day's last edition. In the next fifteen minutes I spoke with (1) a startled witness who had been missed, narrowly, when a masonry slab crashed through the top of a pedestrian walkway at a renovation site and (2) a security guard who allowed me to look at the driver's license of a woman who had been struck by the slab when it smashed through to the sidewalk. Also, I saw the woman lying there on the sidewalk and I could see that she was seriously injured. "I could hear it coming, rumbling," my witness had said. "It sounded like a tornado. It could have been me." I dashed back across the street, typed the story into the computer and made the deadline.

Normally, that would be enough to justify your salary and satisfy you and your editors. But editors, like nature, abhor a vacuum. A reporter whose work is finished and has nothing to do is a worrisome soul. Thus, the early reporter may wind up the day either writing a story for the next day's paper or doing research for a story due for Sunday.

The fact is that when editors *ask* you to write, they are usually *telling* you, but nicely. Usually your proper response is to pick up a notepad and write down instructions without balking. In some cases, however, it is reasonable to say, candidly and sincerely, that the editor might do better asking some reporter who is a bit more fresh. This is simply a gentle way of suggesting what the editor may have forgotten: that you have been on the job since 5 or 6 o'clock in the morning, and it has been a long, long day.

3

Everyday Problems and Who Solves Them

Each day, a newspaper publishes enough words to make a novel. But unlike the novelist, the journalist cannot work alone. The newspaper is like a great ship that cannot sail without a crew whose members work at different assignments.

Generally, there are three main categories of news staff writers contributing stories to the day's pages: the *general assignment* reporter, the *beat* reporter, and the *special assignment* writer.

As a *general assignment* reporter, you usually start the day not knowing where you will be or what you will be writing about. The city editor calls upon general assignment reporters, often without a moment's notice, to write about whatever comes up, as in The Date with Death. You learn to work your wits when rushing off with only enough time to grab a pen and notebook. Frequently, expense money needs to be improvised in a hurry for cab fares and even airplane tickets.

If you are a *beat* reporter, you know *where* you will be, usually, because you make a routine of visiting the same buildings and seeing many of the same men and women there each day. But you often do not know exactly *what* you will be reporting, although you can be sure that you'll find *something* newsworthy. Perhaps on one day your routine yields a short story about an employee honored for heroism; the next day you may discover a front-page scoop, as in The Night the Women Got Loose.

On *special assignment,* as in The Case of Ron and Lou, or The Panamanian Marines, you have the advantage of knowing in advance where you will be and what you will be writing about. You can therefore plan better and write with more time and care.

The General Assignment Reporter:
the Date with Death

Many reporters begin their careers on general assignment, at least until the city editor can evaluate them. The best preparation for this work is mental alertness, a curiosity about all things, and a readiness to start using the telephone soon after you are given an assignment. One day your editor may ask you to interview a toothless stunt man passing through town with a collection of snapshots of celebrities who posed with him. The next day you may be sent to a housing project where a woman has been stabbed to death on her porch and you will have to interview the survivors. On general assignment you learn to expect the unexpected and to solve problems quickly, as illustrated by The Date with Death.

Sometimes you will be assigned a major story simply because there is nobody else to do it. There was no other explanation for my city editor's sending me to cover the execution of John Spenkelink.

Actually, it was his second date with death. Spenkelink had been convicted of murder in Florida and his execution was to be the first in the eastern United States in more than a decade. As such, the case was a *cause célèbre,* and the state prison became a rallying point for advocates and opponents of capital punishment, many of whom camped in a cow pasture across the road from the prison. The major American newspapers and television networks had sent correspondents. Hours before the scheduled execution a federal judge delayed it indefinitely. Nobody knew it was only a seventy-two-hour delay.

Three mornings later, according to my day log (Teel/Date with Death), I was the leadoff general assignment reporter on the early morning shift. I came to work at 5 A.M. and expected that I would do what I usually did on that shift, that is, write one or two stories about events that had occurred overnight and finish them in time for the 7 A.M. deadline. On the way to work I listened to the radio newscast, and when I got to my desk I read the morning newspaper; the major news story overnight was that federal judges had refused any further delay of Spenkelink's sentence, and the governor of Florida had hurried up the execution, setting it for 10 A.M. that day.

On most newspapers, decisions to send reporters out of state are not made lightly, since they involve hundreds of dollars in expenses. But by the time I got to the office, the night city editor, a former foreign correspondent named Mike Duffy, had decided that our newspaper needed a reporter at the scene again. Our reporters had come home three days earlier when the electrocution had been delayed, and nobody was covering.

"You're it," Duffy said, summoning me to the city desk.

"But I'm not the prison reporter. Montgomery's been keeping up with this. He'd love to go." I was serious. Bill Montgomery wrote many of our most gruesome stories; he specialized in crime.

Of course, for such a story you don't need to be an expert. A general assignment reporter can become knowledgeable in a short period of time by fast reading of background information, including previously published stories. Another thing to remember is that when the specialist on a subject is at home asleep, a city editor will almost always assign an urgent story to a reporter who happens to be on hand.

"You're it," Duffy repeated.

Such an assignment requires thorough but quick planning. You know that you have to arrange to fly, to rent a car, to dictate over some distant telephone. You know you will need money. Duffy made an announcement in the newsroom and within five minutes the various editors on the early morning shift had contributed $50 cash. Meanwhile I telephoned for an airline reservation, and the airline arranged for a rental car to be waiting for me when I landed in Florida. The nearest airport to the state prison was at Jacksonville, and that meant, according to my map, a drive of about 100 miles to that cow pasture. A taxi rushed me to the airport in about twenty minutes.

On such a mission you find that you have bursts of rushing around followed by short lulls. I had a few minutes to relax as I sat in the plane taking off for Florida. Then I got busy again and read the morning newspaper reports and some of the newspaper clippings from our news library. Just after I had telephoned for a cab, I had asked the newspaper librarian to round up all the earlier reports on the case. By the time I landed in Jacksonville I had read the background I needed.

Reporters on out-of-town assignments need to keep in communication with the editors at home. This is especially true in covering such an uncertain event as an on-again–off-again execution. When I landed in Jacksonville, while the rental-car clerks were processing my forms, I telephoned the city desk for any fresh instructions from the day city editor, who had just come to work. He confirmed that the execution was still going ahead at 10 A.M. Also, he advised me not to worry about writing the main news story. He wanted me to concentrate on a news-feature story describing the scene outside the prison, with comments from the people who were for and against the execution. He would depend on the wire services, the Associated Press and United Press International, for the main news stories. He also wanted me to write a second story, a feature for the Sunday paper.

On the road, I turned to a radio station for some later information. A disc jockey on a rock music station gave the whole affair an altogether different air; he approached the execution as he would a countdown for one of Florida's space launches: "T-minus one hour and thirty minutes," he said. I jotted that down as I drove.

An hour later, still half an hour before the execution, I drove into the crowded cow pasture, thick with television news vans and hundreds of other people who had camped there. It looked as if a carnival had set up. One man demonstrated his support of executions; atop his van he had strapped a coffin marked with Spenkelink's name. Across the way you could hear drumbeats from the forces opposed to capital punishment, who marched in a circle while a man beat on a large barrel.

In such a situation you discover hidden resources within yourself. What might seem almost impossible becomes possible. Charged with adrenalin, working against a pressing deadline, you quickly stop people who seem to know what's going on, and talk to them. The trick is to keep moving, and to talk to more than one person. Within fifteen minutes you have enough raw quotes in the notebook to build the base of your story.

The one problem I had not yet solved was locating a telephone. I made the decision to get my information first and then worry about finding a telephone when I had something to say. Now I had fifteen minutes before the appointed time of execution. I asked directions, was told about a nearby store, and drove south on the totally unfamiliar Starke-MacClenny Road. It seemed that I passed miles of pine trees before I saw that little store on the left and the pay phone stuck against the wall out front. Luckily, nobody was using it, and within a minute I was talking to a dictationist back in Atlanta. Everything I dictated was to be stored as background paragraphs. After the execution I would telephone again and send the beginning of the story by the 11 o'clock deadline. I raced back to the cow pasture and arrived exactly at 10 o'clock.

No matter how much planning you do, there is usually something that you can't anticipate. I had not imagined that the execution might be delayed. Like everyone else in that cow pasture, I waited for a signal that the switch had been pulled. Actually, Spenkelink did not die at 10 A.M. Minutes passed. It was 10:25 A.M. when the news media witnesses came out of the prison to share what they had seen. Now I had only thirty minutes for everything—about fifteen minutes to listen and another fifteen to find a phone.

There were several witnesses. Some talked about the delay. One suggested that Spenkelink had fought the guards. Did they drug him? What was the reason for the mouth gag the witnesses saw on him when the guards lifted the venetian blinds to reveal the chair? Some said the gag was drawn so tightly it pulled his face out of shape. They got a look at his eyes and one witness said she saw a tear. Then a hood was flipped down over the condemned man's face and the switches were thrown. One newsman stood there in the cow pasture and said he had seen smoke rising from Spenkelink's leg. Everyone agreed that the prison doctor had checked Spenkelink's body three times, after each of three jolts of electricity, and then declared him dead.

In such a situation you hope that the most interesting things are said before you have to leave for a phone. I had no choice. If I didn't find a telephone it wouldn't matter what great observations I collected.

Finding that phone was harder than before. As I suspected, the pay phone at the little store was in use; people were lined up to use it. I drove on. Someone back at the pasture had said that there were more stores to the south on the Starke-MacClenny Road.

With time so limited, you learn to compose the lead paragraphs in your mind as you sit behind the wheel. I had tried several possible leads by the time my eyes spotted an auto body shop. I pulled up to the shop and went looking for the owner. He was a short, dark-haired, and pleasant man who was well aware that Spenkelink was supposed to die that morning. I told him what had happened and offered him five dollars for the use of his telephone. I assured him that I would call collect. By telling him the news, I included him in the drama. He responded helpfully, as though he felt he was performing a public service. He led me to the telephone and left me alone with my notebook. My telephone connection went through at once, and the dictationist accepted the call. As usual, I rewrote some phrases as I dictated, and this is the story that came out:

> STARKE, Fla.—Kris Revilleot had just witnessed the execution of John Spenkelink, and she stood crowded by 100 reporters, reading from a spiral notebook what she had jotted down in the minutes before and the minutes after.
>
> "The first surge of electricity came at 10:12," she read nervously. "The doctor checked him three times. The last time was at 10:18, and he took his pulse and he checked his eyes, and I guess that would be the time of death."
>
> Near the wooden shelter built especially for this press conference, in the pasture near the road across from Florida State Prison, stood a man who hopes this is not the last execution.
>
> Bill Thomas of Orange Park, Fla., and his son had come to wait with others, and talk about another condemned man, Patrick Anthony Brewer, 20, who is on the same Death Row for the murder of Thomas's wife, Tsuyako, Feb. 15, 1978.
>
> "The victim is forgotten by everybody else, except the family remembers," Thomas said.
>
> A quarter-mile from Thomas, across the pasture, a neatly dressed young woman stood on the third rung of a wire fence and shouted, "Killers!" in the direction of the sheriff's deputies across the road and the pale, hospital-green walls of the prison.
>
> A young man joined her, and a minister put a comforting hand on him and said, "Don't fall to that level. We've got 130 more over there."
>
> The minister was referring to the men still on Death Row. . . .

I finished dictating the story by 11:15 A.M. Normally, the city editor would have cut me off at 11 A.M., but he stretched the deadline for this story.

The rush was over. For the second time in six hours, I felt I could relax briefly. My next assignment was to compose a Sunday story with a different perspective and more facts. I began working on that story the minute I stepped out of the office of that auto body shop. The owner was waiting for me and wanted to hear more, as did the few other men who stood around the cars parked there.

You do well to listen to your instincts. In this instance, my instincts told me that these men and their thoughts about the historic execution would make interesting reading in my Sunday story. Although I needed to get back to the cow pasture and hear more of the witnesses' accounts, I stayed several minutes to get their viewpoints. None of the outsiders at the pasture that day said so clearly what the people in that neighborhood felt. The owner of the auto shop, for instance, favored the death sentence; he believed the electrocution would be a lesson to other drifters who came to Florida.

Back at the pasture, I talked for two hours with the witnesses. Some of them lingered just to talk, as if talking eased their minds of what they had seen. From their several accounts, I pieced together a minute-by-minute countdown. At some point I realized that my first paragraph would be about the rock station disc jockey announcing the countdown in his strange fashion.

All that was necessary now was to get home. Despite what you may have imagined about the glamour of expenses-paid assignments, reporters on out-of-town missions frequently are under such pressure that they neglect their own well-being. Except for the five dollars paid to use the auto shop phone, I had not spent anything. It was well past 2 P.M. when I returned to the Jacksonville airport. I was hungry and tired. If I had been at home, it would have been quitting time and I certainly would already have had lunch. I checked in the rental car and went to the airport restaurant and ordered the best steak they had. At the table I began writing my Sunday story, which I finished on the plane. Back at the office, I typed the finished piece into the word processor:

STARKE, Fla.—Since the Cape Canaveral launches, Florida has been known for countdowns, and one Jacksonville radio disc jockey got into that frame of mind just before the electrocution of John A. Spenkelink.

"It's T-minus 1:34," he broadcast just before playing a cheerful record at 8:26 A.M. Friday.

Spenkelink had been set to die at 10 A.M. Next to the death chamber, with the electric chair hidden by three venetian blinds, the witnesses were seated and waiting. Most were nervous, silent except for heavy breathing. By their watches the countdown was over and the time had arrived for the first execution in the East in more than a decade.

But the electrocution was not as punctual as the rocket countdowns. It was twelve minutes late.

Across the two-lane Starke-MacClenny Road, protesters in the pasture thought Spenkelink was dead at 10:08 A.M.

"Killers!" one woman cried toward the sheriff's deputies across the road in front of the prison. Actually, Spenkelink was still being guided toward the electric chair by a half dozen prison officers. He was being strapped securely with leather bonds and a mask so he would not be able to move his chest or say a word or scream.

Beyond the closed venetian blinds, each of the witnesses had a slightly different view. ABC newsman Al Dale sat where he could see through the narrow gaps in the blinds.

"He sat down. There was no struggle," Dale recalled. "Two men were leading him, holding him lightly by the arms. And he just sat down. Then I lost sight of him."

At exactly 10 A.M., the phone rang in the chamber behind the closed blinds. Among the witnesses, David Kendall, the Washington lawyer who had won previous delays for Spenkelink, whispered, "Oh, please, God." "He was obviously hoping it was a stay of some sort," said newsman Ike Seaman, another witness.

In the next eleven minutes there was a hushed, nervous suspense. "The witnesses started getting nervous," Seaman said, "because the venetian blinds hadn't been raised, and it was five after, and six after and seven after 10. And one man could see through the crack of the blinds and said, 'My God, they're putting the straps around him. I can see the skull cap going on him.'"

Through the crack, Dale was watching. "Oh, they must have worked on him for 15 minutes. Very methodical thing, you could see through the blinds. This guy—one guy with huge rubber and leather gloves, apparently the electrician—screwed the bolt down on the thing. A very businesslike thing. It was really eerie, like this wasn't a human being, like putting some machinery together.

"And then there were blurs of movement, like there must have been seven or eight people in there. In the meantime there were a couple of sessions of loud rattling of cell doors. They knew what time it was back in the prison. Rumble, rumble, rumble, rumble."

At 10:11 the venetian blinds were raised, slowly. Some witnesses gasped. "It was like watching a stage play beginning, and there was Spenkelink in the middle," Seaman said. "As he sat there he was tightly bound into this wooden chair. He had a leather skull cap on his head with a large electrical wire coming out of it. He had on a leather gag that covered his mouth so he couldn't speak. . . . His eyes . . . were just large and absolutely terrifying.

"His eyes darted all over the room. There were only two men in the room that he could have recognized." They were his minister, Rev. Thomas Feamster, and his lawyer, who had been reading the 23rd Psalm.

They [the witnesses] had been told by a prison spokesman that

Spenkelink probably would make a final statement. The tight gag was a little startling to Dale.

"The upper part of his cheeks and his eyes were flushed—I don't know whether from the tightness of the gag or just because he was scared, but his eyes were, darting, flashing, I mean they really looked like fireworks," Dale said. "And his mouth twitched a couple of times. Either he was trying to speak or he was hurt by the gag. It was very tight."

For only about 30 seconds, the witnesses and Spenkelink looked at each other. Kris Revilleot, Seaman, Dale and other reporters wrote in their notebooks without looking away from him. Ms. Revilleot, who said she was scared, noted a tear in Spenkelink's eye.

"A minute after those blinds went up," Seaman said, "they pulled a shroud over his face so we couldn't see it."

At 10:12 there was a click. "We saw his body lurch slightly to the right and . . . his right fist clenched and his index finger slowly moved and pointed to his body, and stayed there," one witness recalled. Ms. Revilleot said, "He only really moved once. You could see his pants, his legs move." Tom Slaughter, an Associated Press reporter, said he saw "smoke rising from the right calf" where an electrode was strapped.

In the next six minutes the witnesses counted two more surges of electricity and after each one they watched a doctor check Spenkelink's chest with a stethoscope.

At 10:15 Rev. Feamster, at the back of the room, suddenly boomed out to no one in particular, "I hope you pray this is merciful, in the name of God, for our souls' sake."

A minute later the venetian blinds were lowered, slowly.

Some distance down the Starke-MacClenny Road, a mechanic at an auto body shop said he believed this would be a lesson to other lawbreaking drifters who come to Florida by the thousands. Spenkelink had been one of them; he had escaped from a California prison and while in Florida had shot and beat to death another drifter, a parole violator from Ohio.

"This has to be," said Bill Thomas of Orange Park, Fla., one of the pro–death penalty group gathered in the pasture opposite the prison. He explained that his wife had been stabbed to death in her sandwich shop by one of the other 129 men on Florida's Death Row.

"Justice," he said, "must be served. It was served this morning. I feel sorry for [Spenkelink's] family."

Spenkelink's lawyer predicted a trend away from capital punishment. "I think that the death penalty in another generation will be a thing of the past and that our children will have all the incomprehension of this barbaric utility that we now have for segregated restrooms and burnings of witches."

The story was finished in the computer. I had arrived at work at 5 A.M. and the story had kept me going, non-stop, for fourteen hours, from before sunrise until past sunset, across two states by taxi, rental car, and airplane. I found my own car in the lot and dragged on home.

The Beat Reporter:
the Night the Women Got Loose

As a beat reporter, you are held responsible for a certain territory or subject. One city editor, in assigning a staffer to cover the federal government beat, said it was like covering third base, considering how suddenly lawsuits are filed and how unexpectedly judges' rulings are filed. On such a beat you need quick reaction time. There is no substitute for preparedness, for knowing the people on your beat well, and knowing what is scheduled to happen in the next week. The more you know, the less likely you are to be caught by surprises or scooped by competitors.

Most newspapers have two general types of beats. The first and oldest type is the government beat, which usually requires daily visits to such places as the city hall, the police and fire stations, the county commission offices, and the courthouse, the board of education, or the federal courts. The second type of beat is far more general. Your responsibility is for a certain subject: for instance, environment, science, or medicine. Usually such a beat carries a reporter all over town and frequently out of town, such as when the science writer travels to report the launching of the space shuttle.

The overall advantage of covering a beat is that it gives you some control over your working day. Knowing what meetings need to be covered, you can plan ahead. Days in advance of writing a story, you can lay its groundwork. You have the joy of discovery when you find stories on your beat—or when some "contact" on the beat telephones you with a news tip. Also, your news stories are often on the front pages, because most city editors give priority to news from the beats.

The disadvantage, if you can call it that, is that you are held liable if your competitors scoop you. One of the most sinking feelings for a professional journalist is to hear or read a major story on your beat, one that your city editor will wish was in your newspaper first. The best response in such a case is to get to work immediately and find something new about the same story and publish your new improved version the same day.

Although many beat stories tend to be written about routine events and meetings, you will be looking constantly for the unusual story. Such uncommon stories spice the life of the beat reporter. The reporter on the education beat of the *Fort Lauderdale News* stumbled onto his best story when he was told confidentially that the county's teachers were planning to go on strike. Similarly, two government reporters for the *Atlanta Journal,* Mike Schwartz and Fred Hiatt, were inspired to go beyond the routine when they learned that a suburban county commission chairman had used his influential position to amass a personal fortune in real estate. The reporters spent extra hours in order to detail how the chairman bought large acreage and then managed to have county highway funds allocated so that roads served the land and thereby increased its value. After a series of outstanding stories, Schwartz was promoted to assistant city editor and Hiatt became a reporter for the *Washington Post*.

Some of the best beat stories chronicle some individual struggle against government bureaucracy. Such was the drama of Poozikala Chako Zachariah, a U.S.-trained energy scientist. The U.S. Immigration Service was trying to deport him back to India on the grounds that there was no job for him here that could not be filled as ably by a U.S. citizen. He filed a lawsuit in Federal court, saying that the U.S. actually had a shortage of people in his speciality: fusion energy science. The problem, he claimed, was that he had been misclassified by the bureaucrats in the Labor Department, who had no bureaucratic category for fusion energy science.

A Federal judge, realizing that Zachariah was right, ruled in his favor. In all, the beat reporter got three good stories out of the unfolding soap opera, one of which was reprinted in India.

One of the least appreciated and most demanding routines is the prison beat. Most newspapers do not assign a reporter to cover prisons as a full-time job. Prison reporting tends to be "on demand"—where there is a riot or escape or when an inmate is found slain in his cell. The city editor usually is not eager to have a reporter making the rounds of prisons when they are quiet. Yet that is precisely when a reporter ought to be making personal contacts with the wardens and deputy wardens—when the atmosphere inside the walls is one of relatively calm routine. Once a riot occurs, the warden obviously has no time to socialize with a new reporter; an already familiar name has more of a chance of getting through on the telephone.

The richest vein of story material in prison reporting is found in the lives of the inmates. And one of the standard ways of communicating with them is by letters. Prisoners are true pen pals. Exchanging letters is also a convenient way of covering a prison beat with a minimum investment of time. There are two things to keep in mind, however: (1) censorship of letters is common, so you need to keep in mind that anything you write may be read in the warden's office, and (2) most inmates' stories (including tales about their own innocence) must be regarded with a harsh skepticism. Whatever the case, their letters make interesting reading and can lead occasionally to a good story.

One meeting with an inmate in the state women's prison led to a front-page story about The Night the Women Got Loose. That bizarre story gave readers of the *Atlanta Journal* a rare look at what happened one night inside the remote women's prison when cells were supposed to be locked and the lights were supposed to be out.

According to my records (Teel/Women's Prison), the story started out as an honest effort to write about something altogether different—a survey of the various types of crimes for which women were sentenced to prison in Georgia. After studying the computerized inmate rolls in Atlanta, I set out to see the inmates at the state's only women's prison. Two hours from Atlanta, over country roads and through small towns, I found the prison, a facility once used to house psychotics.

I spoke with several of the women in private interviews. One was serving fifteen years for shooting her husband in a cornfield; she contended that she shot him in self-defense before he could shoot her, as he threatened to do. A six-months-pregnant woman was serving time for passing worthless checks; she said the only reason she wrote the bad checks was to buy food for her other child. Another woman from Detroit was serving fifteen years for manslaughter; she had killed another woman, an accomplice, in a dispute over some missing drugs.

The next inmate was a very young woman who called herself Angyl Jensen. She was blond, was about five feet, five inches tall, and had tattoos on one arm. She walked with a lazy prison shuffle into the room.

She had been arrested while hitchhiking through Georgia. In Florida she had met a young man; he had stolen a credit card and used it to rent a motel room. While he was in the motel room shower, there was a knock at the door. Angyl Jensen opened the door. It was the police. She was now serving a year in the prison for credit card theft.

She looked like a child, so much younger in face than the check-writing pregnant mother or the two women serving time for manslaughter. I did not know until much later that Angyl Jensen had lied to the authorities about her name and her age in order to keep her mother from being told.

You learn to flow with the person you're interviewing. With prisoners, you hope that they will trust you enough to talk unguardedly and truthfully. Angyl Jensen insisted on telling me about conditions in the prison. It was not the subject I planned to talk about—I wanted to know how the women got there—but I let her go on. At last, she practically commanded me to write about the women in the other prison building down the hill, where the disciplinary violators were kept in closer confinement. She said I ought to ask the warden what happened one night over there.

"What did happen?" I asked automatically.

"Just ask them. Ask them about the girls that OD'd."

One of the hardest tasks facing a reporter is separating truth from fiction. The problem is: Whom do you believe, the inmates or the warden? As in other instances, you must often trust your instincts, at least until they are proven wrong. My instincts led me to believe Angyl Jensen. She projected an innocent tell-it-like-it-is attitude. Of course, I planned to check out her story with the authorities afterwards, but I let her talk without contradiction from me, and I took notes. The note taking encouraged her, as it does most people in confinement, and made her understand that I took her seriously.

Angyl Jensen's offhand remarks eventually led to a story very unlike the one I had gone in search of. The story was played at the top of page one and the headline read, 29 IN WOMEN'S PRISON GO ON BIZARRE DRUG BINGE. The story began:

MILLEDGEVILLE—State prison investigators have pieced together a story of one bizarre night inside the security unit at the state women's prison during which women were freed from their lockups, wandered through the building and disposed of about 200 tranquilizers and barbiturates taken from the medicine room.

Three women prisoners, one of them unconscious, were hospitalized for treatment of overdoses, and the lone male officer on duty that night resigned during the investigation, according to the state prison commissioner, Dr. Allen L. Ault.

The incident happened during the night shift of Nov. 13–14, and the results of the investigation were disclosed to the *Atlanta Journal* Thursday.

While stories about what happened vary, prison officials generally agree that the correctional officer, working alone without the usual supervising matron, disobeyed orders, went into the dormitory area and unlocked one dormitory door. Before the incident ended, investigators say, all or most of the 29 women were loose from their lockups, some of them thinking about escape and some getting "high" on medications.

Commissioner Ault said the incident could have been avoided if the prison had enough male and female staff. He said the prison staff is "stretched thinner" because of the increasing number of women being sent to prison.

According to investigators, the correctional officer on duty in the segregation unit admitted that he disobeyed instructions to stay out of the dormitory area while he was on duty alone. They say he admitted he opened one dormitory door.

The officer, a former state policeman, said in a telephone interview Thursday that he opened the door to allow one woman, a bed wetter, to go to the clothing room in the front of the building for a change of clothes.

"I let that one out," he said. "I felt sorry for her."

The officer said that as he was returning the woman to the dormitory, she asked for cough syrup. He said he took her to the medicine room for two APC pain relief tablets. He said he does not know how the medications were distributed to the women and he said he does not know how the other women got out of their locked dormitories. . . .

You will often hear much more than you can prove or need to print. I could not print all Angyl Jensen told me because it was so wild and uncorroborated. She said, for instance, that she had lured the guard into a compromising position by offering to perform an act of sodomy. From what I later learned about Angyl Jensen I tended to believe her, particularly since everything else she disclosed to me, within the scope of her prison experiences, proved true. There were hospital records, for instance, showing that three women in fact were treated for drug overdoses that night.

But the major problem you face before you can publish such stories is getting comment from the authorities. In this case I needed to confirm the inmates' stories. There is an artful way of proceeding, and it often works very effectively. I decided to go straight to the top, to the commissioner himself. I telephoned him from a pay phone along the road on my way back to Atlanta. I told him I had been to the prison and that I had something I wanted to discuss with him the next day. That was all I told him. I didn't want him to prepare too much; I wanted to see the expression on his face when I mentioned the incident, to see what I could read in his look. He said right away that he could see me at 8 A.M.

In cases like these, it pays to have a reputation for being an accurate reporter and an understanding one. As soon as I mentioned what I was working on the commissioner reacted openly. He summoned the prison investigator, who had all the records of the incident. The commissioner told him to share the records with me just to make sure I had my facts straight. That put my story on a solid foundation. Angyl Jensen's role in the escapade was never established adequately, but I have no doubt that *she* was the one who got the keys from the guard and passed them to the other women.

After that, more stories flowed from the women's prison, and all of them found their way to the front pages. Angyl Jensen filled a notebook I had left her. She made daily jottings about life in her cellblock. She turned the diary over to me, and it, together with other diaries and letters, formed the basis for a three-part series on women in prison. One of the diary writers, the young woman from Detroit, needed no encouragement from me. When she got out of prison, two years later, she turned over to me a six-year diary of so many pages that I worked for two months to scale it down to a three-part series detailing her life in prison. By comparison, Angyl Jensen's diary was extremely short, but poignant. She lived in fear of being sent to the isolation unit, the "hole" that looms in her nightmares:

> I hope to be getting out pretty soon. Why? Because these past couple of nights I've dreamed of being free. Usually, I dream of going to court or going to the "hole" or something in that line of thought.
>
> I think these past couple of nights are the first times I've dreamed of being free since I've been locked up. One year now.

As a beat reporter you are always alert for follow-up stories, and there was one last story about Angyl Jensen. She was freed soon afterwards. She finally broke down and told her prison matrons that she was not Angyl Jensen and that she was not twenty years old. They took her to a south

Georgia judge. He granted her special consideration after he learned that, when sentenced, she had been only fifteen, a juvenile.

She telephoned me for the last time from a pay phone.

"Guess what? I'm free. My aunt is here, and I'm going home."

To her family, she had been a missing person for a year. They were delighted and relieved to find her and forgive her. Before she hung up, I got from her the name of the judge who freed her. I wished her luck. Then I telephoned the judge and he confirmed the whole story. Angyl Jensen proved to be the rare example of a truthful convict. She had never lied to me. She never saw the last story about herself, a fifteen-year-old girl who spent a year in the state women's prison, but it was also on page one.

The Beat Reporter on Special Assignment:
the Case of Ron and Lou

Very often the beat reporter discovers a story that needs extra time to research and write. If you're lucky, the city editor will free you to do it by assigning someone else to cover your beat.

According to my log (Teel/Congressman's son), I was given a week off the beat to work on The Case of Ron and Lou. The story originally came from the police department. I was a metro beat reporter for Washington's *Evening Star* in Montgomery County, Maryland—a suburb of Washington, D.C. A young man had been arrested for carrying a pound of marijuana as he rode on the back of a motorcycle. It turned out that he was the son of a New Hampshire Congressman. It was a good story, and all the newspapers, radio, and television reporters jumped on it.

What led me further into it was a tip from someone on my beat, a young man who knew the Congressman's son through mutual friends. My informant explained that the young man, named Lou after his father, had moved out of his father's Washington home and was living in a commune near DuPont Circle. There he took on a different identity: He was known as Ron. He preferred the commune, my informant said, but his double life had led to an even greater estrangement from his father the Congressman.

The father–son conflict seemed to be at the heart of Lou's story. But I would have to spend a few days tracking down the boy's past and talking to his father.

In cases like this you would like to take at least a couple of weeks and follow every clue. But more than likely you have only a couple of days, a week at the most, away from your beat.

I would need to make a good presentation to my editor if I were to get the time off the beat to track down this story. I wrote a presentation and asked for three days. The editor loved the father-and-son story beneath the news.

One problem facing every special assignment reporter is how to budget time. Whereas the beat reporter's pace is to write at least one story a day, as a special assignment writer you simply take lots of notes and try to frame ideas. You raise new questions hour by hour. You become more like a hunter following a trail, or like a detective. One clue leads to another. The best advice is to get started as soon as possible.

The trail led me to a house near DuPont Circle. A man answered the door. He was friendly and courteous, and he gave me a chance to explain why I was there. I explained what I was trying to do in terms that I hoped would be successful in gaining information. I said that everyone had already written the story of the Congressman's son from the point of view of his having committed a crime. I wanted to tell a deeper, more sympathetic story of father and son and how their relationship caused Lou Jr. to leave home. I added that I hoped to find the son's side of the story.

To my delight, the members of the commune came forward, one by one, with some insight about Lou Jr., whom they called Ron. None of them referred to him by his family name. He had been their friend, Ron. Now he was living temporarily with his mother back in New Hampshire, pending his return for the court hearing.

When I left the commune, I knew that I had to go next to see the boy's father. The next day I was in a hall of Congress, sending in a message to summon the member from New Hampshire. He was at his desk in the House of Representatives and was participating in a debate. I sent in a message that I wished to speak with him, and during a break he came out. Instead of shying away from my questions, he was eager to talk about his son and how they had grown apart. But he said he really could not explain why or what had caused their estrangement. He was a very sad man.

With such luck, my research was completed in three days, and it took me another day or so to write the story. The unfortunate gap was that I could not interview the young man; he was being protected closely by his mother back home. Nevertheless, the *Evening Star* considered the assignment successful: a very special father-and-son story.

The Special Assignment Reporter: the Panamanian Marines

No writers begin their day in journalism more to the point than those on special assignment. They know *where* they will be and *what* they will be writing. Often they have only a few more facts to confirm before publishing a front-page story. Such was the episode of the Panamanian Marines, which first appeared in the *Atlanta Journal* and later was picked up by the national wire services and television networks. This case involved the U.S. Marine Corps, but it was developed through roundabout contacts—as many stories are—and by coincidence.

The U.S. Immigration and Naturalization Service was one of the quietest offices in the federal government. It rounded up illegal aliens, mostly Mexicans working in the potato and tomato fields. But this enforcement branch was relatively inactive in the South because of a shortage of personnel.

According to my records (Teel/Panamanian Marines), it was a routine telephone conversation about what the agents were *not* doing because of the understaffing that led to the discovery of the Marines story. The enforcement supervisor said his staff was more overworked than ever and I routinely asked why.

"Well, it's because of the Marines," he said. "They've got these Panamanians in South Carolina over at Parris Island, and we've got to go over and process them one by one."

"Panamanians?" I still didn't know what he meant.

"Yeah. From the Canal Zone. They're illegals. They sneaked into the Marines. Some recruiters up in Brooklyn let 'em in."

I was on to something, and the adrenalin was pumping. I hunched over the phone and took notes furiously, trying to restrain my excitement.

"How many?" I asked.

"That's the problem. About 300."

Whenever you discover something like this you wonder if someone else has already found it before you.

"Has this been in any of the papers?"

"No. It's not final yet. We've got to interview every one of them. We've got to keep two of our men over there for weeks. We just got started."

There is nothing quite like the sensation of discovering news of some importance that nobody has yet published. Reporters who have worked on news scoops have testified that they felt at least a little rush of excitement. One reporter said he always felt like grinning, because only he was in the know.

There is also the possibility that your exclusive story could leak out to other writers before you can publish it, and this is guaranteed to make you feel anxious. Whatever your emotions, you need to think clearly, map out a strategy, and get on with it as promptly as possible.

Having assured myself that the Marines story was a national scoop, I immediately planned what I needed to do before I could publish. Should I tell my editors? A beginning reporter might very well dash to the city editor and spill out all the information. An experienced reporter knows that the editor will simply want you to verify the story as soon as possible. So I decided to wait until I spoke with the Immigration agents in person.

I went to the Immigration headquarters and the officers confirmed everything. The remaining obstacle was to get confirmation from the Marine Corps. There was a danger that the Marines might try to announce the information to everybody at once. Another concern was to protect my main source of information at the Immigration Service to preserve that line of communication and protect the agent's job. I did not want to tell the Marine Corps the identity of the person who tipped me off.

Another major problem was the timing. I found out about the story in the afternoon, after our day's editions had already gone to press. If I telephoned the Marines for confirmation in the afternoon, there was the danger that I might actually lose the scoop. I imagined the possibility of the Marines making a general announcement to all news media that afternoon—just in time for the evening television newscasts. The morning newspapers also would be published before my next day's paper. The only choice, therefore, was to wait until the next morning to contact the Marines.

I decided to go ahead and write the story except for the Marines' comment, which I would insert the next morning. Naturally, I would change the story around if the Marines had a totally or substantially different account of what happened.

The next morning, I telephoned Marine headquarters in Washington. I still had not seen a single Panamanian, but I took the tentative position that this was accurate information. The Marine Corps' public information officer answered. I decided that my best approach was to give him the idea that we already had the facts and just wanted his version of it. I wanted to avoid the weak position of asking him if the story was true.

"We have this story ready to print today," I said. "Let me read it to you, and then I'd like to include the Marine Corps' reaction."

There was silence on the other end as I read, and his first reaction was: "How did you find out?"

Perfect, I thought. He's not disputing the facts.

"Well," I said, "it's fairly common knowledge." That was not untrue, since dozens of people knew about it in the Immigration Service, and uncounted others knew about it at Parris Island.

"I'll have to get a response from the Commandant," he said. The information officer said he would not confirm anything. He said it might take some time for him to get back to me.

I wanted him to realize that we were going to print the story right away—even if we did not get the Marines' comment. Otherwise he might stall too long. After all, the Marines had been guarding this secret for weeks.

"Hurry," I said.

Now that my hunch was confirmed, I showed the story to the assistant managing editor and the city editor. They got supremely excited. They made room on the front page. I told them I was waiting for the Marines' response.

They decided to run the story based on my judgment that my Immigration sources were solid, and then add the Marines' comment later. We put in a paragraph saying that the Marines were expected to comment later.

"Are we sure of the numbers?" the assistant managing editor asked.

I told him I believed they were accurate.

The story appeared on the front page of the second edition. We had our scoop.

It took two hours before the Marines issued a statement authorized by the Commandant. By that time we were putting out the third edition of the day. As I had imagined, the Marines released the story to everyone in Washington, and it quickly became a national story carried by the wire services. That evening, network television anchormen reported the exotic story of the alien intrusion into the proud Marines. One of the networks, NBC, sent a camera crew to Parris Island two days later.

My special assignment continued for two more days. The original story had been written entirely on the strength of secondary sources—I had not seen a single Panamanian Marine. Because of the distance between Parris Island and Atlanta, there had been not enough time for travel if the newspaper was to have a news scoop. Now, however, I packed up and, accompanied by a photographer, went to Parris Island.

We were greeted by a military barricade. The Commandant of the training base agreed to speak with us—now that the story was public—but he refused to allow us to speak with the Panamanian aliens. He maintained that since they were in our country they were sheltered by the Constitution and had a right to protection under the federal Privacy Act.

One axiom for the successful journalist is that for every problem there is a solution. You must expect obstacles. The reporter simply learns to be a problem solver. In The Panamanian Marines, the solution I came up with was to give the Panamanians an optional questionnaire that they could fill in as they wished. It would be anonymous, so it would not violate their privacy. As I had hoped, the Commandant consented. The questionnaire was typed on the spot, and photocopies were made by the Marines to be given to a select group of only about a dozen.

The Marines even allowed me to see the Panamanians as a group. I wanted to explain to them that the questionnaire was voluntary, and to encourage them to fill it out.

At last, I was taken to a room where the Panamanians had been assembled around a table. It was one of those times when I was glad that I had studied foreign languages. I assured them in Spanish that this was voluntary and anonymous. Then I left them to write. When they finished, the Marines handed me the questionnaires, and I realized that the experiment had been a success: I had some interesting statements, written in broken English. It was precious material:

- "I always wanted to be a military soldier, so I decided to join the best force there is, USMC."
- "This private wanted to be a United States Marine because from in my young days I've been watching war pictures and also the television."
- "I love the military life. My dreams is to be a soldier."
- "I always admire this country and the way of living. I love democracy. . . . The Marines are the most disciplinary branch in the armed forces. And being in the U.S. I thought that was very good idea to serve the country."
- "This private wanted to become a United States citizen because this private believe in this country, democracy, especially for his leadership. Also, this private believe in freedom and this country fights for this cause of rights."

The questionnaire had overcome the Privacy Act obstacle. I had seen the Marines and I had quotes.

The next day the story was played on page one under the headline: "A FEW GOOD MEN" MAY BE ILLEGAL ALIENS.

There were more stories as the case unfolded: Recruiters were prosecuted for having filled their enlistment quotas with illegal aliens. Many of the aliens were deported to Panama by the overworked Immigration agents who had been my original source. In the end, the Commandant kept some of the Panamanian Marines—those who proved to be "good men."

4

Ideas and Assignments

When you begin in journalism, you almost always will be working on other people's ideas. If you're lucky, their ideas will be solid and interesting, worthy of your time and energy. Whatever the case, one of the trade secrets of the journalist is the ability to "get interested" in something that half an hour earlier was of absolutely no interest. There is no substitute for this sort of blank-check enthusiasm: If you don't have it, life gets less exciting when you're suddenly assigned to interview the toothless man on a cross-country trip collecting autographs of the celebrities. In fact, if you can't get interested in other people's ideas, you ought to reconsider your choice of career.

You will have ideas of your own, of course, as you learn more about your city and its people. At the same time you will be learning what stories your editors think are worthy of space. Then you can begin offering your own suggestions for stories. Remember, of course, that your editor may like your idea and assign someone else to write it. Coming up with ideas does not make you an assignment editor.

One day's newspaper may contain dozens of local stories. Where did they all come from? Who thought of them, and how did they become assignments?

Although editors make assignments, they do not think of all the ideas. The average editor is so bound up with the responsibilities of managing personnel and organizing the flow of business that he or she has little time to go out and mix with the world. The average editor does read a lot, however. Today's news itself will suggest follow-up stories.

One of the main sources of story ideas is the reporting staff. Beat reporters in particular know what is going on in their areas of responsibility: city hall, courthouses, state legislature, police precinct houses, and schools.

The difference between an idea and an assignment is commitment. When a city editor assigns an idea to you, he or she is committing the newspaper's money and, of course, your time. Thus, although an idea may seem valuable to you, it is relatively worthless in the newsroom until some editor dignifies it with a place on a list of assignments.

After an idea matures into an assignment, editors soon list it on a budget. On many newspapers, the budget is the list of stories expected either for the next edition, or for tomorrow, or for Sunday.

The budget itself is a publication of limited circulation. Editors write and circulate their budgets to other editors so that the newspaper's lineup of stories can be evaluated for length and position in the paper. The budget normally includes a notation about in which edition the story will begin running. Like household pets, each story is christened with a name and is called by that name on the budget and in conversations about the progress of that story. The name is termed a *slug* and is usually quite short; a story about jaywalkers might be slugged "Jays." With so many stories moving through the newsroom, the editor and reporter can quickly get on the same wavelength by referring at the outset to the familiar name. Finally, the budget includes a brief summary of what the story is about, as well as a note about who is writing it and whether there are any illustrations (referred to as "art"). Often written with a tongue-in-cheek flair by the city editor or by one of the assistant city editors, the budget usually lists a wide assortment of assignments being handled by beat reporters, general assignment reporters, and special writers.

The Budget

The budget system is used extensively in newsrooms. On a major metropolitan daily, such as the *Atlanta Journal,* editors commonly revise their budgets for later editions of the paper. The editor who writes a budget attempts to put the forthcoming story in some perspective for the other editors. The following is a typically thorough budget for one edition of the *Atlanta Journal,* complete with story slugs, summaries, and assigned reporters' names. The story labeled "Kids" refers to the *Journal*'s early coverage of what eventually became known nationally as the Atlanta child murders, or the Wayne Williams murder case.

METRO REPORT—Friday, Aug. 22, 1980
COBB—Just in time for the runoff, grand jury says Cobb Western District

commissioner is not guilty of anything illegal such as using county machinery on his land—Milstein.

DEAN—Dr. James Glenn, the new dean of Emory University's medical school, says he'll remain on medicine's front line, doing surgery, and still maintain control of the troops in the trenches; an interview with the new dean—Seabrook.

DEBATE—This is the rubber match between Zell and Herman and sparks are likely to fly as the candidates get in their digs—Hayslett.

JUDGE—How the judges rate the debate—Berkeley.

DISCLOS—Financial disclosure reports reveal that several hundred agriculture workers contributed $15 to the Talmadge campaign all on the same day in what apparently was a gentle nudge from Tommy Irvin—Christensen.

KIDS—There are several similarities in the killings of six children and there are also numerous differences—we take a look at the situation, what the police have been able to determine in an effort to crack the case—Richardson.

KNIGHTS—Knights of Columbus come out against abortion, ERA, gun control, etc.; they simply made a copy of the Republican platform—Speed.

BABY—Little Diablito Wade is reunited with her mother in an emotional occasion at her home—Hughes—w/Art.

DOT—State department of transportation approves $700 million and train service between Atlanta and Savannah—Palmer.

CONSULT—Works with DISCLOS—One of Talmadge's black consultants is proving elusive; in three days he's changed his phone number three times—Christensen.

SUIT—City of Jefferson files suit in school funds dispute—Dolezal.

WHORE—*Gallery* [a men's magazine] listed an Atlanta phone number as a dial-a-whore service. Only trouble is, it isn't. It's a plastics company—Bryans.

AHA—Housing authority blocks some contracts until questions about minority hiring are resolved, sets hearing for Robert Barnett, the staffer fired for protesting the Noragem contract—Scott.

BILLY—Billy says he's hurt himself but not his brother in his dealings with Libya—Woolner.

GSU—One of three Georgia State U. professors accused of diverting university teaching fees to their private firm resigns—Berkeley.

Budgets are not meant to be full-blown stories, and you need some explanation to make full sense of the entries. The "Debate" story, for instance, came from coverage of the final debate in a series between candidates Herman Talmadge and Zell Miller in their campaign for a seat in the U.S. Senate. "Disclos" and "Consult" were scoops of sorts picked up by reporters covering the race. "Cobb," "AHA," and "GSU" were stories filed by beat reporters covering ongoing controversies in the areas of city and county governments and higher education. "Baby" was another scoop associated with a continuing story of the disappearance of a child. "Billy" was the latest chapter in the troubles of Billy Carter of Plains, Georgia, President Jimmy Carter's brother, over his involvement with the government of Libya. "Whore" was a "brite" (an entertaining feature) picked up when the owner of the plastics company called to complain about his business's being listed as a prostitution service in *Gallery* magazine.

Where do all these stories originate? Often, most budgeted stories come from the beats that the newspaper covers—city hall, the county courthouse, the state capitol, the federal courts and federal agencies, police, education, and health and science. Other assignments grow out of reporters' ideas, gleaned from what they have found to be happening around them; they may have heard about something from an anonymous caller or been told something in a restaurant, in a bar, or on the street. A few telephone calls can nail down whether there is any truth or substance in a rumor.

Follow-ups to the news contribute more stories to the lineup. Editors often keep date files in which they put newspaper clippings or notes so that they will remember to inquire about the subject in six months or a year. Perhaps one story in a hundred comes to the budget from the managing editor.

Different sections of the paper have different budgets. Whereas the news desk lists a majority of hard, or breaking, news stories, the feature department editors include fashion, travel, books, and television stories. Naturally, the sports budget would include interviews with players, as well as accounts of games.

Ideas

After you have been writing about other people's ideas for months or years, you begin to develop your own. Your success in making ideas become assignments depends greatly on how these ideas are presented. This section aims to show you how to create your own assignments so that you will often be writing about subjects that interest you. The assumption is that the best interests of a newspaper are served when the paper's needs and the writer's interests coincide.

There are eight steps that can help you refine the skill of developing and presenting your own ideas:

- List fifty ideas for stories you would like to do.
- Underline the ones you know about *and* care about.
- Whittle the list down to ten. Are some more timely? Will some be worthless if not done soon?

- Pick the best three.

- Make a list of contacts for each of the three ideas: List people who can help with information or referrals. Make sure you call them to find out timely *news* angles on each story idea. Of course, if you discover a *scoop*, give the story idea a higher rating and more urgency.

- Write a *brief* memorandum to your section editor. Just list a slug (for example, CHEF) and then a short sentence or two explaining the potential story (Chef of the most expensive, most talked-about restaurant in town is quitting to open his own restaurant). Or, MARINES: Illegal aliens from Panama discovered at Parris Island, S.C., after enlisting in U.S. Marines.

- Try to write a few headlines that sum up your stories.

- *Important:* Do not hang around your editor for immediate replies. Just turn in the memo of story ideas (you may have submitted only one idea, of course) and go about your business until your editor has considered the ideas. If your editor doesn't mention your memorandum in a day or two, just ask if he or she had a chance to read it. In this way, you will find out what the editor thinks without giving the impression that you must have an immediate reaction to every brainchild. After all, the editor has ideas, too, and ideas coming from others. Be prepared for your editor to say that the story idea is a good one, and so-and-so has been asked to do it. Often another reporter ends up working on your idea because it touches on that reporter's beat or expertise. The editor usually will be grateful for a sound and developed idea. If you keep sending ideas, eventually you will be working on a number of them yourself. Be sure to keep copies of all ideas in case, in the often chaotic newsroom, your memorandum is thrown into a waste basket.

In order to generate ideas and assignments, you do not necessarily have to be an original thinker or a genius. But you must keep your eyes and ears open. The sources of many ideas are the people you meet, and it is essential for anyone hoping to generate ideas to communicate with many different types of people. Even a buffoon has his truth, so they say, and in fact you should not necessarily ignore a contact or source who looks and talks like a fool.

Your contacts with people will improve with time, and as people become more comfortable with you, they will begin to tell you more. Sometimes you will feel that you can't say hello to one more person; think of the effort as an investment in your future. Your acquaintances will increase in number and quality, and eventually you will have a pleasant and steady flow of story ideas and assignments for yourself and others. Your cup will run over.

5

Sources and Resources

Every story begins as a stream does—from a source, obvious or hidden. The source can be as open and plainly seen as a public meeting of the city council, or it can be as private and confidential as the legendary "informed source" who wants to meet in a shadowy bar or parking garage.

When working with sources of the second kind, the successful journalist soon learns to "consider the source"—to make a judgment about the bias, or point of view, that motivates a person or group to want a story in the newspaper. The judging of sources is a critical cornerstone in the building of a career in journalism, and the ability does not always come without experience and error. One thing is clear: The journalist who does not question the motives of sources can fall into traps as surely as an animal in the wild. Without a healthy and protective skepticism about people, you will likely find your career blemished by embarrassment and, ultimately, by premature termination. In accepting information, as in buying anything, let the buyer beware.

The motives of sources are not always easy to determine. They can be complex, or multiple. One source may be obviously self-serving, as when one political candidate maligns another. Sources can be public-spirited, with no consideration of personal gain, as when a faithful public employee tells you about some abuse of power or some waste of taxpayers' money or some foolish duplication of effort. Frequently, your sources will have a combination of interests, both public and private, as in an exposé of Veterans Administration hospitals.

One of the national scandals of the era after World War II and the Korean War was the sad condition of veterans' hospitals. Newspapers and magazines across the country looked into the conditions in the hospitals and found them run down and understaffed for the great patient load. This entire tidal wave of publicity began with one source, a Congressional press secretary, who had tipped off the Washington journalists. If the journalists questioned his motives, it was not for long; they certainly couldn't question the facts. Photographs documented the national disgrace: Veterans who had answered the nation's ultimate summons to war were lying in beds in pathetic hospital wards.

Congress reacted immediately by authorizing more funds for the veterans' hospitals. The Congressional press secretary and his boss, a Congressman whose interest was in obtaining a sharp increase in funds for the hospitals, had succeeded in their enterprise. They got what they wanted by using the power of the press, by leveraging that power with the appeal to patriotism and national outrage. The result was that they competed successfully with other Congressmen so that veterans got a bigger share of the nation's revenues.

The genius of the endeavor was that nobody could deny the facts. Yet, if the Congressman had spoken publicly on the floor of the House of Representatives, the impact would have been lost. His speech would have been discounted as self-serving. By contrast, the sharing of *confidential* information, disclosed in private by a trusted and dependable authority figure, gave journalists a special sense of exclusivity and mission. The media, not the Congressman, would get credit for bringing the scandal to the public's attention. Such stories stimulated people to buy newspapers and magazines and at the same time stimulated Congress to upgrade the hospitals immediately. Since the scandal was indeed based on truth, it would presumably have been publicized by someone at some future time. By contacting the national media, the press secretary not only speeded up the process, he seized the initiative. If there was to be a scandal, his action in informing the press shifted the blame from the hospitals to Congress. The press secretary succeeded in giving the impression that the hospital administrators were not trying to hush up or hide the scandal. It was a master stroke of manipulating the press, and no journalist evidently saw any serious problem in the fact that the stories also served the Congressman's particular interests.

Journalists rely on dependable sources. One of the trade secrets of any journalist is the contact with people who confide what is happening in their realms of work and interest, whether in politics, business, or society. As such, sources are as necessary as notebooks.

In practice, journalists sooner or later learn how to manipulate sources. Here are some suggestions passed down from years of experience:

• Use sources as starting points for stories. Be sure to double-check and triple-check with other public and private sources. Do your research and find the supporting facts. Edward Sears, a managing editor for the

Atlanta newspapers, was fond of observing, "To an experienced reporter, a source quote is a tool. To an inexperienced reporter, it's a crutch."

• Maintain a skeptical attitude. Don't be reluctant to discard sources' tips if they can't be substantiated.

• Be careful with confidential sources. One reporter used to say he would pick up his hat and leave the room whenever a public official specified that his comments be "off the record." In practice, however, you will sometimes hear certain things *only* if you agree to go off the record and listen *without* quoting. If what the source says is true, you can verify it later by other sources. But if you don't listen at all, you won't know what to investigate. Once you have promised to keep a source's comments confidential, don't break your promise. Be careful not to blunder into suggesting who your source is by some inadvertent reference that can be traced to the source.

Some men and women have lost their jobs in government or business because they talked with reporters. They were traced and identified because of some published detail that only a few people could have known. In business or government bureaucracy, anyone who leaks information to a journalist is considered a disloyal troublemaker, a "whistleblower." This can happen regardless of the truth of the source's allegations, and despite the fact that the allegations might relate to a matter of important public concern. Superiors will try to locate troublemakers and either fire them or shuffle them off to some demeaning job, perhaps in a distant city, much as the Soviets occasionally send a "dissident" into exile in the walled city of Gorky far from friends. Of course, the American does not have to move, but the alternative is that he or she must quit the job.

Developing Your Sources

As you meet more people and learn your community, you should be continually alert for the people who keep up with what is happening. Develop a bookkeeping method for keeping track of these people. While methods differ, here is one you can try until you perhaps develop your personal system:

• Keep a file box of 3 × 5 cards. Use one card for each source. Be sure to list the telephone numbers for both office and home. Or, keep the same information in a small notebook you can carry with you. Or use both the file and notebook.

• Review your file cards or notebook from time to time. This helps to refresh your memory about the people you have met. If you haven't talked to a source in weeks or months, you might telephone the person, even if it's only to ask how things are going and say you're still there.

- Protect confidential sources. You may want to keep a separate file for sources who insist on confidentiality.

- Don't forget secretaries. Write down their names and numbers. Secretaries consider themselves, often rightfully, as the moving forces behind executives. If they don't *do* the executive's work, they often make sure it *gets* done. Yet secretaries are often ignored and regarded as less than professionals. The fact is that they can help you or hinder you in your efforts to reach their boss when you *need* the boss—before deadline. A helpful secretary can interrupt a meeting and put a note in front of the boss so that he or she has the opportunity of calling you at once. On the other hand, the secretary can wait until the meeting is over and your deadline is past. If the boss is out of town, the helpful secretary may tell you not only where the boss is but also give phone numbers and schedules so you can track him or her down in minutes rather than hours.

Resources and Research

Whether you are writing about a national scandal or about a local fad, the basic rule is: The more information you discover, the sounder will be your judgments and the more accurate your story. No amount of cute writing can gloss over a failure to attend to the foundations of a story through systematic research.

The need for solid research does not necessarily slow you down to a snail's pace on deadline. Today's newspapers are equipped with systematic information retrieval, often computerized for increased speed and ease. A modern newspaper's librarians are trained to be fast as well as thorough. A questionable statement or a perceived misspelling of a name can be checked quite rapidly, with the answer usually coming back before the story is finished. In any case, it is better not to publish than to publish in error. If at deadline you have some unsolved problem or unanswered question, talk to your editor about it. It is not the reporter's place to gamble.

Distinguished reporting is frequently characterized by obvious research. The journalist not only reports on what is happening, but on how the event fits in with what has gone before. Sometimes the writer includes many paragraphs of historical background. Other times, all the research has been used to put the story in perspective, but very little of the background is used. Ernest Hemingway referred to this second technique as the iceberg effect: One-eighth of what you know is showing, and seven-eighths, while quite real and important to the whole, is nevertheless submerged.

Some journalists will tell you that too much research ruins a good story. For one thing, they argue, you can gather more material than you can logically organize, and the story loses focus. Others, especially editors, contend that it is easy to over-research and delay completing the work. There are no easy answers. You must judge for yourself, because in the end your writing will be judged for speed, accuracy, and significance. After double-checking the obvious problems, you must trust your instincts about when to stop researching and start writing to beat the deadline. One writer said he knew to start writing when he started knowing more about the subject than the people he was interviewing.

The modern newspaper has a tempting array of tools for research, and librarians are rapidly adding new acquisitions to the toolbox. Here are some basic resources:

• Photocopy. Your sources often have printed materials that they can share with you to substantiate their arguments and provide you with a history of the problem. The photocopy machine has saved innumerable hours of hand copying and made it possible to rush to deadline with masses of information in hand. If you can't take the materials to the office to be copied, as with certain court and administrative papers, photocopy them near the source and put the cost on your expense account.

• Look for previous news stories about the same subject. Your newspaper's library will have them filed or on microfilm. You should read these clips before going to an interview. If you're away from the office, telephone the library, and with luck the clippings will be on your desk when you get back. You can, of course, have the facts read over the phone.

• Magazine articles can also be helpful. Some large newspapers subscribe to a computer service that quickly lists many articles published recently on your subject and tells you where to find them. Two older catalogues of previously published articles are the *Reader's Guide to Periodical Literature* and *The New York Times Index*.

• Books can be a major help in giving the reporter depth of understanding and perspective. Your library has a variety of reference books, from encyclopedias to college handbooks.

• Government agencies are often of service, particularly since almost no field of human interest is ignored by city, county, state, or federal governments. Government agencies often have a specialist doing research on your subject. Agencies also have libraries. The U.S. government publishes everything from the federal budget to a handbook on what to do if a nuclear war breaks out.

To illustrate how a reporter builds up a research file, here are two short examples and one long one:

• *The Jaywalkers.* An otherwise one-dimensional story about a promised police crackdown on jaywalkers was given some historical perspective after the reporter heard that another crackdown had occurred thirty years earlier. The librarian found the old newspaper stories on microfilm and made photocopies. In the story, the reporter practiced the iceberg technique, including only one paragraph about the earlier crackdown. The one reference was enough to make the point: The police have so much to do that their efforts against jaywalkers are few and far between.

• *The Latchkey Kids.* The story was about young children who let themselves into the house after school and stay alone until their parents return from work. From his own sources, the reporter had interviewed parents and their children, but he lacked a national perspective. The day before he finished his story, he found a national magazine quoting a husband-and-wife team of experts in Washington. A telephone call did the trick. After an hour's conversation, the reporter had all the statistics and trend information he needed. He had located the only national researcher who was systematically interviewing hundreds of latchkey kids, urban and rural, rich and poor.

• *The Alimony Seekers.* This story began on an editor's hunch that judges might be changing their views on alimony just as society's view of sex roles was changing. The newspaper's library turned up a survey of articles written recently about alimony. There were also stories about the newly created "palimony" granted to women who were not married but had been live-in lovers of the men they were suing.

The newspaper librarian provided three computer printouts. The first listed stories specifically about alimony. "Black women to be hurt more by 'reverse alimony' " was a piece published by *Jet* magazine on June 14, 1979. The *New York Times* published on March 6, 1979: "High court voids alimony laws requiring only husbands to pay." That referred to the case of *Orr v. Orr*. The *New York Times* on May 3, 1980, had another relevant story on property settlements in divorce suits. Also, "Who should pay alimony?" was an article by a divorce lawyer, Doris Sasower, in *People* magazine of March 28, 1977. The *Wall Street Journal* on November 21, 1979, carried an article headlined: " 'Additional alimony,' said their divorce pact. But those were only words." And the *New York Times* published a piece on July 2, 1979: "Census study backs divorce-trend rise; estimated four of 10 marriages will end if current levels persist."

The second and third computer printouts listed twenty articles about the most celebrated "palimony" case, the publicized contest between the actor Lee Marvin and his live-in lover, Michelle Triola Marvin. There were other stories about Ms. Marvin's pioneering lawyer, Marvin Mitchelson. The articles included those written at the time of the alimony trial and some written afterward:

- "The paladin of paramours" appeared in *Time* on January 15, 1979.
- "The bonds that tie" was a *New York Times* piece on February 25, 1979.
- "Palimony revisited" appeared July 20, 1979, in the *New York Times*.
- "Overview of the Marvin ruling; no grand guidelines set" was in the *Christian Science Monitor* of April 20, 1979.
- "Divorce Mitchelson Style," based on an interview with the lawyer, was in the *New York Times* on January 6, 1980, almost a year after the trial.
- "Marvin Mitchelson; having made 'palimony' a household threat, this legal beagle is the sultan of split" was in *People* magazine on December 24, 1979.
- "Marvin Mitchelson has progressed from 'palimony' to 'petromony': Soraya Khashoggi is suing for $2 billion" was featured in *People* on August 27, 1979.
- "Lifting of its law on cohabitation is recommended by Swiss state" was in the *New York Times* on March 22, 1980.

Finally, on the last printout were stories that dealt with strictly legal decisions and legislation regarding alimony property settlement:

- A bill before the New York state legislature would permit courts to distribute property in divorce cases in accordance with ten specific criteria, ranging from the length of marriage to the financial prospects of each spouse. The story was in the *New York Times* of May 3, 1980.
- The Maryland senate's passage of a bill allowing judges to award alimony for fixed periods of time, geared to a program of making the recipient self-sufficient, was reported in the *Washington Post* on March 9, 1980.
- West German males were suing for equal rights; divorce courts were ordering working women to support ex-husbands. This was in the *Christian Science Monitor* on February 27, 1980.
- William B. Orr, who won a Supreme Court decision establishing husbands as legal equals in divorce disputes, filed a new appeal because he gained nothing through his victory. That was carried in the *New York Times* on November 27, 1979. The index also showed: "Orr still owes former wife, Lillian, $3,312 in tardy alimony even though law under which payment was imposed was struck down by court; Lillian got Alabama court to uphold divorce decree before William could challenge it."

The librarian photocopied the *New York Times* articles from microfilm, among them the *Orr* v. *Orr* Supreme Court story, the census study article, the property settlement update, and the article about Orr's being back in court contending that his constitutional victory had gained him nothing.

There was a related local divorce case, according to the local files. In the local case, the husband was seeking alimony from the wife and had won a preliminary alimony order from the judge.

To fill in some legal gaps in the story, a lawyer supplied copies of the forms he asks divorce clients to fill in, among them a "Financial Data Sheet" and one listing the "Financial Needs of Wife and Children." This same attorney gave references to three other lawyers. One contact thus led to others.

One of those lawyers described a man she had urged to sue for alimony, how he had blushed and said he wouldn't, and how she had convinced him it was good strategy to scare off the aggressive wife.

A second lawyer provided important documents, among them the new state Divorce and Alimony law, which, among other things, ruled out "palimony" for live-in lovers. He also provided a common-sense background about alimony settlements. Finally, he shared two legal reference services he subscribed to and made photocopies of a *National Law Journal* article about an unmarried live-in lover in New Jersey who was allowed to sue for loss of consortium when her man was injured, and of two cases testing property settlements in "common law" marriages.

With this kind of research, you quickly learn the subject and ask the right questions. Based on the research technology of the computerized library, plus the professional resources of the legal profession, the story began like this:

> "Alimony?" said the woman lawyer outside the courthouse after a divorce hearing. "There's not much of that anymore."
>
> She credited the decline of alimony to "male judges," and she added, "I think it's a backlash from the women's movement."
>
> Even male judges agree somewhat. The movement for equal rights for women—and for jobs with better pay—has led to fewer gains of alimony.
>
> The fact is that alimony for the wife's support only—traditionally one of the court-ordered comforts of divorce—is no longer something to be counted on.

The alimony story, because of the wide reach of the research, developed into a story with more than local significance. Indeed, stories of national significance often are developed in just this way through thorough research that leads to justifiable generalizations.

Whether the scope of your story is local or national, this combination of dependable sources and painstaking research makes for solid journalism.

6

Covering Government

A clever Associated Press writer once demonstrated that from the moment we open our eyes in the morning until we close them at night, our lives are regulated by government. Ordinances, laws, and regulations govern the broadcast that comes over the alarm clock radio and the packaging of the food in our midnight snack.

It comes as no surprise that the journalist sooner or later must learn how government works and how it serves people or regulates them. Throughout a reporter's career, hardly a story comes along that does not connect to some council or board or court or agency on the great government tree. The sooner you learn how government works and who pulls which strings, the easier your work will become.

While some reporters merely look for connections between their stories and government agencies, the government reporter works from the inside out, having been trained to discover how government will affect the person in the street. Whether at the city police station, county courthouse, the state court, or a federal agency, the government reporter has one main challenge every day: to uncomplicate his or her subject and translate it speedily into terms understandable wherever the newspaper is read.

The beginning reporter who is assigned to report the actions of this huge government might easily be overwhelmed by the immensity of the beast. Federal bureaucrats, for instance, count by the trillions and casually regard millions as "drops in the bucket." Many city halls can also count to a million.

What protects the beginning reporter from massive confusion is his or her own personal routine. All governments proceed according to a certain routine, and so must the government reporter. Those journalists who have successfully organized their work into a *system* have ended up understanding more about government than most of the people working there.

Tools of the Trade

Whatever your governmental beat, there is no substitute for good organization. You will save yourself countless hours and catch an unexpected story now and then if you are organized in mind and have at your immediate use a box of fundamental tools.

First among the journalist's tools is the notebook. On government beats, notebooks, like tax records, must be accurate and ought to be kept in some sort of filing system. You can refer to them weeks or even months after the story has been written. Legible handwriting is important. Whether you use pen or pencil is a personal matter; most reporters use pens.

Your ability to locate governmental officials when you need them, day or night, will depend largely on how well you have kept an index file of telephone numbers for their offices and homes. One way to accumulate office numbers in a hurry is to ask your governmental unit for its directory of employees. The directory of federal employees, for example, lists every agency and its various employees according to function, such as: Department of Justice/Immigration and Naturalization Service/Deportation Section/Joe Browne, Director, 555-0001. Home numbers are usually not provided, so it is your task to collect them. There are few tasks more frustrating than trying to locate a public official when you are on deadline and he or she has gone home for the weekend.

If your governmental agency has no directory, you must build a name/phone file from scratch. Add to your collection of names as you make your daily rounds of key offices. One simple way to build a file is to buy a 3 × 5 index card file box and use one card for each name. By filing the names by agency, you will soon know different players on the same team. It is important to consider which of these contacts are special sources you will rely on frequently. When other reporters ask you for numbers and you can give them, you know you've done your homework properly. Don't hesitate to ask the city editor and other reporters to share their telephone numbers.

The city telephone book is an obvious tool. Less obvious is the city street directory. If you know *where* a fire occurred, for example, you can look up the listing for that street and block and call the telephone numbers of the people who live in the same apartment building or across the street. In this manner, one reporter was able to get quick eyewitness accounts of the action outside a bank where tellers were held hostage by two robbers.

One other tool will help you to organize time: the futures file. Organized by month and day, it holds your notes about upcoming meetings, hearings, and other events. You simply open it to the date and pull out the reminders.

Separation of Powers

The American system of checks and balances in government separates the roles of various governmental officials. The city, county, state, and federal governments all divide power and authority, with certain officials authorized to perform three essentially different functions: executive (or administrative), legislative (lawmaking), and judicial (the courts). This separation of powers works to the advantage of the reporter. The executive branch is sometimes at odds with the legislative branch, and there are times when both are at odds with the judicial. A government reporter can develop an interesting story by showing how the branches of government disagree with one another—a healthy sign of the *balance of power*. On the other hand, beware of the limitations of your story if you have not sought to discover any conflicts between branches of government. The exciting new ideas of the education commissioner, for instance, may be immediately opposed by the governor.

At the federal level, the chief executive is the president of the United States, and the president's authority is represented in every city outside Washington by appointed executive bureaucrats. The federal legislative branch, the Congress, is also visible on the local level wherever the local Congressman has an office. The federal judicial branch is headed by the nine justices of the U.S. Supreme Court, but throughout the nation there are other lower federal courts: the courts of appeal, the district courts, and, lowest of all, the magistrate courts.

At the state level, the executive branch is headed by the governor, whose appointees head the state bureaucracy. The legislative branch is the state legislature, which hires hundreds more state employees accountable directly to the legislature. The state judicial system is headed by the state supreme court, and beneath that are tiers of appeals courts and criminal and civil courts.

On the county level, the executive and legislative branches are often uniquely combined in a *county commission* headed by a commission chairman. In some jurisdictions, however, a *county executive* is appointed by the commission or elected to handle day-to-day administration of the county government. Whether appointed or elected, the county executive generally follows the legislative policy set by the commissioners. The judicial branch is represented by the county courts.

What follows is a panoramic view of the four levels of government (city, county, state, and federal) and the various branches you are likely to encounter as you cover the government.

City Government

POLICE AND FIRE DEPARTMENTS.   The city police department and fire department usually are the first two agencies you deal with as a beginning reporter. They are sometimes merged into a public safety department.

In the police department, there is no substitute for "making the rounds," from the radio room to the police chief's office. Listening to the police radio regularly is an almost certain way of hearing about trouble as it happens. The sooner you alert your newsroom, the quicker the editors can assign a photographer to the crime scene. On your rounds, you need to talk with police officers and read their crime reports to discover less obvious developments. Similarly, check with the detectives on their investigations of murders, thefts, and flim-flams. Don't forget to talk to the victims of the crimes, and even to the accused when possible.

Fire departments can be covered less exhaustively. They don't have much going on when there is no fire, and when there *is* a fire, they attract attention by making a lot of noise. Regular telephone calls to the fire departments will tell you whether there's been a fire worth reporting.

COURT.   The types of cases handled by the city court vary, but frequently these are of two basic categories: (1) serious crimes, such as murder and rape, which are quickly passed on ("bound over") to the jurisdiction of a higher court—usually a state superior court or circuit court—and (2) minor felonies and misdemeanors, such as aggravated assault and battery and public drunkenness, and violations of the city housing code. Some cities have special traffic courts to handle traffic violations.

CITY HALL.   The city hall reporters are concerned with politics as much as with hard news. The reporter tries to learn not only what has been done but also who is behind it and why the mayor or city council vote the way they do.

COUNCIL.   Most stories about the city are written about public action taken in open meetings—along with what the various council members said before and after. Never draw back from approaching a council member to ask whether you heard him or her correctly or to ask whether he or she will clarify a stated position for you.

The city hall reporter frequently writes stories about the council, which in some jurisdictions is called the board of aldermen or city commission. Beginning with something the reporter has learned at a council meeting, he or she can ask questions and develop a "follow up" to the remarks. Also, during political years, there are occasional stories involving election politics, as council members jockey for other political offices, such as that of mayor.

MAYOR.   In most large cities, the mayor is the head of the government and chief executive of the city bureaucracy of various departments—from the police and fire departments to the departments of parks, streets, and finance. In other cities, an appointed city manager is hired to run the bureaucracy. Still other cities have city commissioners who run various segments of the bureaucracy.

Sometimes a newspaper assigns one reporter to cover only the mayor's office, to watch who goes in and out, and to follow the mayor and chief aides on some of the mayor's speaking engagements.

Bureaucracies tend to confuse, even at the city level. In the city bureaucracy there are hundreds of employees, each one working for a higher official who ultimately reports to the mayor. The best way to handle the city bureaucracy is to get a city government directory complete with names and telephone numbers and keep it handy. When you meet a new bureaucrat, enter his or her name in your notebook and remember when that person can be of help. Remember, one bureaucrat can refer you to another one who can be of more help.

BOARD OF EDUCATION.   Perhaps no beat in government offers as much variety as the board of education and the school system. One day you will be writing about the board of education meeting; the next day you will be visiting children in classrooms to see how the school system identifies its gifted learners. Parents want to know how the school is teaching their children, and parents and all taxpayers want to be told how much they are being taxed and where the taxes are going. The fleet of school buses, the availability of school lunches, the school's policies about cigarette smoking, honors programs, and job training—these and many more stories are generated by the education beat. Perhaps no other beat requires that so many different viewpoints be considered—from the school board and superintendent's views to those of teachers, students, and parents, to those of secretaries, custodians, cafeteria workers, and school-bus drivers.

In recent years, boards of education in large cities have spent thousands of hours correcting the effects of racial desegregation. Busing of children, quality education, hiring of black teachers in predominantly white schools, and hiring of black principals—all of these matters have been subjects for numerous stories. Some cases have been in the courts, and it has been necessary for the education writer to learn his or her way around the court system to find out when the judge makes a decision that will affect the city's school system.

County Government

THE COUNTY COMMISSION. The county commission may vary in size from one person to a group of five or more. The commission is charged with governing all parts of the county not included in a city—the "unincorporated" areas of the county.

Covering the county commission and its staff can be a full-time job. County commission meetings, like city council meetings, require careful attention and some advance homework. With both, you can check to see what is coming up on the agenda, and you are likely to have a story in *advance* of the meeting, telling your readers what is expected to be considered. Never make the mistake of predicting what the commission (or council) will do.

Be alert for hidden politics. One alert reporter uncovered a series of land deals in which the county commission chairman used his influence to have roads built across his land.

BUREAUCRACY. The county, like the city, is often organized by departments. Counties are responsible for property tax appraisals and tax collections. The county assessor and the county collector therefore are two sources of stories that probably will be well read. Likewise, the county zoning board (cities also have zoning boards, usually) is a source of stories about people who want zoning changes and are pitted against others who battle to retain the existing zoning. The county building office is where you can find statistics on whether construction of houses is decreasing or increasing—one of the measures of recession or boom.

POLICE, FIRE, AND SHERIFF'S DEPARTMENTS. The county public safety authorities patrol and keep the peace in areas of the county outside the incorporated cities. Where there is a county police department, the sheriff's department is usually responsible only for running the jail and serving court papers for the judges. If there is no county police agency, the sheriff is the main law enforcement officer in the unincorporated county. County fire departments vary a great deal, and their main problem is being responsible for an area that is often very large, which necessitates their having to answer calls in remote places. Often counties also rely on volunteer firemen.

BOARD OF EDUCATION. The county board of education, much like the city board, is a focal point for many types of stories. The alert reporter at a board meeting will think of several story ideas that can be followed up after the meeting. One offhand remark by a concerned parent can lead to a major story; the reporter has only to get the name of the parent and the phone number and follow up after the meeting.

State Government

GOVERNOR'S OFFICE.   Usually one of the most reliable journalists is assigned to the Capitol beat to cover the governor's office. Very often it is a reporter who is also qualified to write about politics, about the legislature, and about the state supreme court. This is logical, because an action by the governor almost always affects the legislature or the courts, or both, and it is beneficial for the reporter to explain the impact of the action.

The Capitol beat focuses on the governor when the legislature is not in session. Sometimes the Capitol reporter travels with the governor.

BUREAUCRACY.   The machinery of the state government grinds on whether the governor is in or out of town. The state's bureaucrats, organized around functions such as health, education, transportation, and labor, have their own work to do carrying out the existing laws and enforcing them.

POLICE OR HIGHWAY PATROL.   The state police are a central source of information for the entire state. They tabulate traffic statistics, including the death tolls on weekends and holidays. They have a statewide radio network and can be helpful in writing statewide stories, such as those of the escape of a prisoner or the approach of a winter storm.

At headquarters, the state police usually operate a crime laboratory for the analysis of crime evidence.

LEGISLATURE.   A Southern thinker once said that when the state legislature is in session, making laws and voting taxes, no one's life or property is safe. It is true that a legislator can pass a bill faster than a quarterback can pass a football if the proper political pressures are being applied. So it takes an alert and able reporter to cover this territory.

In some states, the legislature meets year round. In others, the session is held for only forty to ninety days each year, and the legislators work furiously toward the end of the session to pass their favorite bills. A major newspaper will send a staff of several reporters to cover different aspects of the legislative session. It takes a quick and informed writer to size up who is pushing a bill. The legislative reporter keeps his or her lines of communication open to sources in the governor's office to learn as much as possible about what the governor wants or does not want in the way of legislation.

COURTS. State courts are generally divided into two levels. The lower court handles the wide range of civil matters, from lawsuits to marriages and divorces. This branch of the courthouse is also the repository for property deeds and other records. The second branch is usually called the superior court, and this is where serious felony cases are tried. Murder trials are held in such state courts. If convicted, the defendant appeals to a state court of appeals and, after that, to the state supreme court.

There are at least three ways to make sure you have not missed a major story in superior court:

1. Each day check the new civil lawsuits being filed by individual citizens.

2. Check regularly with the various court clerks and with the secretary of each of the judges for the list of upcoming trials, both civil and criminal.

3. Visit the district attorney—the usual title of the chief public prosecutor—to find out what sorts of cases his or her lawyers are preparing for trial. Get to know the assistant district attorneys. If they learn to trust you, they will often tell you about a case "off the record." Even though you cannot print what they tell you off the record, the information will be invaluable to you as background and will keep you from making some naïve mistake. Some judges will speak with reporters, but almost always off the record. They fear that something they say might jeopardize a case; more often, judges simply do not discuss a case pending before their courts.

One of the continuing debates concerning court coverage is the "fair trial vs. free press" controversy. Simply put, this is the conflict between the reporter's right to know and the judicial sanctity of the courtroom. Down through the years, some judges have imposed gag rules barring newspeople from reporting some aspects of trials. In other cases, reporters have been barred from the trial entirely. Judges have fined and jailed reporters for various perceived threats to a fair trial.

Each case is different, and your managing editor eventually will be the one who decides what to do. But it is important to remember that there is a tightrope you walk between reporting the news and violating the legal rights of a defendant. In court, all men and women are judged equal before the bar of justice, even if they've been caught red-handed. Double check your facts. You cannot take too many pains to verify your information. One court reporter wrote a story about a jury verdict after receiving information by telephone. The headline the next morning read: KILGORE CONVICTED. The truth was that Kilgore had not been convicted. The judge had declared a mistrial, and Kilgore had to be tried again. Six months later, another jury brought back a verdict that at last justified the KILGORE CONVICTED head-line. But by then the unfortunate reporter had been reassigned to a suburban beat.

Federal Government

THE FEDERAL BUREAUCRACY.   The federal government reaches into every locality with the long arms of its bureaucracy. Its thousands of federal bureaucrats in each state work for middle bureaucrats who in turn answer to Washington bureaucrats who report to the president.

Here again, as with city hall and the state bureaucracy, the reporter needs a directory with names, job titles, and telephone numbers, as well as his or her own index file of who does what and who is most helpful.

Hardly any aspect of human life, from poverty and education to nuclear energy and military defense, is overlooked by the federal government. The federal government regulates radio and television broadcasts, collects the largest share of taxes of any government, and spends more money than any of them. There are endless numbers of stories for the ambitious and energetic reporter. Very often, the federal beat reporter will turn up a national story because the agency in his or her local jurisdiction is almost always operating on a national directive. What the agency does in any locality often mirrors the overall national orders.

Federal agencies possess exhaustive amounts of background materials for almost any story. Federal employees are usually willing to photocopy documents and mail booklets and other materials that you need for background.

U.S. MAGISTRATE'S COURT.   This is the lowest court in the federal court system, and one of the most helpful for the reporter. It is the intake court, to which a newly charged defendant is first brought by federal authorities to hear the charges and to make application for a bond. In such major federal cases as air piracy, drug smuggling, and counterfeiting, the reporter learns at this one hearing all that's needed for the first day's story. First, the defendant is there to be seen. Second, the defendant is told the exact nature of the alleged crime. And third, the defendant must reveal personal and financial history in order to qualify to be given a bail bond. All this helps the reporter's story immensely. In addition, federal agents must file affidavits describing certain circumstances about the crime. In one such affidavit, Federal Bureau of Investigation agents said that the accused bank robber had flown to Atlanta, drunk a couple of Bloody Marys for lunch, then robbed the bank and changed clothes in a university library before taking the plane home again to Tampa. That sort of detailed background guaranteed a front-page story about this casual caper. In state court there is no guarantee of such a preliminary hearing because bond is often set informally, without such rules of disclosure. After the federal bond hearing, the U.S. Magistrate handles preliminary matters until the case is ready to be referred for trial in the next higher court, U.S. District Court.

U.S. DISTRICT COURT.   This is the court in which criminal cases are tried before juries. It is also the court where civilians sue under federal law for recovery of accident damages (as when injured by a Secret Service agent's car) or copyright infringements or violation of civil rights.

The major trials in U.S. court history have occurred here, trials concerned with such interstate crimes as mail fraud, kidnapping, murder of federal postal employees, acceptance of bribes, counterfeiting, and air piracy.

U.S. COURT OF APPEALS.   Quiet and tame by comparison with the lower courts, the U.S. Court of Appeals is a forum for lawyers only. Defendants seldom, if ever, appear. Often they are in prison in another state, hoping that their appeals will be heard favorably. The appeals judges customarily have read the trial transcripts, and they can ask the lawyers any questions that may arise. This is a court for quiet, dispassionate judicial review of a conviction.

The U.S. Court of Appeals also hears *civil* cases, such as utility rates disputes, in which damages—but no crime—are at stake.

An important thing to remember is that the U.S. Court of Appeals is a *deliberative* court of *judges*, not of juries. The judges make no quick decisions; they issue their verdicts weeks or months after hearings. The alert reporter will keep in touch with the clerk of the court about particular decisions. When the U.S. Court of Appeals overturns a jury verdict of the U.S. District Court, the reporter often has a good story, as when the court rejected the first jury conviction of the kidnapper of the former *Atlanta Constitution* editor Reg Murphy.

U.S. ATTORNEY.   As on the state level, it is important to make regular visits to the lawyers who prosecute criminal cases and assist in investigations. At the federal level, this is the office of the United States Attorney. Although not able to divulge the tactics of the office's team of prosecutors, the U.S. Attorney can discuss the general strategy of his or her administration and tell you when certain cases can be expected to go to trial.

MEMBERS OF CONGRESS.   Naturally, the closest coverage of your Representative will be done by the Washington reporters. But members of Congress maintain local offices, which they visit occasionally, and it is helpful to meet them and the local staff. Even if your beat is not the federal government, your Representative is a source of a world of information that is virtually yours for the asking. Sometimes you can get what you need by talking with the press secretary or aides.

U.S. SENATOR.   Since there are only two U.S. Senators for each state, they tend to be harder to reach. But it is worth the effort to try for a Senator's comments. If the Senator does talk with you occasionally, your stories will carry a certain weight and flavor.

These, then, are the main divisions of government in the United States. Learning the forms is clearly important, but the beginning reporter on any of these beats may sense that there is a significant difference between the forms and the actual *working* of government. Experience teaches the reporter that the determining ingredient in every community, at every level of government, is always the character of the individual men and women who run the legislature, the courts, or city hall. On the national level, it is easier to understand that the character of the government is very much set by the president. But this is true as well at the state, county, and local levels. Learning who is supposed to do what is only the beginning of the work of the government reporter.

7

Allied Arts

Newspapers have been publishing photographs for more than one hundred years. What was once a revolutionary novelty has become one of the most common elements of modern journalism, successful and indispensable. With few exceptions, editors every day search for the best photographs to illustrate dozens of stories. Their aim is to turn out newspaper pages with an attractive and effective mix of bold headlines, masses of type, and eye-catching images. Usually there is no shortage of photographs. Most newspapers hire photographers and subscribe to wirephoto services that transmit images electronically from around the world.

There are several reasons why the writer needs to learn as much as possible about the world of photography. For instance, very often editors elevate a story to centerpiece position on a front page because it has the best art—it is the best illustrated of the stories that could possibly be displayed there. Another equally important story may thus often be placed on an inside page mainly because the photography was not as good.

Writers ought not to be handicapped by ignorance of the visual arts, particularly photography. Naturally, the reporter will concentrate hardest on words. Specialization of labor does not mean, however, that one cannot take an interest—if not an active role—in how the illustrations for stories are planned and carried out.

As you will see, there are many opportunities for the writer and the photographer to become allies in the art of journalism. Often, photographers welcome the reporter's comments about what the main points of the story will be; the more information the photographer has, the more alert he or she can be to the possibilities in a situation. Frequently the best solution is for the two to travel together.

The pictures can be a definite help to the reporter while he or she is still writing. The camera is not faster than the eye, but it does freeze the action and allow for careful study of a scene. It is not untrue that a picture is worth a thousand words. Look at photographs as you would evidence, and let them generate words for your stories.

Photography is just one of the allied arts that newspapers employ to heighten the force of the writer's words. Where photographers are forbidden to go, as for instance they are in some states' courtrooms, editors frequently turn to sketch artists. Slipping quietly into the spectators' seats, the artist uses dozens of pencils to sketch the drama.

Another device for illustrating stories is the graph. Economic stories frequently are easier to explain with a graph, as, for instance, the article about a two-year low in the stock market's Dow Jones Industrial Average.

Maps, too, can be helpful in illustrating the exact location of out-of-the-way towns. The crash of a jetliner at New Hope, Georgia, for instance, required the publication of a map showing where New Hope was in relation to the nearest big city, Atlanta.

But by far the most appealing and effective illustration is the photograph. The presentation of such visual reality establishes an immediate bond of believability and familiarity with the reader of the printed page. Photographs bring to the reader's eye the faces of people who might otherwise never be so widely seen.

The reporter who hopes that his or her own stories will have the greatest possible impact and be prominently displayed ought to pay attention to all these allied arts—the sketch, the graph, the map, and, most importantly, the photograph. The reporter who is always alert for the possibilities of illustrating the story will be more valuable to the editor, just as a versatile athlete is more valuable to the coach and the team.

Following are some rules that can help you in becoming more aware of how to illustrate your stories as you go about your main task of research and writing.

1. Ask yourself from the beginning of any assignment: How can this story be illustrated? List the principal characters as you proceed. Which ones should you try to have photographed? The sooner you can answer these questions, the better for the story. A remarkable photograph can win a center display for the story even before the article is finished.

2. Give the photographer as much information as possible about your story, except of course on highly sensitive or secretive assignments. If assignment cards are used, fill it in with the names of the important subjects, as well as the types of poses or candid shots you want. Don't forget to write down directions on how to find houses; addresses are often not enough. Include a telephone number.

3. Arrange to go with the photographer, or meet him or her at the scene, and work as a team if possible. You will discover that teamwork tends to improve your story as well as the photographs, partly because you are seeing your story from one other viewpoint, through the eyes of a photojournalist. The photographer can question you as you go along. Often, a situation develops that offers unforeseen picture possibilities. Don't forget that you can suggest some shots. You need only to stay out of the camera's way when the photographer is busy.

4. Study photography. You will never regret the expense of buying a camera, or the time spent studying the art involved with composition, or the technology of the different lenses, wide-angle to telephoto. The photographer usually will be glad to give you a tip or two.

5. Don't interfere with the photographer. Trying to boss one is like trying to grab the steering wheel from a driver. The photographer is likely to pull away and resent your amateurish interference. Don't suggest that you could have taken better photographs, although you may have reason to believe it to be true. Certainly if you feel strongly about a certain shot, there are ways of bringing it to the photographer's attention tactfully. So much depends on your working relationship. You can, of course, beg, or ask for a personal favor. You can even offer to pay for the picture. If you have a camera and see a good picture that will help you in your writing, take the photograph yourself, quietly, without fanfare. The amateur who competes with the professional runs into trouble quickly. Your reputation will travel.

The following are some cases in which photography made a difference. The result was a good package of words and pictures.

• *The Photogenic Clerk.* For a story about the half-dozen fleabag hotels in Atlanta's downtown area, the reporter visited them before making a photographic assignment. Then he accompanied the photographer, explaining as they went what he had found at each place and whom they were likely to encounter. Inside each lobby, the reporter went about interviewing people and the photographer was on his own to snap the shots that caught the mood. By luck, they encountered a white-bearded desk clerk who agreed to pose on the balcony of the run-down Falcon Hotel. It was a splendid portrait that would never have been taken if the reporter and photographer, Michael Crain, had not worked as a team. Of all the pictures taken, that was the one the editors preferred.

• *The Underexposed Team.* At a high school where the boys' basketball team nearly always won the championship, the girls' team was constantly neglected, even during its best year. It was not a routine sports story but a feature. The writer worked with different photographers on three

Joe Benton/the *Atlanta Journal*

occasions, two practice sessions and a game. At halftime, Joe Benton, the photographer, was permitted to shoot while the coach talked to the girls in their locker room. The combination provided an intimate and exciting look at female athletes on the way toward a championship of their own.

   • *The Razing of the Ritz.* This was a follow up to the fleabag hotel story. The owners of one of the old places suddenly ordered its demolition to make way for a revenue-producing parking lot. It was another instance of teamwork. The photographer took pictures of the rubble and was about to leave. The reporter took one last look, poking his head past the demolished front door. It was then he noticed that the hotel sign, which distinguished the building, was dangling just behind the front wall. It was twisted but clearly readable. The photographer, Cheryl Bray, stretched inside and got the perfectly evocative and symbolic picture of the rubble in the background and, in the foreground, this battered sign with the name "Ritz" and only the "Ho" of "Hotel." It was this last picture that the editors thought told the whole story.

   • *The Lone Reindeer.* Sometimes the mission fails because the photographer doesn't succeed in perceiving the essence of the story. A second-

Cheryl Bray/the *Atlanta Journal*

grade writing class had written some Christmas stories, and the reporter was selecting parts of them for a holiday feature. The photographer asked the children to line up in a row, and the pictures were rejected by the editor because the kids looked too posed and stiff. A second photographer, Jerome McClendon, got into the mood of the story. He relaxed the kids by squatting on the floor. He took pictures as they read, and these caught the spirit:

cute faces but also intent, absorbed minds engrossed in storytelling and listening.

• *The Moving Truck.* Often the reporter can help the photographer in more than one way when a picture possibility occurs spontaneously. In this case, photographer Joe Benton was driving a car when he saw a photograph he wanted to shoot—the scene in the moving pickup truck ahead of him. He asked the reporter to hand him a telephoto lens and he snapped the lens while guiding the steering wheel with his knees. While he took the several shots, the reporter reached over and lent a hand to steady the wheel.

• *The Punctual Pigeons.* This story was about pigeons in a downtown park. It is another example of the value of planning. The reporter staked out the park and watched the people. Each morning he noticed that a man in a tweed hat arrived with a bag of food for the birds. He came each morning punctually at about 8:15. The pigeons evidently recognized him; some picked him out from half a block away. On the fourth day, photographer Nancy Mangiafico was also there. She picked the best spot to wait. There would be only a few seconds in which to get the best picture— hundreds of pigeons flying down from the ledges, darkening the sky. The photographer decided to use a motor-driven camera. The reporter kept a lookout for the man in the tweed hat. When the birds flew, she fired the motor and quickly shot several frames. The best of the pictures delighted the editors. The picture showed the mass of birds in different phases of soaring

Joe Benton/the *Atlanta Journal*

and landing, their wings forming various feathered configurations against the morning sky.

• *The High Stockbroker.* A reporter writing about stockbrokers soon realized that their offices were all high in the skyscrapers. When it was time to photograph one of the main characters, the reporter suggested that the photographer try to show *both* the broker and the view from his twenty-seventh-floor window.

• *Working in the Dark.* A writer wanted to convey the feeling of Atlanta's downtown in the two hours before dawn when people are just beginning to stir. One photographer attempted the assignment, but he used a flash attachment, which tended to brighten the natural scenes, alter the mood, and produce pictures of sleepy but startled people. Far more successful was Louie Favorite, who used a tripod and a slow shutter speed; his best photograph showed the line of the street lights against the dark sky. One man was crossing the shadowy street, evidently on his way to work with his lunch bag, and another figure stood calmly in the middle of the street while one car passed.

• *Little Nell.* The story was to show how churches had not abandoned Atlanta's downtown. One congregation, for instance, helped the poor through a free children's medical clinic. On the way to the church, the reporter told the photographer that he hoped they would find a poor child much like the Charles Dickens character Little Nell. The photographer, George Clark, found such a girl and took an unposed picture of her curled in her father's arms.

Louie Favorite/the *Atlanta Journal*

• *Strangers in a Strange Land.* There is a world of difference between candid photographs and posed ones. Even when the subjects know they are being photographed, there is an opportunity for spontaneous shots. The arrival of a Laotian refugee family in rural south Georgia was the occasion for a story in the *Thomasville Times-Enterprise.* While the reporter interviewed the strangers about their long journey, the photographer wandered around the room and got a touching portrait of the gentle father and his watchful daughter.

• *The Professor.* Sir Angus Wilson, the British novelist, came to America as a visiting professor at various universities during the 1970s. He taught the English novel at Georgia State University in Atlanta, and the *Atlanta Journal-Constitution* devoted half a page to a question-and-answer interview with him. Sir Angus's responses during the interview were wonderfully candid—about how he began by writing short stories on weekends, how he sometimes writes outdoors with the birds—and it was important to have an equally candid photograph. The writer on the story and the photographer, Minla Linn, worked together, conferring before she went to take his picture. Linn took a serious interest in the assignment, and her photo-

Minla Linn/the *Atlanta Journal*

graph of Sir Angus, while he was lecturing in class, suggests that he was practically unconscious of her ranging around the room. Afterwards he said it was one of the best photographs ever taken of him.

• *Election Day.* Photographs sometimes can tell a story without words (almost). In November, 1980, reporters and photographers stationed themselves at the hometown of President Jimmy Carter in Plains, Georgia.

Jerome McClendon/the *Atlanta Journal*

Among the photographers was Jerome McClendon of the *Atlanta Journal.* "It was the dawn of election day," McClendon recalled, "and an exhausted president had returned to his tiny hometown to vote. Only a handful of people knew what Jimmy Carter knew when he spoke to a group of supporters at the old Plains train depot. His closest advisers had told him that the latest polls showed he would be defeated. Carter told the crowd, 'I've tried to honor my commitment . . .' Grimacing to fight back tears, he continued, '. . . to you. God bless you. Thank you.'" McClendon's stunning portrait of a defeated president was published that afternoon, before the polls closed. From the *Atlanta Journal,* the Associated Press circulated it around the country and across the Atlantic, where it appeared in AP member newspapers across Europe the next day. Subsequently, it was published by *Life* magazine at the end of the year and was judged a winner of a national Associated Press award. McClendon's photograph showed more than words could say: The president knew before the polls had opened that he had lost.

• *The Unexpected Visitors.* Jack Potts had become a celebrity in the media as a convicted murderer who was not resisting his death sentence. His execution was to be the first in Georgia in almost twenty years. Well before the scheduled execution, prison officials permitted reporters and photographers to visit the prison and photograph the electric chair. An *Atlanta Constitution* reporter, Chester Goolrick, and a photographer, Louie Favorite, also toured the rest of the prison. On a quiet upstairs floor, in an isolated cell, they saw a man they recognized as Potts. Potts invited them to photograph him inside his cell, and the prison officer did not object. The photograph portrayed the restricted world of the condemned man: his attention to religion, with the crucifix and rosary on the walls, and his attention to communication, evidenced by a tape recorder, radio, headphones, writing materials, and snapshots near the bed. Weeks after the picture was taken, Potts changed his mind and lawyers succeeded in blocking his date with the electric chair.

• *The Whiskered Woman.* Sometimes there is no way to predict what sort of pictures to take. In writing about the people who come to the city's bail bond district, a reporter discovered that the mood of the neighborhood was different every time he went. It depended on the weather and which of the transient people appeared there by chance. He went with two photographers. On a sunny day, they found a man named Honey who leaned against one of the buildings and talked about having seen spirits. The photographer snapped a stunning portrait of Honey with the bonding house window behind him. On another day, when it was raining, a second photographer went along and they found no one on the sidewalks. But inside a pool hall they found a whiskered woman named Coot. She smiled for the picture, which showed two men in the background playing pool. The two different character studies of Honey and Coot guaranteed that people would notice the story.

- *The Unknown Convicts.* Some assignments are so vague that it is a waste of time to take a photographer until the story can be focused. Such was the assignment to write a story about a prison graveyard. The reporter spent two hours walking between rows of graves. The prison chaplain showed him a few markers overgrown with grass. Pushing back the grass, the reporter found his story and his picture: a grave marked: "UNKNOWN 1926." In filling out the photo assignment, the reporter said he wanted an extreme closeup of only that marker and a portrait of the chaplain who would lead him to the spot.

- *Country Boy in the City.* This was the story of a man who led two lives: He had left the country to find work in the city, and for thirty years he had been going back to his country church, many miles distant. In the city he was a downtown streetsweeper. In his church, to which he traveled one Sunday a month, he was a deacon. The reporter accompanied the same photographer to take pictures of the streetsweeper on his city route, and the deacon peering into his church in the country.

- *The Vanishing Mourner.* As mentioned previously, it is often important for the reporter to have a camera and be able to use it. A reporter was assigned to write about a downtown liquor store where the manager and his assistant had been killed in a weekend holdup. At the liquor store, an old man happened to come by and was told that the manager had been killed. The old man's eyes opened wide and his mouth dropped: "God-damn! Why does a man want to kill two good men like that? . . . And killed 'Shorty' too? He needs burning, whoever did this. I don't care if it's my brother." The old man's shock made him the focal point for the story about the two victims. The reporter took pictures of the old man with the liquor store behind him. The old man soon wandered off. He couldn't be kept there until a staff photographer arrived. The editor was glad to have the reporter's photographs.

Very often the most effective illustration is drawn art. In the following cases, the editors chose to publish drawings, charts, and maps.

- *The Prison Journal.* Prisoners seldom want their photographs published in newspapers. At best, they sometimes consent to a back-of-the-head portrait or a silhouette, neither of which is particularly desirable. One inmate at a state women's prison was so concerned with protecting her anonymity that she chose a fictional name for a series of stories featuring excerpts from her detailed diary. In this case, a newspaper staff artist drew a graphic design that could be used to identify each day's installment in the series. With the two words "Prison Journal," it showed prison bars in the background. In the foreground was a woman's hand writing in her diary.

• *The Composite Courtroom.* Judges usually do not permit cameras in their courtrooms. The courtroom has long been the realm of the sketch artist. Actually, such journalistic artists have developed the skill to a high degree and can render more than one aspect of the courtroom in the same sketch. They can rearrange the participants for a more effective composition, as did an artist who drew portraits of the three defendants in a murder trial; the artist portrayed them each in perfect profile. In another case, the same artist arranged a composite of three interesting elements: the judge, the defendant who was charged with armed robbery, and, in a circled inset, the revolver admitted into evidence. The revolver in the inset was drawn in detail with the evidence tag attached by a string to the trigger guard.

• *The Morning Mass.* The dark interior of a Catholic church during early morning mass would pose a problem for a photographer. Such a low-light situation would call for either flashbulbs or a tripod, both of which would be out of place during worship. The sketch artist, Guy Robinson, could draw quietly without disturbing the congregation. He concentrated on three elements: an old woman kneeling in her pew, a sketch of the church's inside chapel behind her, and an exterior view of the church spire with the moon setting just before dawn.

• *The Toll Gate.* The economics writer Paul W. MacAvoy once proposed in the *New York Times* that the United States ought to consider a tax on imports of crude oil. David G. Klein, a staff artist, caught the spirit of the article with his illustration of an oil tanker being stopped at a toll gate.

• *The Before and After Composer.* To illustrate an essay about what makes composers stop composing, John Howard gave the *New York Times* a two-paneled drawing. On the left was the composer Gioacchino Rossini in full vigor, standing with his pen poised during the creative period when he wrote thirty-nine operas in two decades. In the right-hand panel, Howard depicted the composer seated and musing, pen idly under his hand. The paper is blank.

Statistics tend to confuse the reader. Very often business stories about economic trends are best explained by graphics: charts, bar graphs, and line graphs.

• *The Price of Gold.* A simple story, "Gold Plunges $12 Before Recovery," was illustrated by an Associated Press line graph showing the generally downward trend of gold prices in London during the previous thirteen months.

• *The Smoking Gun.* Cigars and cigarettes sell by the billions. The important difference is that cigar sales have been declining since the 1930s, while cigarette sales, despite publicity about health dangers, have increased significantly. For a *New York Times* business article, "The Curse on Cigars," Dan Miller drew two clever drawings with line graphs. One drawing depicted an opened cigar box with the graph on the lid. The other graph was placed on a drawing of a pack of cigarettes. He relied on two sources: the Cigar Association of America and the Tobacco Merchants Association. By converting the statistics to graphs, he showed the nature of the two trends. The decline of cigars had been steady and continuous. Cigarette sales, on the other hand, had dropped by as many as 20 billion cigarettes every three or four years—but each time surged upwards to more than compensate for the loss.

• *The Five Waves.* One of the most difficult tasks is relating economic information from different sources. In one such instance, the *New York Times* placed five line graphs, one above another, under the headline: THE GREAT REPRESSION: THE ECONOMY'S PRESSURE POINTS. The five charts showed the downward trend of factory utilization (according to the Federal Reserve Board), the upward movement of business failures (according to Dun & Bradstreet), the rising line of unemployment (according to the U.S. Bureau of Labor Statistics), the decline in housing starts (according to the U.S. Commerce Department), and the wildly fluttering pulse of the Stock Market's Dow Jones Industrial Average, which had fallen again (according to the brokerage house Smith Barney, Harris Upham & Company).

There are times when charts are more helpful than graphs, such as when the writer wants to convey information as well as numbers, or when there are so many categories of numbers that they would confuse the reader.

• *Free Advice.* For a story about the changing consumer costs of banking services, the *Atlanta Journal* published a chart under the headline WHAT'S STILL FREE. It listed seven categories from checking accounts to money orders and named which banking institutions offered free services and on what conditions.

• *American Eating Habits.* The U.S. Agriculture Department was the primary source of statistics for a chart in the *New York Times* under the headline: AMERICANS EAT LESS: CUTTING DOWN: CHANGES IN PER CAPITA CONSUMPTION OF MAJOR FOODS. The chart tracked eight major foods across five years, and the reader could easily see that when Americans cut back on beef temporarily, they ate more pork and poultry. Then they reversed themselves two years later. The overall effect was a decrease of about 1 percent in total eating.

- *The Divided Dollar.* When showing how governments or corporations spend their money, artists frequently divide a dollar coin into slices. The same idea has been applied to a picture of a dollar bill. For a story titled WHERE THE CORPORATE CULTURAL DOLLAR GOES, an *Atlanta Constitution* artist divided a dollar bill into ten sections, with the largest amount (twenty-one cents) spent on miscellaneous art forms, the next largest on museums (nineteen cents), and the smallest on purchases of art (two cents).

- *Patterns of Crime.* Ever since the detective novel became popular, readers have been aware of the police practice of plotting crimes on maps in the belief that some pattern will be discovered. Since law-enforcement officers seldom share their innermost discoveries, newspaper reporters often must plot the crimes independently. In the Atlanta child murders case, *Atlanta Journal* reporters spent uncounted hours charting information about the victims, most of whom lived on Atlanta's south side. This map work indicated in part that bodies had been dropped from bridges into the Chattahoochee River. The man who was convicted in the case was eventually caught at a bridge. He was caught in a police stakeout about 2 o'clock one morning after police under one of the bridges heard a splash in the water.

- *The Firebug's Path.* Similarly, a reporter for the same newspaper reported a wave of arson fires, underscoring the proximity of the fires with a neighborhood map. The numbers on the map were cued to an accompanying chart that told of the loss of life and property in each case.

One other graphic technique—a "logo" or a "sig"—is frequently used to distinguish a series of stories or to help the reader identify favorite features and columnists. For the columnist, the design frequently includes the writer's face and name. For a series of articles, some aspect of the subject matter can be highlighted—such as prison bars for prison stories or a microscope for a science series.

8

Interviewing and Note Taking

To find out, the reporter must ask. Hardly ever is a reporter a participant in events and infrequently is he or she even a direct observer of the full development of events. When reporters arrive, often as not, the house is already on fire, the bank has already been robbed, the secret deals have already been made. More commonly, then, you will be the interrogator of participants and witnesses, the collector of testimony. It is by interviewing people that you learn what has happened and what might happen. From interviews come the details and explanations that make reliable stories.

Getting interviews can be difficult, especially in this age of paranoia when most things are viewed with suspicion, including the press. The interviewer therefore must be imaginative. Some situations may require the gall of a snake oil salesman; others, the honest sympathy of a priest. The interviewer labors between two competing factors: (1) The public has the right to know most information, and you are one of the primary people responsible for getting it for them, yet (2) nobody is legally required to talk to you. Hence, one must sometimes play certain games.

Merely arranging an interview can be like disconnecting a bomb. Anyone in possession of power and great sums of money—often the people most worthy of scrutiny and most reluctant to talk to you—may have a phalanx of protective secretaries and public relations people. Other times you will deal with people so accustomed to abuse and deprivation that they are suspicious of anyone asking questions.

Therefore, let us look first at a few techniques for getting your foot stuck inside the entranceway just before the door slams:

• *The direct approach.* Pick up the telephone and call the person. Tell the person what you want. "Hello, I'm Scoop Smith from the *Kumquat Enterprise,* and I'd like to talk with you about plastic fruit."

• *The end-around.* At businesses and government offices, secretaries routinely will try to give you the brush-off, even if the boss wants to talk with you. (It's just habit.) Make the secretary—or any other protector— your friend and ally. Tell the person, "It's really important that I talk with Ms. Skunkliver." If you're pressed for time, say it's urgent, but don't cry wolf too often.

• *The face-off.* Faced with repeated failure to reach a person by telephone, or if the person is so blessed as to not have one, go to his or her hideout and, with as much apology as seems necessary, barge in.

• *The sit-in.* If you really need to see a person, and the protectors insist that the boss just doesn't have time to see you today, tell them you'll wait. Bringing a lunch helps to emphasize your determination.

• *The assault.* Glimpsing the reluctant prospective interviewee passing anywhere within running distance, you make your appeal as quickly and as strongly as possible: "Oh, Ms. Skunkliver, we have information that could get you executed. Do you care to comment?"

• *But be courteous.* People accustomed to being jerked around are often overwhelmed by simple kindnesses: "We know there are two sides to every story, and we want to hear yours."

• *Beg.* Sometimes nothing works like an appeal to a person's sympathies. Reporters often must interview survivors of a tragedy, and you may succeed by explaining sincerely that you feel uncomfortable asking questions and that you feel sorry, but "Could you please tell us what Johnny was like, and do you have a picture?"

More often than not, the direct approach gets the initial job done. Even people who never read newspapers or loathe them seem impressed by the idea that someone wants to hear what they have to say. Most people will at least agree to an interview, but that is no assurance that they will talk to you when you arrive.

It certainly helps to be informed about your subject to some degree before you go to the interview. One of the easiest put-downs a public official can use against you is: "I've covered that a thousand times." Another is: "I've made my position clear on that issue already." Advance research in the newspaper's library also gives you an opportunity to size up the person you are to interview. Is the person normally surly and difficult? Or does the person like to babble on? Such information helps you know whether to prepare for an ordeal or enjoyable conversation.

Planning also makes the interviewee's escape more difficult. The co-author of this book, Leonard Ray Teel, a veteran of the prison beat and a superb interviewer, used to keep a list of several penitentiary inmates and their identification numbers. The information became a valuable tool when he went one day to interview the warden about a cache of prison-made weapons found in various cells in the Atlanta Pen. The warden's assistant, known for his obstinance in dealing with the press, told Teel that the warden was not available. Fine, said Teel, he would wait. But the warden was far away, somewhere inaccessible in the prison, said the assistant. Teel said he didn't mind waiting, showed a brown bag, and said he had brought his lunch. The assistant reiterated his claim that the warden was unavailable. Well, said Teel, while I'm here, I'd like to see so-and-so, writing down the name of an inmate and his prison number. Normally, a reporter must give twenty-four-hour notice before attempting to see an inmate, but Teel, being acquainted with the rules, knew he could "respectfully request" a waiver of that rule. Temporarily defeated, the assistant went back to see if the inmate would agree to talk with Teel. He would not, the assistant reported back some time later. Teel wrote out another inmate's name and number, scribbling out the official request that is required. Irritated, the assistant went back into the cell block again. The second inmate didn't want to talk either. Teel scribbled out another name and number and a hand-written request torn from his notebook. The process continued for well over an hour until Teel spied the unavailable warden strolling in his direction. Actually, the warden had been in his office nearby and finally had to come out to go to the bathroom. Teel seized the opportunity and the warden. Rather than appear to be obviously ducking the reporter, the warden granted a full interview in his office, and Teel got a substantial story on the weapons— with photographs of the prison-made daggers.

Persistence doesn't always pay off, but it certainly provides more returns than no persistence at all. After a sadly routine interview with the bereaved parents of a murdered little girl, Ron Taylor learned that the police had arrested an uncle of the girl's for the murder, but authorities would not release the name. It was not Taylor but the photographer he was with, a former private detective, Bud Skinner, who thought of the next move, which added immensely to the story. The family, he said, surely would give out the uncle's name. They went back to their house. Not only did they give out the name, but Taylor and the photographer captured them at a moment of outrage and gut emotion. "He sat at our table and ate our food," one aunt cried. A cousin threatened to kill the uncle at the first opportunity. Thus what was already a story of human tragedy evolved into one of a family bent on revenge, shattered by the knowledge that one of their own had committed the horrible crime.

In that case and others, the families involved in tragedy did talk freely when given the opportunity, as if they needed to pour out their feelings to a stranger. This unexpected attitude can transform a difficult assignment. A general assignment reporter in Atlanta was sent to interview the parents of a boy who was one of many young victims of a homosexual killer who lived in Houston, Texas. The parents' grief was heightened by the fact that the police had shipped them the wrong body. Instead of turning away the reporter, the parents spoke with the reporter at length, glad to have someone with whom to share their heartbreak and outrage.

Similarly, a college intern reporting for the *Miami Herald* was sent into the boondocks to find the family of a farm worker who had just been charged with the murder of a ten-year-old girl. His first problem was to find the mobile home amid the fields, which took about an hour. He walked to the door, knocked, and said to the woman who answered that he was a reporter and was trying to get the other side of the story. She would not speak with him, and she closed the door politely. He walked to his car and thought it over. He was just sitting there wondering what to do next when someone in the house beckoned to him to come back. He found that the accused man's family had held a discussion while he had been waiting in the car and had decided to tell the other side of the story. The accused man was portrayed as the kind babysitter of the girl. The reporter listened for the better part of an hour, then drove excitedly to the first telephone he could find along the main road and called the office. As a result of this one interview, the intern reporter was hired for a full-time job after he was graduated from college. One success had launched his career.

News, in its simplest form, is that which is out of the ordinary. Therefore, just watching is often as helpful as any other technique for the interviewer. To the trained, alert eyes, the significant can come into focus from just a glimpse of a crowd. This is especially true for reporters experienced at doing *color* stories, which is what editors call stories designed to relate the mood, pageantry, or eccentricities surrounding a particular event. The veteran observer may seize on the falling balloons and juvenile chants at a political rally or the dancing chickens and gullible gamblers at a county fair. Assigned to do a color story on a Billy Graham Crusade, Ron Taylor was walking outside Atlanta Stadium when he spotted a one-legged beggar holding a paper cup. Taylor walked past him several times, enough to notice that he was getting hardly any money at all from the abundant crowd of worshippers. Finally, he went over to talk with him about this apparent absence of charity. The resulting story provided an intriguing sidebar to the main piece about Graham's message on Christian love and brotherhood.

Conducting the Interview

Telling someone how to interview is like telling someone how to conduct a conversation. We all do it a little differently. Some people are naturally direct and aggressive, which helps. But shyness is no serious handicap. People tend to tell secrets to shy people.

Reporters do not necessarily grow up interrupting their mothers, as Norman Mailer once suggested. But you do have to ask questions, and sometimes you have to annoy the interviewee a trifle. If you are not intrinsically curious and inquisitive, the business of journalism probably is not for you. Asking questions, however, is only half the job. Your aim, after all, is to get answers. The skill comes in getting the answers. But, again, there seem to be no absolutes in how to do this. Reporters tend to use whatever technique works best for them in a given situation. Techniques—situations—vary.

Conducting the interview, like arranging the interview, can become a game of sorts. The experienced reporter generally can size up a person with some reliability in a matter of seconds. Is the person a nut? Is the person honest? What's he hustling? What's she going to try to hide? Does he want you to pull the answers out of him like impacted wisdom teeth? What you read in the person's eyes, in the mannerisms, often is a reliable clue to how the interview must be handled.

Preparation, of course, helps. One frequent suggestion for the novice reporter is to draw up a list of ten questions. This is not a bad idea. But keep in mind that interviews rarely go as they are supposed to. In a hasty telephone interview, you may find your questions abruptly rendered irrelevant by more important elements the interviewee introduces. Let the interview take its natural course, and above all else, *listen*. You may come to an interview ready to put the person behind bars with your probing questions, only to find out that the interviewee has considerable evidence of innocence. Never let your eagerness for a scandal cause you to ignore the facts as they unfold. Also, there will be times when you have only a slight idea of what you are looking for. This is especially true in dealing with broad feature subjects. Do not be afraid to admit that you are, more or less, searching blindly. In that case, outline briefly your general subject, and don't hesitate to ask naïvely, "Is there anything you can tell me that might help me?" You will be surprised how often such a question will evoke significant details and a secret or two to set you on the path you need to follow in your research.

Interviewing, as we have indicated, requires a lot of instinct. Instinct, of course, needs help occasionally. So here are ten hints about the interviewing process:

• Try to be on time. You will be surprised to find how many important people really have nothing else to do during the day but talk to you. Still, they like to think that their duties are overwhelming and will often make a display of irritation if you show up late.

• Outline your reason for being there. Unless you are working on something so sensitive that you can't give the faintest clue, bring the interviewee up to date on what it is you are looking for. If you already have considerable information, it might help to tell the person so as to limit repetition.

• Usually, it is best to start with a broad question. This is not an absolute, especially if you're pressed for time. But such an approach achieves two functions: (1) It gives you time to size up the person and collect your thoughts, and (2) it offers an opportunity to receive information you may not have anticipated and to assess any new direction the interview should take.

• Save your interruptions until the person has had a chance to relax. Making an interviewee uncomfortable at the outset is of little value, unless the person is belligerent and you already have the information you need anyway. Often as not, the interviewee who feels most comfortable with you will be most helpful.

• But stick to the subject. Allowing the person to ramble on about his or her kids and the decline of society is okay up to a point, helping to establish rapport. But such chit-chat is also a common trick of evasion. Once you realize that the interviewee has taken you into the snow-covered valley, extricate yourself gently but quickly: "Speaking of your wife's garden club, does she know what the grand jury has accused you of?"

• Grunt and chuckle occasionally. No verbalizing human being likes to think that he or she is being ignored. Doodling or writing down a lot of useless information in your notebook can help, too. Those who feel they have important information to impart like to think it is being duly recorded.

• Stifle any intense surges of emotion. You will have to interview people occasionally whose views are anathema to you. Making that obvious does little for your reputation as an objective reporter, nor will it help in completing the interview.

• Listen, listen, listen. Not only does this make the interviewee feel good and wise, but it helps you control the interview. The interviewee might gloss over something that you realize is germane and move abruptly to chit-chat. If you have been listening, you can bring up the matter a while later: "By the way, you said something earlier about the time you were in prison. When was that?"

• Don't leave until you have gotten the basics. How does the person spell his or her name? What is his or her official title? How old is the person? Never assume that you know these things already. In fact, it is good to make the questions among the first you ask, in case the person turns surly before you have time to ask.

• Be understanding. Nobody likes insensitivity. Even crooks you help send to prison will remember whether you were nice to them.

Keep in mind that the interviewee often is more nervous than you are about discussing whatever sin or tragedy you have come to learn about. The person not accustomed to being interviewed can be especially edgy. Help the person relax. That is best accomplished by relaxing yourself, and that is best achieved by being natural. If your mind suddenly goes blank in the middle of a discussion, do not sit numbly and hyperventilate. Admit that you are human. Just say, "Excuse me, but I forgot where we were and what I needed to ask."

In many ways, the reporter must possess the qualities of an anthropologist. And like Margaret Mead squatting with the bush people, the reporter must have some willingness to taste the peculiar food and sample the suspicious brew without noticing all the flies. Particularly in researching the feature story, it helps to *fit in*. That can be as much a part of the interviewing process as the questions. The quotes come from the questions. The color, the feel for the story, come from the experience.

Ron Taylor once worked two days at the Plains, Georgia, service station owned by Billy Carter, President Jimmy Carter's brother, and got as much of a sense of the president's hometown and the people he grew up with as a hundred sidewalk interviews could have given him—simply by watching and listening. Although they knew he was a reporter, the "good ol' boys" who hung out at the station came to accept him as part of their circle, telling him their troubles and their fantasies. But they were not so friendly after they saw their tales in print. They turned against Taylor only after they saw the story. Do not expect to keep many interviewees on your list of friends when you are obligated to tell the truth about them. People are inclined to feel that they have far more assets than can be adequately discussed in the limited space of a newspaper, and most people would prefer that their foibles not be discussed at all.

Note Taking

Note taking is so much a part of interviewing that the two processes cannot be truly separated. But, again, the techniques become quite individualized. Some reporters, including us, are inveterate scribblers, taking down every inanity that is uttered. We have often found in our notes such profundities as "a stitch in time saves nine," "it's not whether you win or lose," and "nothing to fear but fear itself." Journalists perhaps have earned their reputation for written clichés by quoting the people they interview. You save yourself considerable struggle with your notes later by taking down only what is relevant. That is not always possible, for two reasons: (1) People sometimes stop talking when you stop writing, and (2) you don't always know what is relevant until you have written it all down and reviewed it.

Taking copious notes can spare you the burden of an extra phone call to double check something you should have written down from the first interview. Also, it gives you a chance to review the interview later in its abbreviated, though possibly illegible, form.

Some reporters, however, take very few notes, insisting that they remember everything they hear. Before you try that, make sure you have flawless recall. Thinking you remember a quote, then remembering it wrong, can cause you professional embarrassment. For the news story, that recording of the immediate, for-the-record event, taking thorough notes is especially important, since the risk of libel usually is greater.

Taking notes for a feature—or human-interest type—story is more a matter of instinct. Sometimes you take more notes than usual, since you may be trying to capture the essence of dialect or cleverness in a very quotable person's speech. Other times, you may take practically no notes at all, since the mood, the scene, or your personal perceptions of a situation may be a major focus of the story. It is hard to lose what you feel, although scribbling down the color of a dress or the inscription on a tombstone never hurts (and usually helps more than the observer in you realizes at the time).

The tools of note taking have multiplied with the advent of the transistor and the computer chip. The reporter who once had to rely on a stenographer's pad and a chewed pencil can now sit by the phone and type notes furiously upon an electric typewriter or even more furiously upon a Video Display Terminal, a wonder of the computer age that allows the reporter to *store* notes for later use. (Be warned, however, that the computer also can devour your notes if there is an electronic foul-up in the system.) Or, the reporter can lift nary a typing or writing finger except to press the button of a tape recorder that will take notes for you.

Still, the reporter more often than not is caught with nothing more than a leaky pen and his or her notebook, now available with *Reporter's Notebook* printed on the cover—to make it official, we suppose.

So, let us now review some of the finer points of note taking with leaky pen and Reporter's Notebook in mind:

• Write as fast as you can, the best way you know how. Very few reporters know shorthand. Instead, most develop a personalized version of *speed writing,* which involves the heavy use of abbreviations and symbols, such as # for *number* and & for *and,* but you should use whatever seems to work.

• Keep hand and mind together. If the person isn't saying anything significant, it probably isn't worth recording. Listen for key phrases, or for other clues that shout significance. In a speech, a person often will raise his or her voice or slow down when he or she feels that the remarks take on added importance.

• Some great quotes are lost forever. Sometimes you just can't get everything down. A reporter's notebook is more a collection of *cue* words and phrases than of precise sentences. From those words and phrases, the reporter often can put together a precise quote. Sometimes not. Just do your best.

• Label your notes. Have at least the last name of the person you have interviewed written at the beginning of that section of notes, or else you may have great difficulty later trying to determine who said what. Some reporters also jot down the date of the interview.

• Number what you don't have time to spell out. Connecting the quote with the name can be especially difficult when you have interviewed several people simultaneously. A good practice is to get everybody's name at the outset and assign each one a number. That way you can keep track of whether number one, number two, or number three was speaking, then connect the numbers to the names when you review your notes later.

• Don't lose your notes. It is hard to reconstruct material you no longer have. At least write your name and phone number on the notebook's cover to improve the chances that someone will return it to you if it is found.

Tape recorders are harder to lose than notebooks, which may explain why more and more reporters are using them. The jabbering box, constructed in ever smaller and more portable versions, has some other advantages over the Reporter's Notebook and leaky pen:

• Tape recorders provide the verbatim quotes. This is especially valuable when you are dealing with a touchy subject, since the interviewee may decide to recant everything that was said. In feature stories, the tape recorder can capture unusual dialect that might add to the flavor of a story. The tape recorder also is helpful when the interviewee speaks faster than you ordinarily can record in a notebook.

• The tape recorder affords you the opportunity to review the interview in toto.

• The tape recorder practically is a must in conducting interviews for question-and-answer stories, where both your questions and the interviewee's answers are to be written up in that format. Rarely do reporters write down what questions they asked.

But there are also disadvantages. Notebooks never run out of tape or have dead batteries; tape recorders sometimes do. To guard against such disasters when you use a tape recorder, it is a good idea to take written notes as well. One of the biggest tape recorder bugaboos, however, is informational inundation. With everything so neatly and reliably recorded, the frequent tendency is to put all of that information into the story. There is also the tendency to overquote, to pull from your transcription even the most dubious pearls, rather than do the harder job of interpreting and explaining. And transcription is a problem unto itself. You probably could write three stories in the time it may take you to transcribe the tape of one interview.

Our personal prejudice is against the tape recorder, except for question-and-answer items or for the rare interview of the very quotable, whose words are worth saving on tape for posterity. The notebook seems to us a grander tool for listening. You cannot write down that which you do not listen to. But the trend seems to be in favor of the tape recorder, as it is for most of the newer gadgets of the trade.

An important element of note taking is knowing when not to take notes. As we said earlier, the purpose in interviewing is getting answers. If an interviewee clams up at the sight of a notebook or tape recorder, set them aside. Usually the information you get (at least that which you can remember) is more important than the affront to your professional procedures. People not accustomed to being interviewed may be especially ticklish about having you write down what they are saying, even if they are quite willing to be quoted. The tape recorder seems a special deterrent to the casual interview—another of its disadvantages. The magic box seems to make the interviewee automated, too, or to make the person feel that he or she is being watched.

Of course, a reporter can always hide his or her tape recorder from the skittish interviewee, but we question the ethics of doing so. One education reporter did this recently in an interview with a university president, who actually enjoyed being interviewed but tended to lapse into rare silences at the sight of a tape recorder. The results were mixed. She picked up some good quotes, but others were muffled by the distance between him and the reporter's purse, which held the recorder. And midway through the interview, the reporter heard the awful, loud click of the recorder that meant it had run out of tape. Fortunately, she also had made written notes.

Wiring yourself for sound with microphones stuffed down the sleeves of your trenchcoat is a little ridiculous in our business. We are reporters, not detectives. However, reporters frequently do attach what some would consider "bugging" devices to their office phones to record telephone interviews. This is permitted by federal law, but some state laws require that you inform the interviewee that he or she is being recorded. Check with your editors before bugging your phone.

There are ways to recoup what you might feel you have lost in not being able to take notes during an interview. The best procedure, once you are out of view, is to write down immediately everything you can remember from the interview.

It is also a good idea to review any notes you have taken as soon as possible after an interview. There is nothing more frustrating about interviewing than to turn to a book of cold notes days later and realize that you can't read your own handwriting, that the one word that would unlock the mystery of a treasured quote has formed into an ugly, indecipherable squiggle on the page.

Off the Record

Sometimes people will tell you things with the expectation that you will not print the information. When you agree to discuss a subject *off the record,* you should consider yourself honor-bound to keep the information secret. No law says that reporters must honor off-the-record requests, but there is an important tradition that says we do, and your colleagues will expect you to uphold that tradition. However, information obtained off the record usually can be found elsewhere on the record. The off-the-record interview can be a way to find out where to look and who might talk publicly about the issue.

It is best to let the interviewee be the one who suggests that the conversation be off the record. To propose the idea yourself can put you in the position of having to keep secret something that you probably could have gotten on the record had you not raised the convenient shield. People accustomed to dealing with reporters on an off-the-record basis usually are adept at protecting themselves. Often, they will say something like "If you print this, I'll swear I never spoke to you in my life." Against such threats, no amount of notes will help you much with your skeptical editors and skeptical public.

9
Ethics

Before a reporter writes a story, the reporter ponders. The professional journalist may be casual, even slovenly, in dress, habits, and attitudes, but never in the approach to a story.

There is much the reporter must dig through before writing. The interview notes may be lost somewhere among the stack of tape recordings and transcriptions, the library clip files, the volumes of studies and statistics, the letter scrawled in crayon calling the reporter a Communist or a Nazi, and the photograph of someone's dead son. Therefore, the reporter must pause and ponder: What does it all mean, and who am I to deal with it? The professional reporter realizes that what he or she does is frighteningly important.

The beginning reporter usually is surprised, and, ever so briefly, elated to learn that he or she suddenly is a person of influence, a purveyor of wisdom, a molder of opinions, a shaper of society. The first thrill may come when some respected person volunteers, "I read the other day that . . . ," and the information, offered with authority, turns out to be from a story the reporter has written. The first letdown comes when someone charges that newspapers print nothing but lies, or you get your first growling phone call that usually begins, "I just want to let you know what your little story did to (my father, mother, brother, sister, best friend, business partner, candidate, me), and you're not going to get away with such (obscenity)."

The fact is, what you write inevitably touches other people's lives, and newspaper stories really *can* ruin lives, just as they can make celebrities and causes of the obscure and dispossessed. Consequently, no other profession, perhaps, is so obsessed with ethics, nor so roundly condemned for its transgressions. The reason is obvious. Most literate Americans depend on journalists to tell them the truth. So when you sit down for the first time to write a newspaper story, just remember that several million Americans are counting on you.

Fortunately, this is not a burden you will have to shoulder alone. Editors get paid to help save you from your ignorance and your cockiness. The first thing editors look to correct are elements that could get them and their newspaper sued, such as glaring errors of fact. However, editors do not get paid to do your job for you. The reason larger newspapers prefer to hire experienced reporters is that they want reporters who are not prone to beginners' mistakes. Tolerant editors usually will grant beginners one or two minor mistakes, but rarely three or four, and almost never will they excuse a major flub. Even small newspapers will expect you to come to them with a sense of fairness and honesty.

Entire courses are built around teaching the standards and ethics of journalism, and whole books and magazines have been devoted to discussions of their finer points. So, we will not presume here to tell you all you need to know about the subject. But as you sit there pondering your first big story, let us share with you some of the basic ethical considerations that should precede the race to get your byline into print.

Objectivity vs. Subjectivity

Critics who know nothing else about journalism seem to know the difference between objectivity and subjectivity, and inevitably one of them will accuse you of not being objective in your stories. So that you will not be at a disadvantage, let us at least provide you with brief definitions. *Objective* means "detached, impersonal, unprejudiced." *Subjective* means "based on personal bias."

It is our subjective observation that objectivity actually is a fairly recent mandate of American journalism. Newspapers of the nineteenth and early twentieth centuries were as much collections of opinions and sarcasm as they were sources of information. One has only to review the war coverage of those times to learn which side the writer was on.

Nonetheless, among today's journalists, objectivity is the ideal. We have, after all, risen to the level of institution, the Fourth Estate. In the information age, we are the annointed arbiters. You will learn quickly in the business that editors do not take lightly this ordination. You will be allowed your personal opinions, certainly, but not in the news sections.

Simply put, editors will expect you to write your story without personal biases, for they know that the readers expect as much. One reporter learned this lesson years ago, when in a fit of political statement he referred to a pending rally in support of American troops in Vietnam as "a celebration of the Vietnam War, now in its eighth year of hopelessness." The city editor frowned, asked him if he thought he was being objective, and handed the story back with a threatening stare. He went back to his desk and wrote the story straight.

People who study such things, of course, tell us that it is unrealistic to presume that human beings, with their subjective inclinations, can be truly objective. And there are those among the practitioners of the so-called New Journalism who contend that objectivity is an impediment to the real truth. Researchers generally work for universities, and New Journalists usually display their "fact-fiction" in magazines and books. If you work for most any newspaper, you will be expected to make a stab at being impartial, *i.e.*, objective.

Subjectivity cannot help but enter in when one realizes that the reporter, by and large, is the judge of what goes into a story and what doesn't. The reporter is the assembler, the quality controller, the trial judge of information for each story that he or she writes. But the reporter is not let loose on the world without training from those who know the rules. Newspapers, like government, are a fortunate mess of checks and balances. The reporter does not make the journalistic laws that have been passed and amended through years of trial and, yes, error.

Experience usually resolves whatever conflict between objectivity and subjectivity you might have to deal with. After a while in the business, you will find that being subjective comes harder than being objective. The ocean of information in which you will daily swim tends to wash away whatever illusions you might have about the world being simple or very fair. The danger, in fact, is that you will come to agree with everyone and trust no one.

Fairness

The more relevant concern is fairness.

Once you enter a working newsroom as a reporter, you acquire access to one of society's great powers, the power to give or deny information. You may be an insignificant element of that power. Editors, in fact, make the controlling decisions. But you are a part, nonetheless. While objectivity may be one of our wished-for ideals, fairness is a responsibility, one that always attends power in a democratic society.

To put the matter in somewhat lofty terms, you are the eyes and ears of the public. How you present a subject is how the public will see it. They will believe what they see only if they believe you. And, conversely, they will believe you only if they trust what you tell them.

As a reporter, you will deal frequently with matters of controversy, circumstances in which values are in conflict. To sustain trust, you must present the issues fairly. When you sit down to write such a story, you should ask yourself, "Have I given everybody a fair shake? Have I looked at all the variables?" Once you have finished the story, you should ask yourself, "Would I, as a reader, trust this interpretation?"

Any story that deals with anything more touchy than a 4-H Club meeting should be *balanced,* that is, contrasting points of view should be represented. That does not mean quoting everybody. What it means is that no one side of a debated issue should be discussed without at least acknowledging that there is an opposite side. If, for instance, Senator Fatkitty's ex-wife accuses him of stealing tax money, you better be sure that you have Fatkitty's denial, or at least his "no comment."

Be forewarned, budding young investigative reporter, that once you have raked your muck and prepared your indictment against some governmental miscreant, your editor will expect you to confront the person to get his or her side of the story. Under our system of justice, every person has a right to face accusers, and the good reporter has a passion for justice. Facing the person you were about to embarrass in public print not only is a lesson in fairness but in human nature. What you usually will find is that the case against the person is far more gray than black or white, and that criminals can be among the most charming and interesting people you will ever meet. Furthermore, corrupt politicians often are among the most efficient of officials. So don't expect a great deal of satisfaction or public support after reeling in the big fish of scandal, unless you have done your job uncommonly well—and fairly.

We have rarely met a reporter who didn't seem blessed with an innate sense of fair play. But occasionally we all have our temptations to succumb to anger, grief, or personal frustration in the course of preparing a story. For such situations, we have a kind of mental checklist to keep us on the course of fairness that we think is worth considering any time you write a story, especially one that could be controversial:

• Stick to the facts. Never *wish* facts. Stay with the ones you saw or were told, qualifying as much as possible the ones you were told, as in: "The man was shot three times, investigators said." The medical examiner may find later that the man was shot four times, or that he actually was stabbed, but you often have only the changing facts of the moment to rely on. (We will discuss in the writing chapters the problem of *over attributing,* but for now a good rule to follow is: When in doubt, attribute.)

• Never insert your personal opinion. This rule pretty well applies to any story. You may have personal opinions about a story subject. They may even, regrettably, taint the way you write the story. But, for goodness' sake, never come right out and express your opinion in a story. If you do, editors will threaten you and readers, legitimately, will condemn you.

• Be discreet in the use of adjectives. Some journalism instructors tell students to avoid the use of all adjectives. Fortunately, most good editors are able to repair this academic damage. Good writing demands some adjectives. Yes, Hemingway did, too, use adjectives. Some description and color always punch up a story, but be careful. It is not your place to call Congressmen dumb or ugly or senile. Editorial writers and columnists have that privilege, within certain legal bounds. Your job is merely to tell the story. Changing attitudes also make some modifiers taboo. Because of the women's movement, newspapers no longer refer to women as beautiful, comely, seductive, or buxom. But a bereaved mother certainly is different from a happy one.

• Avoid cheap shots. People are prone to say and do truly dumb things. In writing your story, examine whether a person's clumsiness is relevant to the issue. Sen. Fatkitty may pick his nose at press conferences, but that probably has nothing to do with his announcement of a new missile base for Orange County.

• Somebody with something to say deserves a forum. Eccentrics have followers, too. Just because you believe someone in the news is psychotic doesn't mean that you have an absolute right to ignore that person. If your bias is toward fairness, you will realize that seemingly odd individuals make great copy and that events may eventually prove the person saner than the rest of us.

• Assess your alliances. Are you too close to the people involved in an event to be fair? If so, like a good trial judge you should withdraw from the project.

• Remember that you are an observer, not a participant. It is not your war. Fighting on either side can get you in serious trouble with your editors and your readers.

• Listen to your editors—they will fire you if you don't. Editors may have humorous faults, but they usually have experience and wisdom enough to keep you from committing journalistic suicide.

• Remember the children. Even thieves can have families. Try to put yourself in the place of the people you are writing about. Be aware that you could be ruining a person's life, helping send the person away to prison, or having the person be the laughing stock of his or her peers. Empathy is the best aid of fairness.

This does not mean, as we will discuss in the writing chapters, that you should write so cautiously that your stories lack vigor and confidence. A newspaper adage—never proved but never disproved either—says that if your story offends *both* sides of a dispute, you probably have done your job well.

Now that we have made you a fair and passably objective reporter, let us turn to some of the finer points of journalistic ethics.

Fact vs. Truth

The issue of fact versus truth is a philosophical one, but nonetheless one with some relevance to the ethics of journalism.

The issue, more or less, is: What is truth? Its relevance to journalism is that there are those who argue that a mere collection of facts, the journalistic habit, does not provide ultimate truth. That is probably true, since many facts of the moment have needed repair through the years by the truth of history. For example, history seems to have established that the Vietnam War was a demoralizing national mistake. Yet the facts carried in the media for the first few years of the war seemed to indicate that it was an important pursuit. Likewise, for generations in the Deep South, respected newspapers tended to see the civil rights movement as a disruptive and divisive action far more damaging than the institution of segregation. The eventual truth, of course, was quite different.

The problem with truth, unfortunately, is that it comes only with time, time that a reporter often does not have when working against the pressure of a deadline. Fortunately, your primary job is to gather facts, and your responsibility is to get them right. If in the process you record some everlasting truth, so much the better. We make this point not so much to relieve you of the burden of being a diviner of truth, but to warn you against a common beginner's mistake, that of *presumption*. Never, *never* presume that events will turn out a certain way. For your purposes, the facts of the moment govern. Sen. Fatkitty may have a reputation as the most corrupt politician in Washington, and, in truth, he may be indicted in another five years, but if you don't have the facts—the proof—to write about his corruption, for goodness' sake *don't*. In a sense, you are the public's jury for information, and, like any jury, you cannot convict without evidence. If you try to, you can be sued.

Libel

Libel generally is defined as "defamation of character." That means ruining somebody's reputation. If you do that in print with false information, you have committed libel and have probably violated the law. If you do that orally, in a tavern, you have committed slander, which is very much like libel. Since we are dealing here with the printed word, we will concern ourselves only with libel and why you should not commit it.

Libel laws were written to give citizens some protection against the awesome power of the press. Without such laws, of course, journalists could write anything about anyone, no matter how wild, offensive, or utterly false. Libel laws are governments' way of making sure we abide by the ethics we manifest.

Libel laws are infinitely complex and grow more so every year with each new court ruling that addresses some recent variable in the equation. Therefore, we do not pretend here to begin to tell you all you need to know about the subject. Even editors rely extensively on lawyers to handle all but the most routine questions. However, there are some general points to consider.

How, for instance, do you know when you have committed libel? Often you don't. The potential for libel exists in matters so obvious as saying someone has been found guilty of a crime when the individual was, in fact, found innocent, or matters so vague as associating an attorney with the wrong client. (Both situations occurred at a major newspaper we won't name and resulted in retractions.) A legally accepted test for libel is whether the offended party has been threatened with *public ridicule* because of what you have written. Are people laughing at the poor person and saying evil things about him or her in public? If so, you may be in trouble. But not necessarily.

A legal defense against libel is *provable truth*. That is the legal test applied. Since we have spent some time already trying to distinguish between truth and fact, let us be so bold as to say that what the courts generally take into account is whether your story is *factually accurate*, whether the facts are true. If so, you and your legal counsel may stand a good chance of convincing the court that the public ridicule is the plantiff's problem, not yours. In other words, if an FBI investigation, various wire-taps, and eyewitnesses identify Sen. Fatkitty as a cocaine dealer, you are relatively safe in reporting that, even if it does tend to defame his character and hold him up to public ridicule.

That may not be the end of it, however. If Sen. Fatkitty can establish that you had some grudge against him, that you were somehow malicious in your intent, he might still win. *Malice* weighs heavily against factual accuracy, and malicious libel is punishable as a crime in many states.

We offer these examples merely to give you some idea of what libel is about. As we have tried to warn you, libel law is best handled by libel lawyers. The courts have tended to be more lenient with journalists in cases of alleged libel against public figures, and much less so in cases involving private individuals. But even that premise is vulnerable to reams of legal arguments.

One thing is certain. Newspapers do not like to have to deal with libel lawsuits. Some newspapers, in fact, tend to avoid running a story if there is even the remotest possibility of a lawsuit—even if there is a good chance the paper would win. Litigating to win can be almost as expensive as losing. Good newspapers will back you—to a point—even if you err.

Newspapers today regularly run corrections to sort out misinformation that inevitably creeps into some stories. Not so common are outright retractions, which is a newspaper's way of both correcting misinformation and apologizing for it. Newspaper editors do not like to make public apologies. For one thing, it hurts the newspaper's credibility. If you are the cause of a major retraction, you usually are in big trouble and can expect to perhaps be out of a job. Furthermore, people can sue reporters as well as newspapers, and you could find yourself saddled with a judgment that would cost you more than you could make in a lifetime in this business.

It should go without saying, then, that libel is something to be avoided. The risk can be lowered if you make a habit of the following practices, which are fundamental considerations for any story:

- Check your facts, of course. Do not assume that that little squiggle in your notes means something it might not mean. Do not assume that you remember some unrecorded fact that may not be a fact. Do not assume. The best practice is to never write something you don't have backed up by notes, although this is not always possible. Never, *never* write a story of controversy without notes to support it.

- Cross-check your facts. This is a most desirable practice that, nonetheless, has its limits. In any sensitive investigative story, it is a must. The former *Washington Post* investigative reporters Bob Woodward and Carl Bernstein insisted that they never wrote anything without at least two sources verifying the information. Have at least two sources, and make sure that they are reliable. We are not talking about some wino in a bar or what your roommate heard on television. But if some man tells you he is fifty-five years old, chances are you are not going to pull his birth certificate or ask his neighbors if he is lying. As a reporter, you must develop a sense of what is important and what can be disputed. What is important and what can be disputed should always be cross-checked.

- Prefer documents. People will stretch the truth. Documents tend not to. Written proof is just about the best proof you can get, so get it when you can. Be sure to read the documents before you start feeling smug. Any contradictions should be explained—and cross-checked with whatever other sources are available.

- Regard names and addresses as danger zones. Never interview even your own mother without being sure you have her name spelled correctly. Some of the nastiest libel cases have resulted from the mysterious things that can happen with names and addresses. You can get in bad trouble for such things as putting a senator's name with the address of a known criminal, or putting the criminal at the senator's respectable address. Likewise, do not confuse the name and the address of someone who is dead with that of someone who is very much alive. Mental lapses can also lead to such horrendous gaffes as confusing the name of a bank president with that of a known embezzler. In newspapers, names have a sanctity of sorts, since most people, it has been said, get their names in print no more than three times: when they are born, when they are married, and when they die.

• Ditto titles. Usually an error in an official title is a mere slight, but a major foul-up could get you sued. The president of Alcoholics Anonymous is not likely to also be the president of Alcoholics Unanimous.

• When in doubt, attribute. Attributions, such as "police said," "investigators charge," "witnesses reported," can clutter good writing—but they can also save you from litigation. Never put yourself in the position of accuser, even if you can back up the allegations with documents and witnesses. Have the documents and witnesses do the accusing. It is a dangerous thing to say simply: "For the past two years, Sen. Blustrous Fatkitty has helped bankroll cocaine operations in Miami and Chicago." It is quite another, safer thing to say: "For the past two years, Sen. Blustrous Fatkitty has helped bankroll cocaine operations in Miami and Chicago, according to an indictment made public today." And it is better to say, "Editors contend reporters are incompetent and lazy" than merely to declare, "Reporters are incompetent and lazy."

• When in court, allege. *Allege* is probably the most overused word in journalism, but it is a very important one. Most investigative charges against people stand as mere allegations until the suspect (another overused but helpful word) is convicted and safely behind bars. An alleged robber is not nearly so likely to sue you as an unconvicted person you have identified simply as a robber. The *alleged* is not necessary when no name is attached. If a bank has been robbed, you can safely say, "The bandit escaped on foot." But when names are attached to matters yet to be litigated, allege and hedge, as in: "The *alleged* bandit, who escaped on foot, was identified by police as John Doe." For variety, try alleged synonyms, such as *accused, suspected, charged* (if the person has been), or *reputed* (if the dishonorable reputation is publicly declared by law enforcement officials).

• Demand the other side. No sensitive, controversial matter has just one side. And no story on such matters should be written until all sides have been explored. Even convicted felons have interesting excuses, and it is much harder for them to accuse you of libel if those excuses have been duly recorded in public print. Furthermore, some people accused of high crimes are indeed innocent and are usually more than happy to enlighten you if you give them a call. Going the extra mile, trying to track the person down in American Samoa if necessary, will save you a lot of potential grief.

• In legal matters, rely on legal records. A particular hazard is having a person accused of the wrong thing. Having a name attached to a murder charge that belongs to a glue-sniffing charge can get you sued and fired. Scrutinize police records and court records to get the record straight.

• Do not count on police officers for spelling. Police officers are supposed to record names and addresses from official papers, such as drivers' licenses, but they do sometimes make mistakes. Cross-check such information with names and addresses listed in phone books and city directories just to be sure. Seek to clarify any contradictions. This can be a problem in major urban areas, where people are prone to change addresses and phone listings frequently.

• Suspect your own library. Your newspaper library can be an incredible source of background material, but that material can be wrong. A big danger is that by lifting information you will repeat an error in your story that some reporter made years ago. Often there is not time to check the information against other sources. In such hopeless situations, we apply these rules: (1) Don't use what is not supported by at least two articles; (2) use only what appears obviously safe; (3) when names are spelled differently, go with majority rule or the latest clips; and (4) depend on the clips of stories by reporters you know and trust.

• It's better to be vague than specifically wrong. Editors prefer that you name names and give addresses. But if you are not sure of the information you have (if, for instance, you can't recall the exact name of an organization you didn't list in your notes), don't put it in. Better to write circles than to zero in on a falsehood. If, for instance, the Beer Wholesalers Association and the Beer Retailers Association are on opposite sides of an issue, and you can't remember which one is for and which one is against, better to say, "Beverage dealers are split on the issue" than to possibly offend both and risk being sued.

• Remember, any story can be booby-trapped. There are practical limits to how much a story can be checked and cross-checked. If you have a paranoid streak, you may be inclined to go the limit, which could mean spending a lifetime on a single story. Some stories simply aren't worth it. A story about the biggest ear of corn ever grown in Iowa probably will not lead you to a search of international agricultural records for some comparison. It's just a good yarn with good art. But there are always dangers. In a simple capsuling of candidates in a county election years ago, Ron Taylor mentioned that one of the men running was the brother of the county solicitor. That was what he had been told by people who should know, but he never got around to asking the candidate. In fact, the man was the solicitor's first cousin. We ran a retraction—Taylor's last, as he recalls—but the kinship apparently was close enough to save his job.

Bribes

We know of only one case in which a reporter was offered an outright bribe. The reporter was covering a city council meeting in a rural county when the councilmen passed around the hat to collect money, which they promptly offered to the reporter for a "good write-up." To their dismay, she refused the $16.00. The government in that county tended to operate on bribes and kickbacks, but the reporter, fortunately, did not.

You probably will never be offered a direct bribe, but you may be surprised to find how many people want to buy you meals, give you tickets to movies and ballgames, send you bottles of liquor and flowers, and offer you space in their hotel or on their airplane. They may not even like you, but they may like what your access to the reading public can do for them. Therefore, let us warn you now that some people will try to use you. As a professional journalist, you must stay off the take.

The problem is knowing when a gift is trivial exchange between friends, or even a simple courtesy, and when it is an attempt to court your favor. After the Watergate exposés of the early 1970s, when bank accounts and business transactions seemed to become the object of media scrutiny, newspaper publishers became increasingly cautious about the habits of their employees. The logic was reasonable: People who threw stones could not live in glass houses.

Consequently, many newspapers have since established written guidelines on ethics in an effort to spell out what a reporter can and cannot do regarding gifts and associations. Usually such guidelines include warnings against accepting free services—"freebies," as they are sometimes called—that might tend to compromise the integrity of the newspaper. Reporters are encouraged to not accept free trips, hotel rooms, passes to entertainment events, or meals when such perquisites could be construed as attempts to buy influence with the newspaper. The guidelines may not specifically prohibit accepting freebies. Movie reviewers and music critics, for instance, routinely accept free tickets to events that they must cover but might not be able to get into otherwise. The governing principle at many newspapers is to exercise good judgment, fairness, common sense, and propriety in handling favors and to avoid situations that might cause conflicts of interest or that might appear to obligate the newspaper to some person or group.

Such guidelines, of course, are designed primarily to spare newspaper businesses ethical embarrassments, but they also offer reasonable boundaries for developing personal standards for operating within this profession. Obviously, such guidelines cannot cover all the variables that will test your personal ethics and conscience. Some reporters we know, for instance, will accept not a single meal from a news source. Others prefer not to make a scene over meals, enjoying the view that they cannot be bought for chopped steak and five martinis. Not too long ago, editors routinely were given free movie and sports passes to dispense to reporters. Oldtimers mourn the passing of this practice. But benevolent public relations people have found ways to circumvent management worries by periodically offering blanket invitations to tavern and restaurant openings where no passes are needed.

As in all things, the best policy is honesty, and there probably is no other profession where most people count on you to be honest. With the awesome power comes an awesome trust. Only the sleaziest of newspapers will tolerate any action that tends to taint that trust.

Sensationalism

Sensationalism, like not being objective, is something you will inevitably be accused of. What the reader usually means is that, in his or her opinion, you have seized on the most sordid, disgusting aspect of a subject to play up in your story. At some newspapers, this practice is, indeed, encouraged. At all respectable newspapers it is routinely discouraged. If you have an uncommon fixation on beheadings, sexual perversions, ugly personal habits, or cosmic cataclysms you probably should not go to a respectable newspaper.

Life can be lurid, certainly, but few editors will let you depict it in graphic detail. The admirable argument is that mothers, fathers, and children do not need to know that a young woman's liver was whacked out with a knife and stuffed into a mayonnaise jar—an actual occurrence that Atlanta newspaper readers were spared from reading.

Editors will let you know in a hurry when you overstep the bounds of good taste and start approaching the ugly side of sensational. But you can save yourself a chewing out by remembering that some events produce details that are best kept between you and the police. Ron Taylor learned this years ago when he reported to his editor that he had a little item on a fellow who had been arrested for bestiality. The editor told him that our readers would not be interested in whatever affections the man had for his cow.

A standard journalism test in such matters is this: Does the story so assault public sensibilities as to offend? In other words, would it make a normal person queasy? If so, don't write it.

Invasion of Privacy

Most people have the right to be let alone. If you go poking through a person's garbage, start peeking in the person's windows, or begin intercepting the person's mail to get some juicy tidbit, you are in real danger of violating the law. For one thing, intercepting mail not addressed to you is a federal offense, punishable as a felony. For another, invasion of privacy, like libel, can be a legal issue in itself.

Invasion of privacy, however, is far more difficult to establish than libel and involves even more complexities that should be left to lawyers. Courts have tended to be lenient toward the media on the issue, leaving public figures to the fishbowl existence that fame inevitably creates for them. But the courts always are redefining just what "public figures" are. A derelict who discovers the body of a socialite may, for instance, become a public figure, but a bank president discovered with a prostitute may be determined not to be.

It is a safe assumption that someone making news can be written about in a routine story. But if you have gone to some extraordinary length to sensationalize the life of some hermit who will not give you the time of day, there is a risk that you have invaded his or her privacy.

Advocacy Journalism

You are a journalist, not a propagandist. Do not plan to come into the business with causes to fight and crusades to wage. Your job, in fact, often will be to struggle through the propaganda—the glowing publicity and special-interest hype—to get at the honest issues and information.

Few newspapers today practice in their pages what is known as advocacy journalism, the concept of stacking the facts so as to prove one side of an issue or to take a position the newspaper prefers. That duty at most newspapers is left, as we have said before, to editorial writers and featured columnists. That does not mean that some city-desk editor will not suggest a particular slant on a story, expecting you to play up a certain angle he or she considers especially important. In such cases, the editor will usually expect you to muster some objectivity, nonetheless.

If you are overly obsessed with certain points of view, you probably will have trouble in this business and maybe should consider writing political tracts or working for one of several advocacy magazines.

After some conditioning in the newspaper business, you will find that few causes deserve reverence. Not even charities are without their villains. Like so many other things in this business, the inclination to push someone's propaganda usually is healed with experience. Furthermore, editors simply will not let you get away with personal advocacy. They might let you wear a "Stop the War" button (some places definitely won't), but they will not let you rail in print against the "running-dog American imperialists."

Moreover, editors will not let you read people's minds. If somebody didn't say it or you didn't see it, chances are that your editors will not let you write it. Exploring a subject's thoughts and motives, writing about how something might have happened (but maybe didn't) are marvelous literary devices used by New Journalists to give their reporting the tone of novels. But New Journalists write almost exclusively for magazines and book publishers, because their form has not found favor in most newspapers and isn't likely to any time soon.

A related trend is developing, however, in the form of what might be called Stylistic Journalism. Stylistic Journalism emphasizes imaginative, *stylized* writing of stories as an integral part of the reporting process. It represents a departure from the popular idea of newspapers as mere records of events and a renewed faith in the idea of newspapers as the literature of immediate fact. Television, after all, can give us the news, but not the nuances. Increasingly, newspapers are breaking with the bland wire-service formulas for writing and are hiring talented writers who lend personal styles to their stories. Stylistic Journalism, though, does not betray the facts. The difference, ultimately, is in the writer's exhibition of the facts, not in the reporter's devotion to them. Stylistic Journalism, like New Journalism, actually is a return to roots rather than a departure from them. New Journalism, certainly, has its roots in the social reporting that Charles Dickens used for his fiction. And the current form was used as early as the 1930s by James Agee in his *Let Us Now Praise Famous Men,* the written documentary of sharecroppers struggling through the Depression in Alabama. Stylistic Journalism, in many ways, is a return to the days of less than a century ago when newspapers were identified by the spunk and wit of their writers.

If there is a difference, it is in integrity. In this age of information overkill, writers simply can't get away with perpetrating myths, as was sometimes the case in earlier practices of the forms.

Sources

Never promise a source for a story something you cannot or should not deliver. If you promise the source money, chances are he or she will tell someone, and you may be branded a checkbook journalist—one who cannot get information without paying for it. Promise the source anonymity, and you may end up in jail.

Editors are given to cycles of worry, and the latest one has caused them to demand that reporters name their sources. There are legitimate reasons for this. Judges have ruled that in certain sensitive matters, such as a criminal trial, reporters can be held in contempt of court for withholding the names of sources whose information might shed some light on the case. Reporters have spent time in jail for citing a higher commitment. Also, reporters and their employers have been embarrassed when it was discovered that unnamed sources did not exist. In such cases, newspapers have had to apologize and reporters have had to find other lines of work.

So, before you swear on your mother's grave that you will protect the identity of some mysterious soul who hands you an audit of Sen. Fatkitty's Swiss bank account, decide whether you could eat prison food or could spend the rest of your life slinging hash at some all-night diner after you lose your job.

It has been our experience that such tests of resolve almost never occur, but this is a business with infinite surprises. Our advice, frankly, is to not take any risks your employer isn't willing to take for you. Some newspapers will fight your case all the way to the Supreme Court. Some will suggest that you resign and hire your own lawyer.

Lies

Do not lie. If you have entered adulthood, we should not have to tell you this. But the world is full of deceivers, and occasionally one or two of them wind up in the newspaper business. Fortunately, such people usually don't last long.

Even among the usually honest, the temptation to stretch the truth a mite can come when attempting to make a story something extraordinary. That evidently was the case with Janet Cooke, a talented young writer for the *Washington Post*, who applied her imagination to a collection of anecdotes about drug abuse to create a composite eight-year-old heroin addict. "Jimmy's World" became a famous fabrication that brought righteous indignation from editors and cost Cooke her career. The embarrassment was compounded by the fact that the story had won for the *Post* a Pulitzer Prize, which it had to return. A reporter in Atlanta got in deep trouble when he wrote about a cripple who ran in the Peachtree Road Race. The writer later admitted that no such thing had occurred, claiming that the "highly apocryphal" (his words) story was based on an actual event that had occurred in a road race elsewhere. He kept his job by promising to never take such license again. Few reporters who do such things are so lucky.

Editors may occasionally forgive honest error, such as when you are the victim of innocent confusion or of the lies of others. They do not forgive deceit, as they know the readers won't.

Jokes

This may seem like a funny thing to bring up in a chapter on ethics, but, as we said, this is a funny business. And one of the oddest occurrences we have noticed is the number of reporters who have lost their jobs through some manifestation of creative wit.

One of the best reporters we know, a veritable expert on heinous crime, was sacked at a Florida newspaper after he wrote a story announcing a local barkeep's intention to open a tavern on the moon. The barkeep never made such an announcement, nor did the reporter intend for the story to get in the newspaper. But some copy editor picked it up and wrote a headline for it, and there it was in the next day's editions.

Writing parodies, a regular habit among reporters, is a special danger in this age of computers. What is tapped into the Video Display Terminal can always come out in the composing room and wind up being waved in your face by an unforgiving editor.

If you do something dangerously imaginative, keep it to yourself. Another journalist we know wrote a column so that the first letter of each paragraph spelled out his publisher's name and the writer's somewhat libelous opinion of him. He might have gotten away with it had he not bragged to some colleagues. He has not been heard from since.

Practical jokes also can draw the wrong type of attention to yourself. When Jim Naughton was working for the *New York Times,* he got a call from his managing editor wanting to know why Naughton had showed up at one of President Gerald Ford's press conferences on network television wearing a chicken head. Fortunately for Naughton, his managing editor chalked up the escapade to the stress of the campaign trail.

The warning here is not against having fun. Just don't let your private jokes get into public print or under the skin of some ill-tempered editor.

Obscenity

Any schoolyard survey would tell you that more Americans are cussing these days. But few newspapers are letting obscene words or vulgarities get into print.

Editors will sometimes bend the rules if you can establish that certain no-no words are overwhelmingly significant to the story you are writing. Two reporters at the *Atlanta Journal* made just such an argument for a series on policemen and the obscenity-laden world they must travel in. They won what amounted to a quota of expletives: a couple of insults to motherhood, one slang reference to urination, and two vain calls upon God.

But the prevailing rule at most newspapers is: Don't use any word that would make your grandmother blush. The reasonable logic is that newspapers are designed for family consumption, and some families still are shocked at the language that they would hear in most newsrooms that never gets into print.

When Not to Print

This is a decision your editor has to make, but you may have to help the editor arrive at that decision. One of the toughest decisions any editor has to make comes when the public's right to know is in conflict with public security and safety.

Except in cases where national security might truly be violated, the right to know tends to win out with editors. Often, in fact, the arguments against publishing some delicate matter are made by people more interested in job security than public security. Supporters of Richard Nixon argued strenuously, but unconvincingly, that national security was at stake in their shenanigans with burglaries and wiretaps and laundering of payoff money. They mounted a similar argument against the *New York Times*'s publication of the Pentagon Papers. The articles actually served to point up the mismanagement and dubious purpose of the war in Vietnam.

In the late 1970s the *Atlanta Constitution* had to cope with police pressure not to publicize information about a series of lovers' lane killings. Police officials argued that publicity about the investigation would allow the killer to escape detection. *Constitution* editors decided that to publish the information possibly would serve the greater good of warning people away from areas where they might fall victim to the killer. The story ran. The killer was never caught, but no one else was murdered in a lovers' lane.

More recently, the Atlanta newspapers were criticized for their extensive coverage of the murders of twenty-eight young people. Some critics went so far as to accuse the press of creating a pattern killer by emphasizing the cases. The fact is that most big-city newspapers routinely cover murders, especially when the victims are young and their bodies turn up in out-of-the-way places. And in the cases of Atlanta's murdered and missing young people, no emphasis of a possible common killer was made until the police made it. It is true that some killers feed on publicity like a pyromaniac feeds on the sight of fire, but it is equally true that no compulsive killer, especially a psychotic one, has ever stopped killing simply because he or she wasn't getting enough ink. (The flip side of this particular situation is that the Atlanta papers initially were accused of not focusing enough attention on the tragic slayings.)

As we said at the outset of this section, these are not decisions you will have to make. However, you do have a responsibility to keep your editors abreast of information that may be needed to render the decisions. Do not withhold information simply because you alone feel that the subject is too sensitive to publish. Likewise, don't hesitate to make your feelings known if you think your editors would be wrong in publishing something. They may ignore you, but at least you will have cleared your conscience.

Consequences

Always, there are consequences to what you do. If you stay in the business long enough, you will at one time or another be accused of ruining the reputations of people, businesses, neighborhoods, cities, or whole states.

It was Walter Cronkite, one of the most trusted journalists ever to appear on television, who once said that the duty of journalists is to report the news regardless of the consequences. His well-taken point was that a journalist cannot afford to let what *might* happen stand in the way of reporting what *is* happening.

But no journalist should sit down to do a story unmindful that there are consequences. Those squiggles on the notebook or incoherencies on a tape represent lives you will affect in some way. Be careful what you do to them.

10

Journalistic Writing

At some point in your career—probably the first day—you will be expected to take everything we have tried to teach you thus far and apply it to the written word. Let us, then, begin to tell you how to write *journalistically.*

Writing for newspapers is not so hard as many editors and teachers may try to tell you it is, nor is it so easy as it appears on the printed page. But journalistic writing *is* different, different really from any other kind of writing. Charles McDowell, longtime columnist for the *Richmond Times Dispatch* and a frequent lecturer on newspaper writing, contends this is because "newspapers have a thousand ways to make the telling of a simple story complicated." There are reasons for that, also, buried in habit and special needs. The needs, as well as the habits, are slowly fading. There was a time when newspapers provided the first news anybody got, and some traditionalist papers hold to the old forms and constraints required of that age fifty to sixty years ago.

Because we don't know whether you will be going to a newspaper that still insists on calling cars "motor cars" or to one that uses "twisted" in the sense of being zonked on drugs, we are going to endeavor to prepare you for either. This particular chapter will address the traditional forms and discuss some of the constants. In the following two chapters, we will take you over the edge into stylistic writing, with some tips, examples, and appropriate warnings.

The one thing we can assure you of is that writing is incredibly important at any newspaper. Gone are the days when big-city newspapers had "leg men" who merely collected facts and fed them to a "rewrite man" who wrote the stories with flair and, sometimes, exaggeration. Some newspapers still use rewrite people to help rework stories that others have written or have dictated by phone. Some newspapers also have a kind of writing-by-committee system for special projects, whereby several reporters collect information, which is then handed over to one or more writers on the team. But once the project is finished, those people who have done the leg work return to being writer-reporters again. At today's newspapers, a reporter must also be a writer. And it has been our experience that the better you write, the better you will do in this business. Increasingly, editors seek talented writers, grudgingly admitting that the public can, indeed, get its basic news from TV but not in the substantive, interpretive way good newspaper writers can present it.

Before you dash off to the Pulitzer Committee with your treatise on urban potholes, let us start at the beginning, with the fundamentals.

The Constants

Journalistic writing is concise writing. Points are made quickly and briefly. William Faulkner, one of our most honored novelists, would never have made it in the newspaper game. Editors would have yelled at him for his two-page sentences. He would have been frustrated by editors' putting apostrophes and frequent periods into his marvelous visions. Ernest Hemingway, another honored novelist, was also a journalist and wrote like one. His short, snappy paragraphs are in the most durable tradition of journalistic writing. He also shows how much style can be crammed into something simple.

The concise form was born of necessity. Newspapers must tell many stories on any given day, and there is only so much space. If you simply cannot restrain your gushes of prose, you might consider writing magazine articles or books. At newspapers, you will have to write succinctly. Editors will insist that you do. Saying a lot in a little space, unfortunately, is one of the hardest skills to learn in journalism. You will do it well only after much practice and some merciless editing. However, a few arbitrary, but generally accepted, rules can help force this habit of *tight* writing:

• Keep paragraphs short. Any paragraph that runs more than five typewritten lines is too long, usually. Three or four lines are preferred. Editors appropriately refer to newspaper paragraphs as *graphs,* since normally they are not true grammar-textbook paragraphs but paragraph fragments. Rather than being a collection of sentences expressing a complete thought or theme, newspaper graphs often are one- and two-sentence segments of the thought, which is completed after two or three graphs.

As in all things uniquely journalistic, there is a special reason for short paragraphs. They are primarily a newspaper layout tool designed to prevent the newspaper from looking too *gray* because of too many words jammed together. Editors also assume, rightly perhaps, that readers like to get their information in a hurry and don't want to wade through something that looks awesomely long.

• Get to the point in a hurry. Traditionally, this has been done in the first two or three paragraphs, known collectively as the *lead*. Even in stylized stories, where you are setting some scene or telling an anecdote, the point should be established early on, at least by the fifth or sixth paragraphs.

• Use action words. Active verbs add energy and excitement to a story and get it moving in a hurry. A person who *dashed* through a crowd appears more interesting than one who *was running* down the street. In addition, the passive voice tends not only to slow down sentences but often makes them awkward.

• Keep in mind that you are a selector of detail, not a recording secretary. From the mass of information available to you, you are expected to select the most significant and interesting details and present them in a way that will immediately grab the reader's attention and hold it. As you become more experienced as a reporter, you will find that there is much more to be discarded than to be saved. Saving the best and putting it into the proper order of significance is a measure of the newspaper writer's skill.

There is a time, certainly, for written windiness. Knowing when to expound and when to truncate comes with experience, practice, and heartless editing. At most larger newspapers, the good reporter is forced to develop two skill levels: one of speed, brevity, and patterned thinking, and another of imagination and perspective. Most frustrating to novices, certainly, is that they will be called on to exercise the former far more than the latter in the beginning.

In the newspaper business, you must learn to run with the breaking story before you can crawl through the analytical feature. As we will see, there is much about journalism that is backwards. So let us start at the finish line.

The News Story

The news story is what it is all about. You are in the news business, and you will be expected to write news stories.

To know what a news story is, of course, it helps to know what news is. To be candid, news is pretty much whatever your editor decides it is. It may be a triple axe-murder–suicide or your publisher's favorite charity. As in most matters of uncertainty, definitions vary. One we like, picked up from a wise old journalism professor, is this: *News is that which is timely, truthful, and of public interest.* If any of these three elements is missing, chances are you don't have a situation worth presenting to your newspaper's readers. A lot of things are timely and truthful that are not at all interesting. (Your editor, of course, may be aware of some interest that you do not immediately see, such as your publisher's interest in seeing a story in the paper about the favorite charity.) Something that is timely and interesting, of course, might not have a grain of truth to it, and to foist a lie upon the public is the cardinal sin of journalism.

Timeliness is the stock and trade of newspapers, and nowhere is that more pertinent than in the basic news story. The news story deals with the immediate, the facts of the moment, "what's happening." It is the story with adrenalin pumping. It demands the best of reporting (news gathering) skills. It demands that the writer be quick, accurate, and not overly sensitive about his or her *art,* for news stories can be dreadfully, painfully, insufferably *dull* in the hurried rendering. Only the very best of a vanishing breed of backward-thinking geniuses are able to make high drama of upside-down storytelling with any consistency under deadline pressure.

With deadline-panicked editors on his or her back, the journalist writing a news story often must fall back on an acquired bag of tricks in pursuit of abbreviations of description. A bank robber pointing a pistol in the face of a terrified teller becomes "the gunman"; a person standing neck-deep in water (whose name you forget to ask) becomes "one flood victim" or "one stricken resident"; a state representative babbling lunacies at a press conference seconds before your deadline becomes "the controversial legislator." A talented writer often can put an original make on a news story, even under those conditions, but with precious seconds ticking away and libel lawyers waiting in the wings, the veteran journalist is most inclined to handle a news story in ways that are tried and safe.

For the panicked writer there is probably no better form to use than the *inverted pyramid.*

Writing Backwards

The newspaper writer is an assembler of facts in that he or she puts together the parts of the story in an orderly fashion. However, in writing the traditional news story, the proper order actually is a kind of disassembling. We start with the bicycle and wind up with a leftover bolt. Traditional newsstory writing might be considered upside-down writing. You give the punch line, then tell the joke. In academic circles, this has become known as the *inverted pyramid*. Although you may never hear the term used in a news room, editors will assume you know how to use the form. Some purists, in fact, will insist that you use the form regularly because it is something they know how to handle when they don't know how to handle other tricks of writing. What is meant by the inverted pyramid, basically, is that you lay out the facts in *descending* order of importance. It is the standard narrative, inverted. Instead of beginning with a problem, such as a murder in a mystery story, and ending with the resolution, you tell the resolution in the beginning, then move steadily backwards to where the narrative normally would begin. The traditional inverted pyramid form for the news story has three key parts:

• *The lead*. The lead is the first few paragraphs of any story. In the traditional form, the lead is supposed to tell everything earth-shattering that there is to know, as well as the most relevant details. A sufficient lead often can stand by itself as a short story, as do the leads from the Associated Press wire stories that some newspapers compile into *news briefs*. (In some newsrooms, editors are prone to spell the word *lede*, a holdover from hot type days when *lead* was pronounced *led* and meant metal inserted on the plate in the composing room to stretch out a story that was too short.)

• *The middle*. This includes paragraphs to support the lead, to add details that are significant but not essential. The lead on a murder story, for instance, may mention the motive as a "domestic quarrel." In the middle, you probably will want to quote police or witnesses about what the quarrel concerned. You may also want to include more details about where the body was found, how many bullet holes there were, who was in the house, etc.

• *The expendable ending*. A major reason for writing news stories in the inverted pyramid form is so the bottom can be cut without eliminating some crucial detail. Unless you have your editor's word, written in blood, that it won't be cut, never save your best lick for the end. If you do, readers may never see it, for stories almost always are cut a little—often from the bottom—to fit the space. The expendable end should include background information. The murder story, for instance, might include a summary of how many murders the city has had to date. Unless the increase is alarming, in which case the information should go higher in the story, such peripheral matter can be cut without damaging the story.

Regardless of the form—and we shall discuss some others in the following chapters—there are elements that should be included in every story.

The Five Ws, Sometimes H, and a Few Cs

It is true. All stories should include the five Ws: *who, what, when, where, why*. And most stories should include the *how*. The news story, particularly, should have these elements high up in the story. Sometimes overlooked in this traditional equation is that stories also should include some *conjunctions*, those little words that smooth the transitions and keep the sentences hanging together. One oddity of journalistic writing, frowned upon by some purists, is the habit of beginning sentences with such conjunctions as *and* and *but*. Purists hold that these little words can be used only to separate independent clauses in compound sentences. We are not here to argue sentence structure. All we can tell you is that in journalism, it is done. And, another set of words that are indispensable when shifting points is such conjunctive adverbs as *meanwhile, moreover, nevertheless,* and *therefore*.

In the traditional news story, the five Ws come into play early on. At one time, it was considered important to get them all into the first paragraph, certainly somewhere in the first two. This is no longer a rule at most newspapers, although the veteran journalistic writer almost counts them off in his or her head in writing the first few paragraphs, sticking them into sentences, thusly:

* *Who*. This is whom the action is about. Who is talking. Who is dead. Who is stealing. And so forth. Sometimes it is a name, perhaps accompanied by a title: *Mayor Maynard Jackson, Sen. Blustrous Fatkitty, Mary Jane McSwane, Dr. Joyce Brothers*. Sometimes it is a brief description: *A 35-year-old DeKalb County man, a deranged Vietnam war veteran, a psychopathic anti-war leader*.

* *What*. What happened. It usually includes a verb. (Who) *was slain, attacked welfare, shot her boss*. It may also include slight description and detail: Mayor Maynard Jackson *announced the dedication ceremony for the new airport;* a 35-year-old DeKalb County man *died of injuries in a head-on collision;* an irate secretary *shot her boss*.

* *Where*. In Atlanta or Denver? Leaving out where an event occurred confuses readers to no end. In covering city news, you may be expected to include a street address. Often it helps to include a landmark as well. Sometimes the building, house, barn, or whatever is important. An address might not mean so much to the reader as pointing out that the incident occurred *across from Manuel's Tavern*. A decision made at City Hall may be expected, but one made by the city council at Paschal's Restaurant may be unusual. At most larger dailies, the city where you are writing becomes simply *here*, as in: *Former President Jimmy Carter announced here Saturday*

that he finally has finished his memoirs. If your newspaper is in Atlanta and the announcement is occurring in Plains, Georgia, you might still use *here,* but with a dateline preceding the first paragraph, this way:

PLAINS, Ga.—Former President Jimmy Carter announced here Saturday that he finally has finished his memoirs.

- *When.* Simply the day of the week, usually. Like *where,* it is a reference point for the reader. Sometimes, more specific time is important to include. A downtown murder that occurred *shortly after noon during the lunchtime rush hour* takes on more immediacy than one that occurred *Tuesday afternoon.*

- *Why.* Hard to answer sometimes. It usually involves some discussion in the second or third paragraph of why the news event seems to have occurred or why it is significant: *The curbside pickup plan is aimed at helping settle the year-old garbage strike; the accident occurred when Jones lost control of his vehicle.*

- And *sometimes how,* which usually takes care of the story's middle. How does the mayor plan to implement his curbside garbage pickup? How did Mary Jane McSwane wind up dead? How will the president's umpteenth economic recovery plan finally end inflation?

The ending in the traditional, upside-down news story, often as not, should be whatever is left over: *In other action, the council voted to proclaim Thursday "Say Hello to a Stranger" Day.*

The hardest part of writing a story is coming up with a lead. So dreadful is the task to some writers that they write the rest of the story first, then go back to put a top on it. One reason that the lead is so intimidating is that it is quite difficult to summarize a whole story in two or three paragraphs. In the traditional form, that usually is what you are expected to do. The task is made none the easier by the quirks of editors who like to see leads written as they were taught to write them, and each editor seems to have been taught something different. Some editors like the ancient form of cramming everything into the first paragraph. Some editors like brisk five- or six-word leads, with everything else crammed into the second paragraph. And some rare editors will let you do whatever seems to work. In the beginning, it is best to go with tradition. Not only is it easier to write conventional leads, since they fit into standard formulas, but the early habit helps prove to your editors that you are not some crazed journalistic radical. However, once you have made that point, it is generally safe—and wise—to try something daring before you get locked into habits that can impede your eventual progress to a better newspaper.

To that end, we are going to rush through conventional lead writing in the following section so as not to introduce you to too many rules. In fact, we intend for you to have learned to break most of them by the time you have finished the next two chapters. Rules, of course, are marvelous conveniences when you are traveling blindly, and you will find that the conventional lead will serve you well in those moments when the city is afire and you are five minutes from deadline.

Writing the Conventional Lead

Various efforts have been made to label different types of leads. We do not intend to contribute to that confusion. No editor we know is going to accuse you of putting a *question* lead on a story that should have had a *suspended interest* lead, but if the editor's interest is immediately suspended, you will be accused of writing a bad lead instead of a good one. The one label that does seem to have some merit is the *summary* lead. The conventional lead should summarize, certainly. This may be done in the first paragraph, or in the first three or four paragraphs. Since the inverted pyramid form requires that you deal with facts in descending order of importance, the best way to establish what is important is to summarize it at the outset. A good practice for writing a summary lead is to pretend that you are talking to a friend who has an attention span of about five seconds. How do you get that friend to notice that some calamity has occurred? Gene Fowler, a legendary reporter of the 1920s who had been accused by his editors of "backing into" leads, proved he could get attention in a hurry with this classic lead: *Dead. That's what she was.* That lead, of course, does not altogether summarize the event, but it is a fascinating start.

Traditionally, the summary lead is an attempt to get as many of the five Ws as possible into the first and second paragraphs. Here is a good example of how that is done, from a story by the Associated Press, which, like the other wire services, has made summary leads a constant bordering on blandness:

> A 16-year-old girl was critically injured and burned, and her dog was killed when the dog urinated on the wiring of an electrified sign here, the Suffolk County police reported.

Here, we have the *who:* a 16-year-old girl and her dog. We have the *what:* The girl was critically injured and burned; the dog was killed. We have the *where* established as *here,* magnified by the attribution: Suffolk County police. We even have the *why:* The dog urinated on the wiring of an electrified sign. The *when* is mentioned in the second paragraph.

That particular lead also offers us an opportunity to discuss the issue of when to attribute. Since attributions seem almost an interruption, first paragraphs are more readable without them. In this instance, the attribution "Suffolk County police reported" could have been used to begin the second paragraph. But some editors consider a first paragraph incomplete without attribution. They especially like to stick in the newspaper's name where a big scoop is involved, as in: "Payoffs to building inspectors is a common practice in the city, the *Screaming Eagle* has learned." Attribution in the first paragraph is also important if you are dealing with sensitive matters, where you want someone else to be held accountable, as in: "Sen. Fatkitty stole $5 million, FBI investigators have charged." Our rule is: When in doubt, attribute; but don't let your attributions become regular interruptions of the flow of a story.

After a while in the business, you will discover that some conventional leads are so automatic that you practically could plug them into a computer with only a couple of blank spaces to fill in later. One of the most common is the bank robbery story:

> Two masked gunmen robbed the C&S branch bank at 3568 Moreland Avenue Friday afternoon and escaped on foot with an undisclosed amount of cash.

Robbers with any savvy at all usually wear masks and carry guns. Friday afternoon tends to be their favorite time to strike. They normally hit a branch bank. And neither the bank, the police, nor the FBI will tell you how much the robbers took. Actually, robbers usually escape by car, but the last time anybody seems to see them they are still on foot.

The police story becomes a staple for many young reporters, so you probably will run into another standard—the domestic homicide, wherein someone guns down a best friend or spouse. The stories go something like this:

> A 38-year-old Atlanta man was shot to death during a quarrel outside the High Life Bar & Grill Saturday night.
>
> Atlanta police identified the dead man as Wendell Smudwell of 3236 Renaissance Park Avenue SE. Arrested and charged with the murder was John Francis Doe, 32, of 3237 Renaissance Park Avenue SE.
>
> According to Detective Joseph Friday, the two men had been discussing the Falcons' recent losing streak when Doe pulled out a .22 caliber pistol and fired five shots into Smudwell's abdomen.

For some types of stories, such as obituaries, newspapers do, indeed, have what amounts to fill-in-the-blank forms. At the *Atlanta Journal*, standard obituaries begin: "Services for . . ." The second paragraph includes a brief biographical sketch, beginning with the name of the deceased. The third paragraph begins: "Survivors include . . ." Here is one example:

> Services for Harry Rosenberg, 65, of Atlanta will be Thursday at 2 P.M. at Ward's Glenwood Chapel, with burial at Forest Lawn Memorial Park.
> Mr. Rosenberg, a retired Delta maintenance department foreman, died Friday. The New York native was a member of the OX-5 Aviation Engineers.
> Survivors include his wife, Mrs. Rachel Adams Rosenberg; a sister, Mrs. Ross Kohuth of Brooklyn, N.Y.; and a brother, Joe Rosenberg of Wellesley, Mass.

The form, of course, varies from paper to paper, and even changes at a particular paper. *Journal* obituaries used to begin: "Funeral for . . ." They used to end "Surviving are . . ." You shouldn't have much trouble writing obituaries, called *obits* for short, except in making sure you spell all the names right. Nowhere, in fact, is it more imperative to get the names right. Would you want someone to misspell your name if you were getting the last recognition you would ever get on this earth?

Standard obituaries, however, are not the same as celebrity obituaries. Celebrity obits usually are turned over to veterans for what amounts to eulogizing. A notable citizen always is put away with kind, and often effusive, words.

Another thing to keep in mind when writing the conventional lead is to get as much pertinent detail as possible into the first few lines. This can require some straining to inject the peculiar adjective clauses that set apart newspaper writing from other kinds of writing.

Here is how Ron Taylor backed into a lead one time, endeavoring to set a tone before he had made clear what he was talking about:

> When Raymond Sagoes called his mother at 4:45 P.M. Friday, "he was crying and said he was sick and didn't have no money and didn't have nothing to eat."

Taylor was struck by the sadness of the quote from the mother of a man on the run. His editor, fortunately, was struck by the fact that the man had allegedly killed two people. The editor felt that that was a secret worth sharing with our readers at the outset. Here is how the editor fixed it:

> The last time accused double murderer Raymond Sagoes called his mother here at 457 Western Avenue NW was 4:45 P.M. Friday, and "he was crying and said he was sick and didn't have no money and didn't have nothing to eat."

The reason we think it unwise to label leads for convenience' sake is that they are so often dictated by events rather than rules. Some situations seem to invite a certain amount of playfulness. Nothing works so well sometimes as a twist on an old joke or literary reference. To the reader, the familiar is easier to follow, certainly, than the unfamiliar.

Who hasn't heard Johnny Carson and Ed McMahon doing their stock television routine on the weather: "How hot was it? It was so hot . . ."? So why not this lead?

> How hot was it?
>
> It was so hot Thursday that a young woman took the liberty of taking off her clothes in Central City Park in the heart of downtown Atlanta.
>
> After prancing bare-bosomed before a lunch-hour crowd in the park, the woman was arrested.

Given the right circumstances for Christmas, you can always dust off this one:

> The Grinch is not the only one who steals Christmas.
>
> A lot of ordinary Americans walk off with stacks of Yuletide gifts they never bother to pay for, and professional thieves work overtime this time of year.

Be warned, however, that there is nothing worse than a pun or a cliché twist carried off to the nth degree of silliness. Our advice is simple: Be original, even with the unoriginal.

Here is an example of how coincidence invited such a twist:

> One of the first things Sam Lowry was told in a class on delivering babies is that they usually aren't born in the backseat of a taxi.
>
> Well, how about the front seat of a green 1970 Dodge Monaco, in a motel driveway at 12:30 on a Friday afternoon?
>
> That's how Brooke Alan Lowry came into this world, all 7 pounds, 8 ounces and 19½ inches of him.

In this example, you also can see how an unconventional approach can lead to an unconventional rendering of the summary lead. The first paragraph tells us little, but it sets up the next two paragraphs, which tell us everything we need to know before moving on to some elaboration.

A different type of lead, in purpose but not in form, is the *second day* lead. Second-day leads are written for stories in which the main event already has occurred but some action relevant to the event is continuing. Here is a conventional approach to such a second-day story about an ongoing search for a missing person:

> More than 100 volunteers continue to comb a five-county, 125-square-mile area in search of a 43-year-old father of three missing since last Friday.

Here we have summarized the continuing developments in the event, establishing indirectly about whom we are talking, what is going on, and the time frame. We move to the second paragraph for more detail:

> The search began Sunday morning after Donald E. Pinyan of 639 West Ponce de Leon Avenue, Decatur, failed to join a scheduled deer hunt in Monticello Friday night.

There you have your full lead. Then, we move to the middle for some clarification:

> Pinyan's abandoned truck was found near I-20 between Flat Shoals and Candler roads Saturday. The truck was locked with Pinyan's hunting equipment still inside.
>
> Authorities speculated that Pinyan may have stopped to help a woman change a tire. Pinyan's truck and the woman's car, a 1959 or 1960 Dodge, were sighted in the same area Friday afternoon.

That, in essence, is how you apply the formula. The more experienced you become, the more ingredients you can toss into the recipe without having the cake blow up in your face. The more ingredients, or details, you have, the better, for there is thus more to work with.

We will give you some elaborate recipes to work with in the next two chapters, but, first, a few more words about traditional methods and the peculiar language of newspapers.

The Peculiar Language of Newspapers

The language many newspapers are written in today has its roots in the 1920s, '30s, and '40s, the period when newspapers began to standardize the presentation of information to a public that still got most of its news from newspapers. Then, newspaper leads functioned much as the TV and radio summaries of today. The leads essentially were the same as the banked headlines with the articles and qualifiers filled in. Some reporters today, in fact, jot down possible headlines for their stories as a way of outlining elements they want to include.

Actually, the traditional newspaper language is much the language of headlines. As Charles McDowell, the Richmond columnist who is a leading critic of newspapers' "artificial" prose, points out, "We jab, hit, lambast. . . . We have peculiar adjective clauses: 'The red-haired, 25-year-old mother of three.'" It is an instant language that recently has found a home in the most instant of media—television—giving rise to such parodies as: "Soviets launch nuclear attack. Film at 11." It is a language that only gradually, grudgingly is being replaced by a more personal, stylized language aimed at the literate members of television's pervasive audience.

The traditional news story is a form of abbreviation and contraction of sentences. The word *that* is one of the most frequent syntactical interruptions relegated to limbo. Instead of:

Nixon said *that* he was not a crook

you would write:

Nixon said he was not a crook.

Who and *which* suffer similar obscurity in traditional news writing.

The person driving the car . . .

rather than

The person *who was* driving the car . . .

Or, taking abbreviation a step further:

The driver.

The word *on* also tends to disappear. It is

He said Monday . . .

rather than

He said *on* Monday . . .

He may not have *said* "Monday," but that is one of the structural oddities we have been stuck with.

Applying the formula, we can reduce ten words to eight:

She said *on* Monday *that* she was going to Taiwan.

becomes

She said Monday she was going to Taiwan.

Even in your flushes of literary wizardry, you should keep in mind that newspaper writing is not magazine writing and is therefore always shorter and tighter. It is our way of sparing readers our excesses. A story about a university president probably should not begin with the sun rising gently in the east, as was the struggling attempt of one college writer we recall. Once you begin to apply some of the creative touches we will discuss in the following chapters, keep in mind that you still are functioning in a form that demands that the point be made quickly and that the story be told succinctly. Always there are words that can be eliminated and ideas that can be condensed. Only the abusive writer would impose upon the audience something like this:

> Sen. Blustrous Fatkitty was moved to deny he had committed any of the crimes for which he has been arrested and charged,

when it all could be said so simply:

> Sen. Blustrous Fatkitty denies the charges.

In second references to people and things, you can tighten your sentences by using general, usually shorter, terms for the specific. Thus, you would have such things as:

- *legislators* for *members of the House and Senate*
- *the organization* for *the National Association for the Advancement of Colored People*
- *authorities* for *police, sheriff's deputies,* and *FBI agents.*
- *residents* for *people who live in the Morningside community*
- *high court* for *the U.S. Supreme Court*
- *aides* for *the press secretary, administrative assistant,* and *bodyguards*

There are numerous other possibilities that we won't bother to list. Keep in mind, however, that on *first reference* you should be specific to make clear whom and what you are talking about. Furthermore, don't take the preceding list as any sort of absolute. Most nouns have synonyms. Use them generously. *Aides* can become *assistants, advisers, associates,* or *confidantes,* or, in less polite situations, *cronies, henchmen, enforcers.*

Editors and journalism professors' insistence to the contrary, newspapers are not—and never have been—written so that any twelve-year-old can understand them. If that were so, police reporters would not persist in adopting the police habit of calling thugs *perpetrators,* nor would headline writers dig into their Greek vocabulary to identify legislators as *solons.* Furthermore, today's twelve-year-olds, thanks to the ubiquitous television, are exposed daily to wars, royal pregnancies, assassinations, nuclear proliferation, and cereal commercials. Today, editors are less inclined to quibble over the use of such once intimidating words as *microcosm* and *slog,* realizing that even children slog through a microcosm of our troubles every day.

Newspaper stories should, nonetheless, be written simply. But simple writing is not simplistic writing. The best writing, in fact, is simple writing. It is easy to follow, and it communicates; and the business of newspapers is communication. Ernest Hemingway maintained that he wrote for people who moved their lips when they read. He preferred simple declarative sentences. That still is the best way to tell a story.

Now that you know something about the formulas and language of newspaper stories, let's take a brief look at the various forms that come from these techniques.

The News Story (Again)

Sure, we have discussed the news story before, but we told you how to write one, not what it is. What the *news story* is is the foundation upon which all other newspaper writing is based. To solidify its place at the heart of the newspaper scheme of things, editors have given its content macho names, such as *hard news,* to distinguish it from sissy *soft news,* or *spot news,* to give it that we-were-there quality. This is our way of warning you that editors will expect you to be a journalistic aggressor. Only when you prove to be hopelessly talented will they excuse you to pursue flighty objectives.

The Feature Story

For those drawn to journalism not by the sound of alarms and disasters but by the restless urge to write, the outlet is the *feature story.*

The feature story has its different names, too, given by editors fearful that the common term somehow debases the idea that newspapers are solely about the business of news. Hence, we have such recent terms as *news feature* and *soft news,* the latter carrying the connotation that fluff carries import, too. To dare apply electronic terms to the printed word, it might be said that the classic news story is the *play-by-play* and that the feature is the *color* commentary.

Newspapers have had feature stories at least as long as they have had news stories, and the two types are by no means mutually exclusive. In the traditional sense, features are what used to be called *human interest* stories, those wonderful collections of human agonies and victories about everything from the harvest of giant turnips to the joys of panhandling. But the human interest story certainly has its element of news, helping magnify society's current styles and eccentricities. Editors have finally conceded that news at its best is the story of people. *People news,* in fact, became an obsession of newspapers in the 1970s, although few papers have pursued the concept with any consistency.

Features without some link to current events, of course, really belong someplace other than newspapers, and, as we will attempt to show you in the next chapters, any news story can be *featurized.*

Actually, the concepts of news and features have been blended for some time in other types of stories, such as the *interpretive story,* which tries to make sense of complex issues—a considerable writing job—and the *investigative story,* which is insistent in its featured detail of scandalous news.

The Interpretive Story

The *interpretive story,* variously dubbed in the trade, *think piece, explainer, thumb sucker,* and *analysis,* normally seizes on some pressing issue and endeavors to make everyone understand it. You get leads like this: "Inflation is a problem that won't go away, and experts say it will probably get worse." Or: "Can the Peachtree Plaza Hotel withstand a nuclear blast?" And headlines like: WHAT IF A SATELLITE FELL ON ATLANTA? (an actual headline in the *Atlanta Journal,* which prompted a parody from the *Austin Statesman* staff: WHAT IF A BUFFALO FELL ON AUSTIN?). From the various experts and professional talkers, you move to address those burning issues in some detail. The Plaza, for instance, would be vaporized, but some rats in the basement might survive. (Some experts told us so.)

Clarity is especially important in writing the interpretive story, since the subject would not need interpreting if it were readily clear.

In such stories, it is best to do most of the interpreting yourself in the written version, since experts tend to speak expert-ese, a language foreign to non-experts in your audience. It may be helpful for you as a reporter to know the following:

> A nuclear power plant in critical state is reliant upon the proper functioning of the high pressure coolant intake system to prevent the remote possibility of core meltdown.

But it is best explained to your readers in more basic terms:

> Without cold water to cool off the little radioactive rods that boil water in a nuclear generator, the rods could melt, drop through the floor of the plant, and set off radioactive steam that could wipe out a city.

That much readers should be able to understand. It is not your purpose in the interpretive story to establish that you have learned something. It is to help your readers learn something. The interpretive story offers the best opportunity to play teacher to an ignorant world by making simple that which often is so disturbingly complex.

The Investigative Story

The *investigative story* begins with the premise that evil has not been erased from the world. Such stories are best approached with indignation, tempered with as much fairness as is humanly possible. Just laying out the cold, smoking-gun facts often suffices: "Under the guise of promoting dental health, teachers at Daffy Elementary School routinely coerce students into surrendering their candy, which the teachers eat themselves, informed parents say." (Not all investigative stories end presidencies and unpopular wars.)

More than in most stories, attributions are vital in investigative-story writing to lend authority to your discovery and to make clear who is doing the accusing. The reporter never should assume the role of accuser in writing the investigative story, even if his or her facts are backed up by a chorus of eyewitnesses.

Investigative reporting may be the most glamorized position in journalism, but the writing of investigative stories can be deadly dull. When you publicly depict a person or institution as disreputable, you have to back up the claims with irrefutable facts, else the target can claim defamation and sue you. Hence, investigative stories tend to be long and meticulous and filled with qualifiers. When the people under scrutiny are wise enough to offer some public defense to the charges, that should be played high in the story to establish fairness. Because of the delicate nature of the investigative story, it is essential to make clear in your writing that fairness has been strived for. Therefore, any quibblings or alibis, regardless how feeble, that benefit the person or institution being held justly accountable in public print should be duly quoted. That is not to say that the story should be written so cowardly as to obscure completely that something incredibly suspicious has been uncovered. As is the case with any kind of newspaper story, the investigative story should not be written in the first place if nothing important has been found.

Editorials

At larger newspapers, you won't get to write *editorials* until your hair begins to gray. The *editorial pages,* usually distinguished clearly from the news pages, are the primary place where newspapers allow—yea, demand—

opinion. One of the easiest ways to spot a critic who is ignorant of the way newspapers function is to listen for the occasional attack upon the editorial pages as biased, one-sided, subjective, and opinionated. They are; that's what they are supposed to be.

At most large dailies, the editorial pages reflect the reputation and integrity of the publication, as well as the will of the corporation, so publishers do not take lightly the selection of employees to serve the function of writing editorials. Thus, usually only the old and wise are so anointed.

There are two basic kinds of editorials in newspapers. There are the unsigned editorials, usually called *staff editorial* because they represent some consensus among the several members of the *editorial board,* the folks who work in the editorial department, with one writer assigned to go forth and lecture to the public on that issue. Most newspapers run three to five of these staff editorials each day.

Then, there are the *editorial columns.* These are the opinions with bylines and mug shots that identify the person writing them. These editorials amount to short, personal essays. Most large newspapers carry at least one column by a satirist or humorist to mix in with the prophecies of doom. Newspapers also employ a mix of local editorial columnists and *syndicated* columnists. Syndicated columns are distributed by syndication services, which pay the columnists fees based on how many newspapers buy the service. (Syndicates also sell other features to newspapers, such as comics, astrology predictions, how-to-do-it articles, and feature stories.)

Feature Columns

Apart from editorial columns, most large newspapers have general, or feature, columns. The *featured columnist,* as that writer is sometimes called, is allowed the latitude of opinion within certain limits. Such columnists—and some newspapers have several—deal with *human* problems rather than cosmic truths. Such columns magnify some subject merely skirted or perhaps ignored by the news pages. Featured columnists also are prone to write about their pets, children, and old sweethearts. Some featured columnists are funny; some are sentimental; some gossip about their friends and where they hang out.

The feature column is the stuff of which legends and acclaim are made. In the business, becoming a featured columnist practically takes an act of Congress, so don't expect to have to write a column unless most of your coworkers are dead and gone or unless your editors share the high regard you have for your talents. On smaller papers, luck sometimes strikes. On larger newspapers, you have to be both experienced and very good.

Reviews and Criticisms

Reviews and *criticisms* basically are editorials applied to the arts. Reviewers and critics, however, do not so much attack the world as the works of the creative. Practically every newspaper has its reviewers and critics for fine arts, movies, television, and restaurants. Traditionally, a reviewer is more merciful than a critic in that a reviewer merely sums up the subject, whether it be a symphony concert or the latest episode of "Dallas." The critic is prone to ridicule and occasionally praise. However, newspapers tend to use the terms interchangeably and often call them editors, such as *arts editor, music editor, TV editor,* and so on. Increasingly, newspapers employ specialists in these areas rather than grabbing someone in the newsroom who happens to like—or loathe—certain movies, TV, types of music, types of art.

Sports Writing

Sports writing basically is news and feature writing about sports. The intriguing thing about sports writing is that it often brings out the best in newspaper writers. One reason, we suppose, is that sports stories are generally action stories. Knowing how to write action is one of the best skills to have in the newspaper game, and a few of the nation's best *serious* writers have been extricated from newspaper sports departments. Ralph McGill, James Reston, and Tom Wolfe are among the more famous.

Another significant aspect of sports writing is that it has for generations combined the news and feature approaches, telling us first that Bartkowski busted his ribs again, then that the Falcons lost miserably.

Since sports sections tend to be the best-read sections of newspapers, we will move now to instructing you in how to apply the sports writing technique of featurized news to the world's less playful triumphs and disasters.

11

Writing with Style: the Forms

In chasing it [objectivity] we have dulled our stories. We too often made them frightfully boring, plodding unfoldings of events, in which the words, like plowmen plodding their weary way, were strung together like mud balls when they might as well have been pearls.

Ralph McGill, *The Best of Ralph McGill: Selected Columns*

There is an old joke in journalism about the newspaper reporter who covered the Johnstown, Pennsylvania, flood of 1889 and filed a lead that began with God standing on a mountaintop, looking out over the destruction. His editor wired back: "Forget flood. Get interview with God." Editors, you will find, are very literal-minded people. The reporter may have been overstating the facts a mite, but there was a commendable sense of awe in that approach. It might be said, frankly, that the best newspaper writing always has come from the perspective of God on a mountaintop, that view which is at once detached and involved.

A former city editor of ours used to urge his reporters to "write with a sense of history." It was his way of telling us to render the story significant, to give it the energy of cavalry charging and mortars firing. It was his way of telling us not to write stories that are dull. We give the same advice to you.

Making zoning board meetings seem like Caesar's crossing the Rubicon obviously is not something you can do with ordinary writing, so let us now begin the risky task of telling you how to write with style.

Style is that quality buried in us all which manifests itself as a shout of distinction. Applied to writing, it is that broad stamp upon all the sentences

132

and paragraphs that says, "Mine." The person who has found his or her style leaves some personal mark upon the work.

Good writing is like music. It has its distinctive rhythm, its pace, flow, cadence. It can be hummed. The great stylists seem to have an inner music. But even the not-so-great stylists can learn to play a tune or two with their words.

In searching for your writing style, it is always wise to study the styles of others. Steal if you must, for a style cannot be truly stolen but always has some borrowed parts. In the end, however, you must realize what you do best in order to do it well. There are people who write action well, but not description. There are people who write good funny stories but bad sad stories. It is all a matter of style.

You will find that style actually is not something you plan. It just sort of happens. This is especially true in newspaper writing, where the locomotive of genius often runs into the wall of deadlines. But the more experienced you become, the more naturally you will write the way you write.

Now that you have started searching for your style, let's discuss what to do with it.

Writing, like everything else, has its rules. Your genius of style, therefore, will encounter encumbrances. Journalism, in fact, has a bad habit of tying style into knots. Most newspaper-writing instruction begins with special rules of grammar which presuppose that newspaper writing is somehow above, or below, ordinary writing. It should not be.

However, there are some common writing tips that are worth mentioning—with appropriate reservations. Among them are these:

1. *Avoid the use of adjectives.* Why? Some journalism teachers insist this is true, but we have never seen it proven in actual writing. Try writing a weather story without using *hot* or *cold.* Be discreet with adjectives, however. Judgmental ones are best avoided. Calling people *fat, ugly, deformed, pompous, criminal, homicidal, demented,* or *despicable* can get you in bad trouble. Calling people *beautiful, stunning, sweet, generous, wonderful,* or *magnificent* can make you look silly.

2. *Avoid words ending with -ings and -lys.* See criticism of Rule One. It might be argued that "he sees a psychiatrist" is stronger than "he is seeing a psychiatrist." Then again. The one *-ly* problem we have encountered is when the adverbs are stuck together, as in "she was severely physically handicapped." That is not wrong, but certainly it is awkward. Better to say, "she was severely handicapped physically." Better still, find a different way to state the matter.

3. *Avoid the use of "quite" and "rather."* We'd rather not, but it's quite up to you. The argument against these seemingly harmless words is

that they merely emphasize the obvious: *He was rather nice looking* instead of simply *he was nice looking.* Our position is that there is no harm in emphasizing the obvious. The emphasis can have an ironic value in understatement, as in: *He was quite upset at finding a rattlesnake in his lunchbox.*

4. *Avoid the use of dependent clauses.* When writing long stories, it is hard to avoid using something other than declarative sentences. But don't hang dependent clauses all over the place so that your story is dependent on an interpreter. Dependent clauses are those parenthetical parts of sentences, often beginning with the words *which, when, where,* and *while,* that depend on the rest of the sentence for their meaning. An example: "*While she was at the Macon Beacon,* Mary developed a new way of spelling *paraphernalia.*" Journalistic purists prefer dividing the two ideas into separate sentences. But making a habit of that limits variety. Dependent clauses are often valuable in squeezing an extra idea into a sentence.

5. *Have one idea to a sentence.* Not bad advice, actually, if it were always possible. As we have said, the best sentences are simple declarative sentences—with one idea to the sentence. This is a goal, but not one to be pursued at the expense of variety and clever rhythm.

6. *Avoid any form of the verb "to be."* This warning usually refers to the word *was.* Again, there is some passable merit here. *Was* puts sentences into the passive voice and deprives them of some of their punch. If you are having trouble getting action into your sentences, look for the *wases* and see if you can set them aside. Make "he was driving" into "he drove." Change "she was running" to "she ran."

7. *Put emphatic material at the beginning or end of a paragraph.* Wonderful advice. Sentences, as well as paragraphs, should have anchors. Either seize the reader at the outset ("Dead. That's what she was.") or surprise the reader at the end ("Jerry Galloway said he would never move from in front of the oncoming train. That was *the last thing he never did.*") Every good joke should have a strong lead-in and a strong punch line. Think of writing as a joke.

Think Before You Write

All the while you are researching, you should be writing your story in your head. What you will be disappointed to realize is that the story in your head does not translate directly onto paper. But it is a start. During your research, you should be thinking of what angle the story should take, what quotes will be worth using, and, most importantly, just what it is about the subject that interests you. Somehow you will get the general idea down on paper.

The key point—what this lesson is about, really—is to absorb what is interesting and use it. That is where the stylistic approach should commence. When the words click up on the VDT screen, your lead should focus on that mannerism, that mood, that scene, that set of numbers, that quote, that irony, that conflict which kept flashing again and again in your mind's composition of the story. Obviously, that element is what grabbed your imagination. Chances are it will also grab the reader's imagination.

Seizing on the element of interest often can turn an ordinary story into something not so ordinary. Take the hold-up of a chicken restaurant, for instance. The facts are roughly these: A man walks up to the service window with a shotgun stuffed down his pants; the workers disappear into a back room; police arrive and the man is arrested. The conventional lead might go something like this:

> A would-be robber with a shotgun was arrested Thursday after employees of a fast-food restaurant thwarted his efforts by hiding in a storeroom.

Not bad, actually. But if you make a few phone calls to pick up any extra tidbits and apply that information to what the whole affair must have looked like, especially to the robber, you get something like this:

> A would-be robber with a shotgun stuffed down his pants limped away in disgust from a southwest Atlanta chicken stand Thursday evening after everybody he intended to rob disappeared into a back room.
>
> His obvious frustration was compounded when he walked right into the gun-drawn presence of an Atlanta policeman who had been called to Church's Chicken at 464 Markham St. S.W.
>
> The store's manager, Michael Siplin, has learned to cope with such situations through bad experience. He says he has been robbed four times in the past month and, this week alone, lost six employees who got tired of looking down the barrel of a gun.
>
> "They just walk up to the window, pull out a gun, and walk off with money," complains Siplin.

This is how you begin to stretch within the limitations of the old inverted pyramid. Toss in some color, some legitimate interpretation, a little relevance and you get a story with some action. None of this can be fabricated, of course. In this particular story, the reporter got the information about the limping and the drawn gun from police and the restaurant's manager. The "obvious frustration" was the reporter's interpretation, but what purist would suppose that the would-be robber was happy?

Stylistic journalism, as you can begin to see from this example, has its place in the traditional form. But it also is changing the form. The inverted pyramid is slowly being supplanted by new shapes. The *Wall Street Journal* formula has given us the *diamond,* and even the traditional "feature" has given us the limited use of the *carafe*, the inverted pyramid lead-in followed by a lengthy narrative. Let us now turn to those other forms, with one final word about the inverted pyramid.

The Inverted Pyramid

For the foreseeable future, the inverted pyramid is inescapable in journalistic writing. It has one important characteristic that should be applied to all shapes of journalistic writing. It requires a strong first paragraph. All good stories—all good books, for that matter—have good first paragraphs. The first paragraph is the good writer's way of saying, "Hey, look here. I'm about to tell you something fascinating." In the inverted pyramid, of course, the first paragraph usually summarizes. In other forms the first paragraph may merely introduce a character or zoom in on some odd detail. The first paragraph always should be written with smoothness and confidence, so as to tell the reader that a professional writer is at work. The best first paragraphs make readers see something. With the right detail and images, this can be done sufficiently with the inverted pyramid. For instance:

> Some said it looked like an afternoon stroll—Karl Wallenda's walk in the sky, 541 unusually fast but careful steps across Tallulah Gorge.
>
> The amazing 65-year-old circus star walked 1,000 feet toe-to-heel 700 feet above the jagged bottom of the gorge in 17.7 minutes—22.3 minutes fewer than had been predicted.
>
> Chomping on a piece of candy, he grinned and jabbered into two movie microphones as he traversed the $\frac{13}{16}$-inch cable while a hush settled over the smaller-than-expected crowd.
>
> The throng gasped as Wallenda eased toward the middle of the wire, then smoothly flipped to a headstand and kicked his heels in the air to a round of applause.

This story shows how small details can serve the action. Wallenda's walk is recorded by the clock and the measuring tape. Such things help readers absorb the import of events. The counting of the steps was not only a fine detail, but also a scoop of sorts. The *Atlanta Journal* was the only newspaper that day to print this particular bit of information, a detail that was later reprinted in the *Guinness Book of World Records* for that year.

The Carafe

The *carafe* is a spinoff of the inverted pyramid. It sets the upside-down stuff atop a narrative or chronology, giving a story the shape of a wine-serving bottle. In this form, the traditional lead-in explains the significance and the nut of the issue. Then, developments follow in the classic storytelling form, from beginning to end.

Laurie Baum, a reporter at the *Atlanta Journal,* used this approach in detailing the deliberations of the jury in the trial of Wayne Williams, convicted of killing two young men in Atlanta's string of murdered and missing young people cases. Her story began:

> Once the jury forewoman put her signature on the verdicts declaring Wayne Williams guilty of two counts of murder, the 12 jurors joined hands and prayed as some began to cry out of pity for the Williams family and out of relief that their own ordeal had come to an end.
>
> After listening to nine weeks of testimony from technical fiber evidence to often-contradictory eyewitness accounts and emotional testimony from the defendant and his parents, the jurors assembled at 5:20 P.M. Friday in a courtroom—used instead of a jury room because of the volume of evidence—to begin their 11½-hour deliberations on Williams's fate.

That sets the premise. Then, we have:

> The following is an account of the proceedings based on the recollections of four jurors who agreed to speak with the *Atlanta Journal* but who asked not to be named.

From there, she goes into an hour-by-hour account beginning with the selection of the jury forewoman, the review of the mound of evidence, discussion of Williams's apparent "lies" and of the fiber evidence, the vote shift of a holdout, and the consensus on one case and the continued debate on another. The story ends thusly:

> For them, the reading of the verdict signified the end of an extraordinary experience—one they've called "enlightening, good, highly pressured, and awesome."

The carafe has had its place in newspaper writing for generations, although it has been used sparingly, and the name is ours. It is best applied to extraordinary events where much detailing is required. Before using the form, consider whether the story cannot be better told by weaving the events in some other form. The carafe form risks simply lumping material into easy chunks—easy for the writer but not necessarily easy for the reader.

The Straight Narrative

The *straight narrative,* telling a story from the logical beginning to the logical end, is almost never used in journalism. One reason is that readers have to read all the way to the end to find out what you are talking about.

People simply do not read newspapers as they do books. If you have drawn in the readers properly, they might follow the story to the end even if you have given away the plot with a nut graph (that paragraph high in the story that summarizes the point, or "nut," of the story), but they probably will not read to the end just to find out what the story is about.

However, the narrative does have its place, and some mavericks, such as the columnist Charles McDowell, advocate its greater use. The narrative can work well with a *sidebar,* those shorter stories that relate to some larger story. If the reader already knows what is going on, the reader may want some chronology. Meyer Berger, a Pulitzer Prize–winning writer for the *New York Times,* used the narrative to tell the story of a crazed killer who had gunned down several people on the streets of New York. Berger simply began where the killer had begun, telling the story from the eyewitness accounts of the killer's movements that day.

The narrative is always a shaky approach. Here is an example from the *Minneapolis Tribune* that leaves us begging, for fifteen inches or more, "Who is dead?" It begins like this:

> ARLINGTON, Va.—The humid haze of early summer lay hot and heavy on Washington, D.C., but here across the river, under the oak trees, the air was fresh and cool.
>
> The little girl sat on a folding chair, her mother on one side and her older brother on the other. The child's face was blank and bemused, almost dazed. Around her stood a thousand others. Closer in, a score of men with cameras crept and scuttled and snapped their shutters at her.
>
> In the center of the crowd, just in front of the girl and her brother and her mother, stood six soldiers. They held an American flag stiffly over the casket in which the little girl's father was to be buried.

In the final two paragraphs we learn what is going on:

> Then the little girl and her brother and her mother were taken away, leaving their father and husband under the oak trees with the others who, like him, earned in war their right to lie there.
>
> In a few weeks, he too will have a little headstone, with an inscription like all the thousands of others on the hills and in the hollows under the trees. His will say:
>
> Medgar Evers, Mississippi.

For emotional impact, the story is most effective. Near the end, the writer has this gripping paragraph:

> Now the little girl wept again, and then looking at her mother and seeing her weeping too, sobbed aloud and clung to her uncle's arm. He lifted her into his lap.

The problem, and the only problem as far as we're concerned, is that the reader may have never given the sad drama a reading without knowing early on whom the story was about. Even with the now-you-know ending, probably many of you, children of a different era, don't know that Medgar Evers was a civil rights leader killed in June 1963 in his effort to bring racial equality to his home state of Mississippi. Now, as Paul Harvey says, you know the rest of the story, which the narrative form limited the writer in telling us.

Our advice is to use the narrative only if you understand fully what you are attempting to do.

The Diamond

The *diamond*, too, has been around a while, but the *Wall Street Journal* has elevated it to a newspaper art form. Basically, the form has a narrative introduction, often an anecdote or some personalized image, which leads to the *nut graph*, that paragraph where the point is revealed, followed by a *significance graph*, relating the point to the world scheme of things. The nut and significance graphs lead into the old inverted pyramid, wherein the relevant issues and background are discussed in order of descending importance.

Here is how James P. Gannon, now executive editor of the *Des Moines Register*, did it when he was a reporter for the *Wall Street Journal:*

> LYNCHBURG, Va.—Over a conference table littered with scraps of leather heels and sample shoes, Robert Lockridge shows a visitor a chart with his dark vision of the economy's future: a jagged line sinking down, down, down through 1975 and 1976.
>
> Mr. Lockridge, president of Craddock-Terry Shoe Corp., a footwear maker based here, fingers a point representing June of 1974 and says, "This is where I told our boys to stop buying anything we couldn't use in 30 days." His company is hunkering down for a long siege of hard times, the executive says. "Now is the time for tightening up, for prudent management and for no expansion," he contends.

Now that we have heard Mr. Lockridge's troubles, we move on to the nut graph:

> This batten-down-the-hatches mentality is only one of many signs that the national economic slowdown is beginning really to hit home in this industrial outpost in the foothills of Virginia's Blue Ridge Mountains. Other evidence is abundant: small but spreading layoffs, weakening retail sales, a backing up of inventories, a dramatic disappearance of materials, shortages, and the early signs of eroding prices. In short, the recession has arrived in Lynchburg.

But what of the rest of the world? Comes now the significant graph:

> With its diversified economy of foundries, garment shops, shoe factories, paperboard mills, electronic plants, and other businesses, Lynchburg pretty well reflects broad trends in the economy. Not dependent on any single industry, Lynchburg doesn't swoon when auto sales drop or home building slumps. It's more a barometer of the economy's general health. And right now, Lynchburg's businesses are signaling a creeping, pervasive recession that's spreading from one industry to another like a contagious disease.

There are variations on the formula, certainly. Sometimes, the nut graph may be followed by more anecdotal material before the significance graph is inserted. But the formula is one you will encounter in your work as more and more newspapers imitate the *Journal's* success.

The Goose Egg

When in doubt, write in circles. Actually, stylists are rarely predictable in their approach, and those with experience can start a story almost anywhere and wind up with an interesting presentation. More to the point, the best stories tend to be those that do, in fact, make a circle. By that, we mean a story that starts with a particular premise and then returns to it at the end. The *goose egg* actually is a classic form of storytelling. The scene opens, events unfold, and then the beginning is explained in terms of the moral at the end.

We have discussed the dangers of putting good endings on your stories that your editors might cut. But editors are becoming more attuned to good writing and are willing to struggle to save a good ending with a well-defined point. In the view of Jim Naughton, an assistant managing editor at the *Philadelphia Inquirer,* and a former White House reporter for the *New York Times,* a good ending is the writer's way of rewarding a reader for reading the story all the way through. Stylists also recognize the dramatic effect of good endings and prefer to make a valiant attempt to push them past editors who are inclined to cut from the bottom. In between the grabber beginning and the breathtaking ending, of course, the writer must have woven a tale worth the reader's journey. And, in journalism, that tale must have included important points, significant details, explanations, and background—all those facts that make it news.

One of the leading practitioners of the *goose egg* form is Richard Ben Cramer of the *Philadelphia Inquirer,* the current home of stylistic journalism with its stable of imaginative writers. Here is one example of how he makes his circle in a story about the boyfriend of one of the victims of New York's "Son of Sam" killer. We begin in a tavern:

Johnny Diel rolled into the Ridgewood III just a little bit late for his 6 P.M. bartender shift.

He was lit. His greetings to the regulars around the bar loosed a faint odor of Jagermeister, the German liqueur he favors.

Nobody said anything to him about the Jagermeister or his tardiness. In Ridgewood, a folksy German, Hungarian, and Yugoslav neighborhood on the Queens–Brooklyn border, Johnny is treated gently these days.

Since Jan. 30, Johnny has done little but hang out with the rest of the guys in Ridgewood. He makes no plans. He is often a little bit drunk.

And every once in a while, when he is very drunk, or when visitors come by from the "city," as Ridgewood residents call Manhattan, he talks about Jan. 30.

That is the day Johnny's girl friend, Christine Freund, was shot to death by Son of Sam, as Johnny sat next to her in his car.

At the end, we are back in the tavern. Diel is talking:

> "Right now, we'd be engaged already. We'd be planning our marriage. It'd all be different. I could never love a girl like I loved Chris. We went through our twenties together, and I think that's the most special age there is."
>
> A visitor at the bar said he knew how it must be.
>
> "You don't know," Diel said. "The only ones who know are the ones who live through it. You're out having a good time and some idiot comes along and blasts a part of your life away. You can't know."

Zap. The end.

In between, Cramer, in his simple, almost classic journalistic prose, introduces us to one poignant scene after another. Ultimately, it is not the style that is noticed but the very stylized selection of facts that make a mood. Another example from the middle of the story:

> Now, at 30, with no plans and no ambitions, no loves except for a single dead girl and no hopes of finding one, Johnny Diel is going nowhere.
>
> In his bedroom, as he wakes at noon, his first act is to clasp a chain with a silver "C" around his neck. She had worn the charm sometimes. He wears it always. He smooths his long dark hair and rubs a hand through his bushy beard and mustache while he looks into the mirror on the dresser. The dresser is decked with snapshots: Chris and John at a Christmas party at her house, Chris and John in Mexican costume for Halloween, Chris on the beach, Chris in formal gown . . .
>
> He shows visitors a photo album. It is filled with dozens of pictures of Chris's funeral.
>
> Then he drives the Pontiac to a flower shop, apologizing to a visitor for the lack of air-conditioning. "But I wanted the car right away," he explained. "It was Friday night and I wanted to surprise her, you know, I knew Chris was going to love this car."

In the flower shop, the woman behind the counter knows without asking that Diel wants a dozen red roses to take to the cemetery. As he waits for the flowers, a little gray cat plays with string on the floor.

"You know, Chris and me had this little cat once . . ." Diel says. The cat still lives with Chris Freund's parents. He sees the cat when he visits them every week.

At the cemetery, he exchanges the fresh roses for an earlier batch that has wilted in the August heat. As he kneels in front of the polished black stone, the reflection of his bowed head appears just below her name and the German inscription: "Geliedt and Unvergessen"—beloved and not forgotten.

Throughout the story, we see Cramer's focus on one man's obsession with a personal tragedy. If you look hard enough, you can also see Cramer walking along beside him, absorbing Diel's personal habits, his thoughts, his manner of speech. There should be little doubt that Cramer is the anonymous "visitor" sitting at the bar, trying to offer sympathy and absorbing the response that provides the story's touching ending: "You don't know. . . . You can't know." In the process, Cramer shows us a rare skill among newspaper writers, the ability to inject himself into a story without intruding. He is there, but only as a visitor. The story is as Diel might have told it to us and as only someone of Cramer's sensitivity could have. The best advice we could give you at this point is: Write like that.

Sensitivity and talent are something good writers tend to be born with. But most of us have more ability stored away than we often realize. To help bring out some of your latent genius, let us proceed now to some more detailed points on stylistic writing.

12

Writing with Style: How to Do It

A well-written newspaper story will make the reader see the depth of things. It is a factual vision of our times and places and the people who inhabit them. So let us not *tell* you how to write with style, but try to *show* you.

The following pages include what we regard as some very good examples of what we wish to illustrate. The examples are held up not as the only way, nor even the best way, to handle certain subjects. But they are examples of how some top professionals painted their particular pictures. We also include some of our own articles, not because they were the only ones we could find but because we can show you with some assurance what was being attempted—even if it didn't always work. Read the tips around the stories, certainly, but especially read the stories themselves. As in any craft, there always is something to be learned from the handiwork of others.

Let us mention here that we also are including some final warnings at the end of this chapter. Study them carefully, for they will help you bring realistic focus to unrealistic visions.

In this business, you will work for editors of varying tastes and attitudes. To become established in journalism, you will have to perform according to the standards of your employer. We think the following examples represent the highest of the current writing standards, but be prepared to have your employer disagree.

Looking Out Over History

Let us return now to the mountaintop we talked about at the beginning of the previous chapter. It is from up here that we can see how best to approach certain events of our time. This view from the mountaintop is often applied to stories involving important places and events: historic cities, wars, earthquakes. It is a perspective used by reporters who admit to watching television, to being *visual*. To them, stories are scripts with closeups and cutaways and panning. For the historic city, you can begin with a panorama, then cut to the multitudes in the street. Fade. Next scene.

For an example, let us rejoin Richard Ben Cramer as he looks out from the mountaintop on his first visit to Cairo:

> It is the joy of a visit here that just when you think you must cry for its troubles, this city will teach you to laugh. It is the sorrow of all who know it that just when you have learned to laugh, Cairo will show you more reasons to cry.
>
> Peace is now the dream of Cairo, peace and reconstruction and prosperity for all. Shall we laugh with the Cairenes for the unexpected joy? Or shall we cry for the hopes, the millions of hopes, that peace will not fulfill?

Then Cramer, the writing director, cuts to the multitudes in the streets:

> It is dusk now, in the City of the Dead, in the eastern quarter, where the tombs of Egyptians great and humble stretch on for miles to the base of the bare, dusty Moqattam hills. The call to evening prayers echoes from a mosque off the marble walls.
>
> To the south, the garbage pickers' fires send columns of smoke, black and thick, into the dull orange sky. It looks as if the gates of hell were moved to the cemetery wall to be close to these hundreds of thousands of souls.

Then, the writing camera moves in closer.

> And then, in the half-light, there is the form of a child at play, darting around the edge of a tomb. From beyond comes the sound of a mother calling her young ones in. Two donkey carts creak by, their drivers asleep. The donkeys know the way, because this is home.
>
> The donkeys and their drivers, the mothers and their young, are some of the thousands who live in the City of the Dead. The crypts and tombs for Egyptians of another age have provided homes for uncounted Cairenes for the last 30 years.

Then, we have the *nut graph:*

> In that time Cairo's population has grown from 2 million to 9 million. But Cairo itself has not grown so much as it has bulged. It is now, for the most part, an overburdened slum, with some living on the dead and more living on the living.

As usual, Cramer takes us full circle on his trip. We pick up near the end:

As they accelerated out of the circle, the driver glanced to his left at an intersection where a group of workmen had just dug a trench across the width of the cross street.

"Aha," he said, and began to smile.

The other student followed the driver's glance.

"Aha," he said, and began to giggle. Soon, both were giggling so hard that the driver had to pull over to the curb. Finally, he controlled his laughter enough to explain.

"They had just closed," he announced, as solemnly as he could, "one of the busiest streets in Cairo for an indefinite period of time."

Westerners learn to laugh, or leave.

To show you that any average human can do that, here is Ron Taylor's view from the mountaintop overlooking Plains, Georgia:

> This town would not be much different from any other little south Georgia farming village, except for events of history.
>
> The sun still comes up orange and unobstructed against the haze of autumn morning upon the scrub oaks and yellowing crops.
>
> And pickup trucks pulling queues of farm wagons still thunder like coupling freight trains across the double railroad tracks running through the center of this southwest Georgia town.
>
> It is harvest time, and the men of Plains go to the fields, like fishermen go to the sea. In the peanut fields, they work all night beneath floodlights in the dark.
>
> As they do, a huddle of official-looking cars zip past them along U.S. 280. Jimmy Carter, the local boy who would be president, is home again for awhile.
>
> With the sun comes the clatter of tractors and the harsh ring of hammer against steel wheels banging loose ruptured tires at Billy Carter's Service Station.
>
> Old men made leathery and ragged by their labors, now retired to rest awhile, gather at Billy's to watch the world go by, and it does. There is a procession, almost constant, almost silent, of strange and curious people making the circle through their town.

From the vantage point of the mountaintop, you can carry your readers through fire and snow. For *Atlanta Journal* colleague Bill Montgomery, the occasion was snow:

> It was the week Atlanta was measured for a one-two whammy. A week for the coldest morning of the century, followed in hours by a freezing celestial bucket of rush-hour sleet and snow that turned the city's streets into skating rinks and transformed its highways into ice-bottomed parking lots.
>
> It was a week that will be treasured for months by barroom storytellers and office water cooler yarnspinners. Though the overall hardships hardly

seemed to equal television news images of autos buried to their windows in Buffalo, the ordeal was quite a bit for Scarlett O'Hara's Sun Belt city.

It was a week that brought out the best, and some of the worst, in Atlanta's people. Some folks lent their brawn to push confused motorists, unaccustomed to true winter driving, through the icy spots. Others roamed the city like predators, ripping off batteries, CB radios, and tape decks from abandoned cars.

The week had its light spots, like the guy ice skating in the center lane of Roswell Road, leading a creeping procession of 20-odd cars Tuesday night.

And tragedy: Leonard Gravino, a 35-year-old shoe store manager, suffered a fatal heart attack at the wheel of his car that same night, after fighting traffic for five hours. One of 10 dead attributed to the storm, Gravino is survived by his widow and two young children.

It all happened in Atlanta the week of January 10, 1982.

Cities, of course, are not the only thing you can see from the mountaintop. Another colleague, Mike Christensen, watched the demise of the Equal Rights Amendment in the state legislature:

It was quiet when they buried the Equal Rights Amendment in Georgia—quiet and solemn and final. There will be no more votes, no women dressed in green or red, no rallies on the Capitol steps, no debates.

The boisterous House of Representatives usually is still only when it is praying, but Wednesday afternoon the members sat hardly moving for 90 minutes while ERA ratification was called up, debated, and defeated by a vote of 116–57.

House Speaker Tom Murphy said he didn't want any turmoil, and there was none. Even the spectator-laden galleries looked like a painting. There was silence in the marble halls outside. "It was so serious it could have been a wake," Rep. Peggy Childs of Decatur said.

Thirteen House members, led by ERA sponsor Cathey Steinberg of Atlanta, took the microphone—11 in favor and two opposed—and padded across the carpeting as if they were in church. Each had been limited to 10 minutes, and only Rep. R.A. Dent of Augusta took more, but he is an institution, and it is expected.

In the end the bell rang, the voting board blushed red, and for the fourth time in eight years, the General Assembly turned aside the most emotional issue it has ever faced.

As the members filed out, 68-year-old Rep. Eleanor Richardson of Decatur made her way slowly down the center aisle, her eyes rimmed with tears.

From these examples, we hope we have made the point that one way of writing with a sense of history requires that you make people see in written cinemascope the flow of events around them. From Cramer's laughter and tears about Cairo to Christensen's wake for the ERA, the reader should be able to realize that what is happening is far from trivial.

But this movie you are writing can also start with a closeup. History, after all, is what has happened to people, and sometimes it is best to see it through their eyes. You can give a sense of history by letting the people who were there tell their private stories, as Ron Taylor did with Ceola Miller:

> SELMA, Ala.—The first time Ceola Miller went to register to vote, they wouldn't let her inside the Dallas County courthouse.
>
> The second time she went, they told her she failed to qualify because she left out her middle initial. The third time, they told her she mispronounced words on the literacy test. The fourth time, they told her she had mistakenly included her married name.
>
> The fifth time, she signed her middle initial, pronounced the words right, and listed only her maiden name. They finally said she could vote.
>
> Five times it took her to get her right to vote, and three times after that she walked to the crest of Edmund Pettus Bridge to demand that right for other black people. The first time, she was teargassed and kicked. The second time, she was so scared she could hardly see. The third time, she went on—went on to Montgomery and history. That last march began the morning of March 21, 1965—just 15 years ago Friday.
>
> Ceola Miller sits now in a mobile home bearing the dust of age and unpaved roads, surrounded by her eight children and two grandchildren on the outskirts of Selma. She is a proud and seemingly happy woman, proud of the house trailer with its ragged furniture and of the little piece of land upon which it sits, for they mean ownership, something that was once alien to many black people here.
>
> She pulls from a drawer the bright orange vest kept from dust and harm inside a plastic bag. The vest was the badge of honor for those who marched the 50 miles from Selma to Montgomery those four days in 1965. Only those who walked all the way got them. . . .
>
> She punctuates the sing-song story of those awesome days with self-effacing chuckles. But there are white people in Selma she will never forgive.

Since the best stories are the ones about people, let us now turn to some tips on personalizing the news.

Ordinary People

Every person, it has been said, has at least one good story to tell. The problem is that in the crush of the world's ordinary disasters so few of them get told. But editors increasingly are finding that the best way to tell any story—from earthquakes to zoning disputes—is through the people involved. We are not talking about survey stories here but about another closeup on some representative of the day's events before we pull back for the broader view.

William Serrin, one of the *New York Times*'s best stylists, virtually shouted his intentions in this approach to an economics story.

> The bottom line is not money in the bank. The bottom line is 4729 Conner Street, the unemployment line, next to the Spartan-Atlantic discount house and the United Wig Shop.
>
> Here, in a desolate, rundown shopping center just north of Mack Avenue, is the unemployment center for the Lower East Side. And every day, laid-off automobile workers come by the hundreds to fill out a one-page yellow application, Form MESC 1554 (Rev. 3–78). When claims are approved, they line up every two weeks on a day known as "hit day" to receive in unemployment compensation a maximum of $128.00 a week for a worker with a family of four.
>
> "I've got six or seven people, people I owe bills, calling me for money," says James Lee Gray, 27 years old, of Detroit, standing in the unemployment line. "I'm way behind."

From there, Serrin tells us about the trials of James Lee Gray before moving on to the dull details of Detroit's economic tribulations.

Serrin was even more personal in his approach to a story about a mining disaster in which a woman was killed:

> What he would not forget, after he had left the hospital where she lay, still in her sweatshirt and long underwear and coveralls, on an emergency room cart, was that there was nothing to suggest that she was dead.
>
> The only marks he could see were a small bump and a cut on her temple. A trickle of blood from the cut matted her hair. It was like a scrape from striking a car door or a kitchen cabinet. She looked as she did when she was alive.
>
> There was only one other thing. Her hands.
>
> Her face, like all coal miners' faces, was black with coal. But her hands had been covered with gloves. And, as she lay on the hospital cart, the gloves removed, her hands were as white as snow.
>
> And the coroner came and pronounced her dead.

Often times, the person *is* the story, as we saw in Cramer's piece on Johnny Diel. That was the case in this story by Frank Rossi, another of the *Philadelphia Inquirer*'s stylists:

> QUINTON, N.J.—They're wrecking my house.
>
> That's all 86-year-old Irene Pierce could think of as she watched her dream flattened. With an ear-splitting clamor, the bulldozer methodically smashed the wood-frame building and everything in it to matchsticks.
>
> Two hours before, Irene Pierce had tried to throw herself between the bulldozer and the ancient house in this Salem County community. Somebody

called the state police, and they dragged the kicking and crying woman away from the work area.

Now she was sitting across the street in a weathered rocking chair watching and trying to keep the wrath and the hurt from choking her. Two Quinton Township police officers, who had replaced the state troopers, stood by, waiting to grab her if she tried to get near the bulldozer again.

"God's gonna pay 'em," she said, her voice reflecting despair more than anger. "I ain't gonna hate 'em. I want this soul of mine to have a rest place when I die. I ain't gonna hate nobody."

This story also is an example of another important consideration in good writing: the need to evoke emotion.

Making People Feel

No story, if it is to be written well, can be approached with indifference. Chances are, if there was no emotion involved, the issue wouldn't be news anyway. Although you must maintain your pursuit of objectivity, never write a story so blandly that it will not be read. Remember, you are a reporter, not a recording secretary. You are the public's witness, and no witness sees events without being moved somehow. Where there is hurt, help the reader feel the hurt. Where there is humor, help the reader laugh. If the reader just wants the numbers, the reader can order the government reports.

There are dangers, of course. Portraying the emotions of one troubled person may ignore the emotions of the one who caused the troubles. But we already have discussed fairness, and, if you are truly fair, you will give us two sets of emotions in such instances rather than a distorted view of indifference on either side.

Keep in mind, however, that we are talking about depicting the emotions—and the emotional circumstances—of the people you are writing about, not your own. You are still an observer, a moved observer perhaps, but an observer nonetheless. Step out of the way of your subjects, but tell your readers what you saw when they traveled past.

Usually, stories that cry out for a dash of emotion are by their very nature emotional stories. Among them are stories about murders, natural disasters, deprivation, public buffoonery, and the everyday gaffes that people are going to laugh at anyway. Life is naturally interesting. Apathy is something that is forced upon us. Newspapers should not be the force of apathy.

How can anyone be indifferent about the dead cow problem? Let's face it, dead cows can be funny—to humans, anyway—and Ron Taylor more or less said so when his editors ordered him to explore this burning issue. His story began thusly:

> Last year, in Fulton County, 64 animals weighing more than 200 pounds apiece were hauled away by the government and quietly buried. It is estimated that 90 percent of the animals were cows.
>
> It is not an ordinary problem, the dead cow problem. Some officials deny it is a problem at all. "If they haul 'em up to the landfill, we bury 'em," says Walton County Commission Chairman Robert M. Hawk, dismissing the issue.
>
> But Gil Davis, community development director for Rockdale County, says he gets four, five dead cow reports a week. Just since Jan. 1, neighboring Newton County has buried 41 cows, 17 horses, and one hog. Seems there's a dead horse problem, too.

The dead horse problem, in fact, dominated the second half of Taylor's story, partly because the two people telling him about the situation were so incredibly quotable. After mentioning that the dead horses caused the most grief, he picked up these observations:

> "Most of 'em belong to teenage girls. They're a desperate lot anyway," says Davis. "They think a hearse ought to come out, and that we ought to have flowers and a casket.
>
> "When you drive up with the backhoe, you'll see them draped across the horse, crying their hearts out, threatening to throw themselves under the wheels of the backhoe."
>
> [James] Johnson says the parents of children who have horses that die often will request that they sneak in and bury the thing before the kids get home from school.
>
> One elderly woman, he says, kept them waiting beside a hole they had dug for her horse while she ceremoniously covered it with a blanket.

The way a person tells a story to you obviously can influence the way you write it for the newspaper. There certainly was nothing funny about the mass suicide of 400 members of the People's Temple at Jonestown, Guyana, in 1978. That is, unless you see the tragedy through the mischievous eyes of the lawyer Mark Lane, the conspiracy buff who helped represent Jim Jones's bizarre cult. Consequently, Ron Taylor's meager contribution to the massive coverage of that event turned out like this:

> Up the hill and into the thick jungle of Jonestown, Guyana, they went, two gentleman attorneys fleeing one of the oddest tragedies of modern human history.
>
> As automatic weapon fire rang through the air, 69-year-old Charles Garry bounced along with his stuffed briefcase.

"I said, 'Charles, throw that damn thing away,' " recalls his companion, Mark Lane.

"But I've got all the files on the People's Temple in here," protested Garry. "Mark, I've never lost a file in my life. I have a duty to my client."

"But he just ordered you killed, Charles," Lane reminded him. "I would consider that a termination of contractual agreement."

Garry was adamant. Besides the records, the briefcase contained his electric hair dryer.

"I said, 'Charles, you'll never find a place to plug that in out here in the jungle,' " Lane recalls.

But the briefcase went with them into the high jungle grass.

As Lane spun his tale, Taylor could not keep from laughing, and he saw no reason to keep his readers from laughing. Still, it was a tragedy we were talking about, which Lane acknowledged as Taylor did in this passage:

Lane sits in his Memphis office and chuckles occasionally as he recalls the craziness of it all, but he also remembers vividly how close he came to dying only a week ago. More than 400 people were not so lucky as he. Some were shot dead; most drank poison.

The "so-called" suicide, Lane calls the mass dying of Rev. Jim Jones and the members of his strange sect, the People's Temple, at their 3000-acre hideaway deep in the rain forest of the tiny South American country of Guyana.

"I don't understand how you drip poison into a baby's mouth and call it suicide," says Lane. "That's out-and-out murder. The choice was not whether to die, but how to die—drink poison or be shot."

Some mayhem is just plain funny, as we see in this treatment by Leonard Ray Teel of a story that builds its own case for laughter:

GAINESVILLE, Ga.—The shoot-out at Welchel's Barber Shop along Highway 60 makes people wonder if the hills up here are big enough for both Eddie Joe Ledford and brother-in-law Steve Free.

Because Ledford survived being shot in the abdomen, people can only guess where the feud between the Ledfords and the Frees will end. The last words Ledford was heard telling his brother-in-law were:

"I'll get you for this. I'll get you for this."

So ended Saturday's explosive shooting, slashing, and roughing between three Ledfords and three Frees. The gunfire sent three barbers running to huddle in the locked bathroom of their empty shop and scared the druggist next door and his clerk, who ducked behind a shelf of pharmaceuticals.

Ledford, his wound bleeding, was rushed to the hospital by his 20-year-old wife, Lora Ann, after she got free of the Frees' hands that were pulling her blonde hair.

Nearly hysterical, she drove 120 miles an hour along a two-lane road that looked fuzzy because she lost her glasses when her head was being pulled around.

"Please, you're all that's keeping me holding on. Please calm down," said Ledford, her husband of three months.

In the back seat, Ledford's 70-year-old father, Ernest, with a swollen eye from being knocked down in the 10 minutes of violence, was watching her out of the other eye and urging, "Slow down! Slow down!"

"I was airborne," Lora Ann says. On the way to the hospital she zoomed past the police and ambulance going to Welchel's Barber Shop, where the entire glass front door had been blown out and the three barbers were just beginning to peek out of the bathroom.

Notice, also, in this story the wealth of details and how they are sprinkled throughout.

Just as some things are undeniably funny, others are grievously sad. No event in our society, probably, is sadder than the death of a child, and there is no reason to make it seem less so in writing about it, as in this account:

Little Jeremy Rowe sat on the steps of the Full Gospel Fellowship Church, gingerbread cookie all over his face, and told his granddaddy Friday how he was going that evening to get a Halloween suit.

Children walked by his house at 783 Mercer St. SE Saturday night, going Trick or Treating, but Jeremy was not among them.

He was dead. They hauled his body out of a wooded area at the corner of Mercer and Waldo streets in the Saturday morning rain. He had been murdered, left hanging by his little sweater against a tree. He was just 4 years old.

By their very nature, investigative stories tend to evoke a sense of outrage. After all, the reporter has not done the job unless the facts are laid out so as to make the public feel robbed, deceived, cheated, or repulsed. But it is a feeling that must be conveyed by the facts, not by some trick of literary fancy, for the risks are grand in the investigative story, as we have discussed. But the facts suffice in most matters, as in this story:

Joey Lister never had a chance.

He was brought to the red-brick Children's Building at Central State Hospital in Milledgeville by his stepfather on May 18, 1970, at the age of 6. He carried an ivory-colored suitcase.

"The boy is attractive and cooperative," wrote the evaluating psychiatrist. "[He] asked for his stepfather."

From the first interview, the psychiatrist seemed uncertain what Joey's problem was.

"The boy has been on Ritalin [under outpatient care]," she wrote. "I wonder if he was hyperkinetic, but he does not look [it] now. He looks sad. . . ."

Nevertheless, Joey Lister was admitted to the hospital, formally diagnosed by a second psychiatrist as suffering hyperkinetic reaction of childhood, an intense, though somewhat nebulous, form of hyperactivity.

Joey Lister, the "J.L." of the landmark "J.L. and J.R." class-action lawsuit,* would spend six years at the state's largest mental hospital before a three-judge panel, condemning the state's method of committing youngsters and its lack of "alternative care," would essentially command his release.

In November, 1970, having celebrated his seventh birthday inside the hospital, Joey printed his name to a "notice to voluntary patient of rights to discharge."

It said, in effect, that Joey's discharge might be conditioned on the consent of his adoptive mother and stepfather. They never consented.

The boy's strained signature rests in a closed file as little more than a tragic symbol that his fate was somehow sealed. It was a fate he probably never understood to the day he died last year at the age of 12.

Joey's tortured life did not end even after he was released last April. Through a series of mysterious circumstances, he was returned to his adoptive father, whom he had not known since he was a toddler. The father seemed bent on breaking whatever fight Joey had left.

On Aug. 4, 1976, Joey died at the home of his adoptive father in Thomasville. His body was found in a clothes closet. He apparently had hanged himself.

The story documents at length Joey's stay in the hospital, the bureaucratic bunglings in attempting to place him in a foster home and the eventual trial of his adoptive father, Dr. Joe Lister (a dentist), who was convicted of child abuse.

Following Jim Naughton's dictum, the writer made the effort to end his opus with a dramatic touch:

> During his trial, Lister testified that he tied Joey to his bed on at least three occasions, supposedly to keep him from roaming threateningly around the house at night.
> And it was Lister who testified to the ultimate toughness of the kid he could not handle.

---

*As a result of the class action lawsuit brought on behalf of two young inmates at Georgia's Central State Hospital, identified only as J.L. and J.R., mental health officials were ordered in 1976 to provide "the least restrictive environment" for mental patients. That issue still is under study by federal judges in Georgia and Pennsylvania, where a similar lawsuit was brought. However, the U.S. Supreme Court ruled against the plaintiffs in both states in 1980 on another element of the case, declaring that the states did not have to require legal counsel for minors at commitment hearings. After his death, Joey Lister was identified as the "J.L." in the Georgia case. J.R. was never identified.

"I could always get him to ride his bicycle," Lister said in court, "but toward the end I couldn't make him run."

Setting Scenes

The best stories tend to begin with a scene. Many of the stories we already have shown you have examples of this: Cramer with his laughing-crying Cairo and the hell fires of the City of the Dead; Serrin with the white-handed corpse upon the hospital cart; Christensen with his hushed legislature; and Ron Taylor's effort with the gentleman lawyers huffing and puffing through the jungles.

The great risk in scene setting is that you can get carried away with your own wonderful prose and forget the points you were trying to make. Nothing so antagonizes editors—or other writers who fancy themselves the artistic compressors of information—than the literary reporter who flies off into the colors of wallpaper, the taste of whiskey, the Louis for whom the chair was named, the slant of the sun, and what Truman Capote would have said about it had he known what it was. Avoid tangents that do not connect with some planet. This is not to say that detailed descriptions have no place in journalism. We have spent most of these pages trying to make the opposite point. What we are warning you against here is self-indulgence, the misguided act of journalistic defiance. The inclination comes sometimes to show your editors that journalistic restraint is poppycock. Rather than new forms, which we encourage, you get overwrought scenes spewing adjectives and odors. Our advice is to first consider the point that is to be made, then consider the shortest possible scene—or other method—to take you there.

To show you that nobody's perfect, here's an example of one of Ron Taylor's opening scenes that almost got out of hand:

> Gene Wood leased the little white clapboard grocery store on Flat Shoals Road in southwest DeKalb County back in February and named it for his 7-year-old daughter, Kelly.
> "I'd planned to stay there as long as I could," he says. But now the butter and the cottage cheese and the sandwich spread sit spoiling in the freezer, and half-filled shelves go unstocked. Two weeks ago, Wood decided he couldn't stay any longer. Because of Melvin.
> "I don't want it on my conscience. Melvin had been a good friend of mine for years," Wood said, as he stood outside a rickety shed of tools and greasy motor parts where he now works on cars.
> Looking up at the clear blue sky of the crisp fall morning, Wood said, almost whispering, "Melvin was supposed to go on a hunting trip today."
> It was around 7 P.M. Friday, October 22, when Wood got the call from "Pee Wee," a helper in the store.

Any idea what this story is about, yet?

> "Melvin's been shot," Pee Wee finally blurted out after stammering incoherently at first, Wood recalls.
>
> When Wood arrived, he found Melvin lying behind the counter, clutching a pack of cigarettes—dead.

Now you know. But should it have taken that long to get some hint? The approach can be defended, especially since it's Taylor's story and he's here to defend it. The scene does offer some foreshadowing. We know that for some reason Wood is closing a store he owned, that it is because of Melvin, and that Melvin was supposed to go on a hunting trip. From the look at the sky and Wood's near whisper we should gather that Melvin will miss the hunting trip. But if he could redo the story, Taylor says, "I think I would have waited until later to dwell on the spoiling butter and cheese or to mention that the store was named for Wood's 7-year-old daughter."

See how much faster this story moves along:

> Bernard Bryan can't forget the fire, the awful, awful fire, and all the dead people lying around him, and mostly, the dying, the not-yet dead, and how helpless he felt.
>
> "I heard people hollering, hollering for blankets," he recalls.
>
> Tossed out of the broken, burning airliner onto the muddy earth, Bryan struggled to his feet and walked dazed and weakened toward a house, bent on getting the blankets the dying called for.
>
> He remembers a man beside the driveway, lying there with one leg partially torn away, begging for a tourniquet.
>
> Feebly, Bryan endeavored to remove his necktie, intending to use it to stop the man's bleeding.
>
> "I remember I had difficulty picking up the fellow's leg," he says. After that, the afternoon of Monday, April 4, 1977, is a blur to the 46-year-old Atlanta businessman.

But as airlines tell us, plane crashes are relatively rare. Few stories offer such natural dramatic beginnings as this one. For the ordinary story, you must do what you can do. Just don't overdo it. Often the little touches count most. Here is how one beginner, Karen Harris, punched up one of her stories like a veteran with a sprinkle of description:

> The sound of thumping crutches and scuffling slippers stopped when a wan, bent woman rested against the door of Grady Hospital pharmacy, her hand emerging from a pocket with a scribbled piece of paper.
>
> But before she could hobble to the end of the line at the druggist's counter, a woman guarding the pharmacy entrance threw up her palm like a traffic cop.

"Excuse me, ma'am," Shirley Robinson said. "Are you aware of the new policy here at Grady Hospital? You have to pay full price for your prescription. You have to pay cash because we can no longer bill you. No exceptions. Do you understand?"

The woman's eyes grew wide with surprise, and she said, "This can't be true." But Ms. Robinson nodded, apologized, and handed her a form that explained the new rules.

"Well, don't you know there's going to be a lot of dying people, including me," the woman muttered, and then turned to leave the way she came—empty-handed.

Once you have found your talent, you can do this again and again at the start, as Harris did, again:

In the shadow of The Strip at the half-built MARTA [Metropolitan Atlanta Rapid Transit Authority] Midtown station, a mud-splattered construction worker's callused hands grip a scaffold, much like the nearby businesses that cling to weathered hopes waiting for the trains.

For some merchants who have survived along the Peachtree Street corridor between Eighth and 14th streets, the MARTA depot—when it opens in the spring of 1983—could be the end of the line for bad times wrought by the area's image as a haven for hookers and hoodlums.

Simplify

"If you can't simplify," says Jim Gannon, executive editor of the Des Moines *Register and Tribune,* "you don't understand."

In this complex and frightening world of ours, the newspaper writer's highest duty is to simplify. Understanding is what saved modern societies from the dangers of superstition. Because of enlightenment we no longer burn witches, bleed the sick, shackle the insane, or chop off the heads of people who bear us bad news—a good thing, too, for the newspaper business.

The best way to show your understanding of a subject is to communicate it in a way most people can understand. If your stories are cluttered with the buzz words and computerese of experts, you are having difficulty simplifying. A mistake of novices is to quote what they don't understand. Hence, you have stories about Professor Bogglewoggle's employing rhesus primates to assist in the study of the sensate properties of delta-9-tetrahydrocannabinol as found in cannibas sativa through respiratory manipulation. What the professor is telling us is that he is going to have monkeys smoke dope to see if they get high. The professor may resent that you would put his serious scientific study into such common terms, but your readers will not.

Your duty is not simply to tell the readers that an expert in fire suppression and extinguishment is also a fireman. You must also bring understanding to an issue as a whole. The best way to do this is to relate the issues to something that can be easily grasped, to bring them down to earth, so to speak.

Ron Taylor attempted to do that when his editors got agitated about freight truck drivers' holding a truck race during one of the nation's worst fuel shortages. His lead:

> They burned enough diesel fuel at the Atlanta International Raceway Sunday to haul a load of Georgia chickens all the way to California and bring back a trailer full of avocados.

On a slightly more pressing subject, two reporters at the *Journal* came up with this lead-in on a story attempting to explain the issues in a strike by the Professional Air Traffic Controllers Organization (PATCO):

> Among air traffic controllers, it is jokingly called "allowing extra space for mom and the kids." It generally happens when controllers are about to crack.
> The textbook ideal is to bring airplanes into position for landing as close as possible to a standard three-mile distance between them. But when a controller begins to get shaky, he starts allowing more and more space between aircraft. He begins to doubt his judgment, to have visions of the dots on the radar scope, representing hundreds of people in airplanes, suddenly running together.

Readers can understand airplanes colliding in the sky. Merely saying that stress is one of the issues in the PATCO walk out leaves the reader wondering why. Explaining how controllers see that stress is one way to help readers understand why the issue is important to them.

Explain, but don't overexplain.

Jim Naughton tells of writing a story about President Ford's relaxing in a game of golf and being delighted with a bogey on the eighteenth hole. An editor at the *New York Times*, Naughton recalls, inserted a paragraph directly underneath explaining that bogey is a score in golf meaning one stroke more than par on a hole. Taking that exposition to its illogical extreme, Naughton saw such compounded explainers as these: "Golf is a game invented in Scotland . . ." "Scotland is a country north of England . . ." "England is the governmental center of the United Kingdom . . ." "The United Kingdom. . . ."

Explain only what seems necessary to explain. Assume that your readers have learned something from television. On the other hand, don't forget your five Ws. Make especially clear the *who*. If you are on Sen. Fatkitty's case, make sure you identify whether he is a state or United States senator and what state he is from. In your lofty pursuit of literary excellence in journalism, don't lose sight of the main purpose: to inform.

Weave, Don't Lump

The highest compliment an editor can pay a writer, though rarely is it intended to be such, is to tell the writer that there seems no appropriate place to cut the story. What that usually means is that the story is so tightly written that a single cut would disrupt the flow.

So that you, too, can befuddle your editors, let us tell you that the trick here is a simple one: transition. Ideally, each paragraph spins off another, so that there is a piece of thought from one intertwined with the other. Stories should not be written in lumps. That is, the different ideas should not be so piled in their separate corners as to cause the reader to trip over them. Stories should be woven, with the ideas stitched together through transition. Here is a rather odd example, from a perspective piece on the history of the income tax, where each sentence is appropriately dependent on the one before:

> The income tax, said Chief Justice Melville Fuller in 1894, is discriminatory and "inevitably leads to oppression and to general unrest and disturbance in society."
>
> So it has.
>
> In 1977, FBI statistics showed that 74 percent of all threats and 41 percent of all assaults against federal employees were directed at employees of the Internal Revenue Service. In 1978, 186 IRS employees reported 252 attempts to bribe them.
>
> It didn't help much. Americans still had to cough up $213.1 billion in individual income taxes in 1978.
>
> The income tax we all know and pay grew out of the Panic of 1907, becoming an official part of the U.S. Constitution in 1913, 67 years ago today. Americans have been panicked ever since, especially from the first of January to the 15th of April, that period known to the working population as "tax time."
>
> Blame Tom Watson of Georgia, or the states of Delaware, Wyoming, and New Mexico.
>
> It was Watson's Populist movement, seizing on an anti-corporation fervor, that preached the income tax as a symbol of reform in the late 1800s. It was the legislatures of Delaware, New Mexico, and Wyoming that gave the 16th Amendment, which established the federal income tax, the required three-fourths vote of the states on Feb. 3, 1913.

When the news hit Atlanta the next day, it was overshadowed on the front page of the *Atlanta Constitution* by events at home. The daughter of Julius DeGive, the man who gave the city the DeGive Opera House, had been bitten by mad dogs.

The opera house eventually became the Loew's Grand Theatre, which recently burned to the ground. The income tax survives and shows no signs of perishing.

Which brings us to another general tip on newspaper writing.

Consider Nothing too Trivial

The measure of a good newspaper writer is not so much what he or she can do with the big story but what she or he can do with the trivial, even the silly. Editors have pages to fill, and occasionally they run out of any ideas of what to put in them. That's when they pull out their notes from conversations with neighbors or nuts. Sometimes they assign you their personal peeves and curiosities: What about potholes? This was Ron Taylor's lead:

Nothing so rattles this nation's mobile spirit as the American pothole. It warps the frame and punctures the tires of that great symbol of free travel—the car.

And there are spelling bees to cover:

Which one of these words is misspelled: *redd, pensile, aal, gouache,* or *restauranteur?*
Wrong.

And senior citizen olympics:

Red Stokes's pacemaker is working just fine. He won the third annual Senior Citizens Olympics at Piedmont Park wearing his third pacemaker, and his heart didn't stop once.
It does every now and then.

Or a fellow who gave his girlfriend a surprise wedding:

She was a stewardess with a hurt back and a master's degree in music. He was a physician's assistant who owned a Steinway piano.
One thing led to another.

Then there was the time that Taylor was sent to Bessemer, Alabama, to do a story on the annual exhibit of a mummified body:

There is a certain excitement in this Birmingham suburb every time Hazel Farris comes to visit, although she hasn't been alive now for 70 years.

It's not so much that Bessemer is that kind of town. Hazel simply is a peculiar item, and the Bessemer Hall of History Museum is happy to have her a few weeks each year. She makes money for them, for one thing.

Hazel is frightfully shriveled, bronze-colored, and leathery and is beginning to lose some of her red hair. They say she was pretty once, but death seems to have taken its toll.

Sometimes, of course, you run into something you can sink your teeth into:

Jonathan Herring took the exit off I-85 at Hamilton Mill Road and tried to get to a service station, but the wings wouldn't pass between the exit road signs.

So Herring backed his airplane down the ramp and commenced to explain to an off-duty Gwinnett County cop who had stopped behind him why he was tooling down an interstate highway Sunday afternoon in a Cessna 150.

Bad weather, he says.

In fact, Herring was the second pilot to drop out of the sky onto a major Georgia thoroughfare this weekend. Weather was that bad.

There is a danger in doing well with the trivial, of course. You can get typecast. "Dead cow problem, huh?" the editor will say. "Sounds like a Ron Taylor story." But there are considerable benefits too. If you can turn a story about the world's largest turnip into a weeper about humanity against the earth, editors will begin to look upon you as a *real* writer—maybe a bad reporter, but a real writer. They may think you peculiar, even obstinate, since they may not understand how it is you do what you do, but they will let you get away with some things other reporters can't. That is when you take your final step in stylistic writing.

Experimenting

In an effort to define good writing for a young reporter once, Ron Taylor came up with this formula: Good writing is 20 percent *instinct,* that which you are born knowing how to do; it is 20 percent *soul,* a distinctly Southern term for gut feeling, passion, sensitivity; it is 10 percent *experience,* something that can take a long time to acquire but that is necessary to round off the rough edges; and it is 50 percent *utter gall.* Writing, someone once said, is an act of arrogance. We dare think that what we put on paper is important. Actually, writers tend to be rather insecure people, but their acts must be bold acts if they are to be more than ordinary. Being ordinary is no sin, but being bold can be loads of fun.

The key to writing boldly is letting go. See what you can do and if you can get away with it. Be prepared to fail. Editors sometimes will consider a bizarrely crafted piece an affront to professional standards. Stay within the bounds they set until you can figure out something new to try.

The bold touches often are accident made design. The phrase or the concept pops into view, then you back off and realize, "Hey, that's clever." The boldness comes from sticking to the vision.

Assigned to do a story on strip joints and their menace to Atlanta, Ron Taylor decided to write the story in the form of a memo to his city editor. The form had been suggested by a former managing editor, who had congratulated Taylor for a memo he had composed on a prior occasion to explain his having spent $90 of the company's money on a "bar girl." When a subsequent opportunity arose, Taylor decided to approach the story the same way he had that memo. He never collected his latest loss of $50, but the story began thusly:

> Dear City Editor:
>
> In view of the controversy surrounding the attempt to open a topless go-go club in Buckhead, I am submitting, per your request, this report on the effects of nudity upon the community integrity. As you know, I have done considerable research into the matter over the years and only last week completed some comparative studies.
>
> First, let me explain the $50 I spent on Marilyn.
>
> Her rosy lips and bouncy blonde hair did not hide her sad story. She came here from England just five months ago, and she has two small children, and her best friend got raped, and the guy she was going to marry deserted her, and she, too, wants to be a writer, after she finishes nursing school.
>
> The next thing I know, she was dancing next to me at the bar and taking off her clothes. That cost another $10.
>
> She said she would like to charge me only $5, since I had curly hair and a wonderful laughing face (I don't think she said "laughable") but that her boss would kill her if she shaved the price. Before we had really finished discussing the matter, she was quite naked. I gave her $10. I knew that the company would not want to be responsible for the death of a stripper.

Taylor stored the story in the computers and vanished. When he finally sneaked back into the office, just before the piece was to get its final editing, the editors were predictably grim-faced. "What do you expect me to do with this?" one asked. "I don't know," Taylor said, and vanished again. After many conferences and worried exchanges, the editor decided, that, since the article was to run in our Perspective section and therefore did not have to be *real* news exactly, they would run it. Taylor thanked them for their generosity, not bothering to point out that the memo—or letter—form for telling stories is one of the oldest in modern literature. Perhaps it *was* a trifle unusual to apply the form to a newspaper story about strip joints.

Here is an example of experimentation that is more imaginative from another *Journal* reporter, Chet Fuller, who decided to tell the story of life in public housing through the monologue of a woman tenant:

> "When we first moved out here, my daughter had to learn how to fight. She was 3.
>
> "She got slapped in the face by a 14-year-old girl. Later, my other daughter got cut on the foot when some dude threw a beer bottle and hit her. Another time, she got hit smack between the eyes with a Bama juice bottle. A little boy tore a hole in our screen door and threw it at her.
>
> "I worry all the time that some child is going to hit one of my children, and I'll go out to stop the fight and the other child's mamma will blow my head off. Some people are like that here. A lot of people are uptight. Life's so hard on them. You have to be careful, because it could happen any time. The least little argument, anything can start it. . . ."

Fuller's approach differs from the ill-advised *tape recorder* story wherein quotes merely are regurgitated. He took the quotes from the interview and carefully reorganized their chronology so that the story unfolded with drama. The touch comes in the organization and in the boldness to avoid convention. Such approaches can fail miserably, but here it worked because the woman was articulate and had a special kind of story to tell.

Be prepared to have your most daring stuff rejected. Editors sometimes do not get the point, and so they assume the readers won't either. Here is Ron Taylor's attempt at poetry-prose, an effort to turn one of those trivial assignments we just discussed into a new version of " 'Twas the Night Before Christmas."

> All through the corridors all the people were pushing, sour-faced children and dour-faced yankees, going to grandma's or going to nowhere, but going anyway on big jet planes.
>
> Into the throng at Atlanta's Hartsfield International Airport walked a round little man, smiling and waving. The faces lit up, for an instant, at least, while they passed the strange sight. Who would've thought it? There was St. Nick.
>
> Yep, Santa himself stopped off to pass out some candy while doing what hundreds of thousands of Americans do here every year—waiting to change flights.

Taylor's version didn't fly. His editors changed it to something mundane like "Santa Claus came to Atlanta Friday carrying a bag of goodies for children." But Taylor says, "The next time I have an occasion to meet Santa at the airport, I'll try again. I still like the idea, and maybe I'll eventually find an editor who does, too."

Your experimentation may be limited not only by your editors but also by the language your newspaper uses. If your newspaper is published in English, you may have some trouble.

What Language Is This, Anyway?

American is not English. We ride *elevators*, not *lifts*. We *phone* or *call* our friends; we don't *knock them up*. And while the English were listening to the *wireless*, we already were listening to the *radio*, a term Britons finally accepted.

The American language has its structured grammar, certainly, and that is something we expect you already know. (There are many good books on the subject, if you need a cram course.) But the pure American language, when stripped of its stuffy British inclinations, is a casual language, especially when it is spoken. We are inclined to make verbs of nouns, to create new words, and to alter structure at the drop of a silicone chip. It is a habit that strict speakers urge us to break, but we don't. Newspapers actually are just beginning to loosen their formalities. Until recently, some newspapers still had stylebooks which required that all automobiles, what we call cars, be referred to as *motor cars*, the argument being that it is more specific. But who really uses it, and what other kind of car is there? Those concerned about dull writing in newspapers are encouraging writers and their editors to think American. Charles McDowell accuses newspaper reporters of having tin ears—an inability to hear the American language as it is used. The best American writers have had an ear for the language. And the best American newspaper stories often are those laced with authentically American quotes.

Some editors frown on the use of dialect, contending legitimately that there is the risk of condescension. Certainly there was a time when the use of Afro-American dialect was a form of ridicule in newspapers. Those days no longer exist, nor do the days of writing dialect by phonetics to reinforce the oddity of accents. Today, dialect serves broader purposes, tending to emphasize personality, regional distinctions, and general mood, as in this example:

> Sandra Collins was telling the story again. By now, she seemed to have it memorized. "I heered the shots," she was saying to yet another reporter. "I seen somebody runnin'. It's kind-ly scary. 'Specially with children. They coulda been out walkin'."
>
> As she talked, one of her six children, a boy perhaps 7 or 8 years old, swung two huge, dead rats by their long tails. "Throw those things away," Mrs. Collins shouted, pausing in her story. Yes, she said, rats are a problem. "We kill as many as we can, but we keep findin' more."
>
> Mrs. Collins would worry about the rats some other time. Today, reporters walked on her grass and seemed to consider what she had to say important.

The occasion for this article was the coverage in Lawrenceville, Georgia, of the March, 1978, shooting of the publisher of *Hustler* magazine, Larry

Flynt. Dialect was used to establish the irony that this woman's humble, rat-plagued life was suddenly the subject of interest because she was a witness to something deemed important.

Here is an example of how dialect helped capture the sad mood of an old man whose dog, a mutt that regularly showed up with him at important functions in Atlanta, had died:

> "If it hadn't been for Sandy, I'da been just another old man in town," Fenuel P. Jones says wistfully. "There are thousands and thousands of old men in this town that nobody ever knowed."

Quotes—with or without dialect—are invaluable in depicting personality. Such quotes can be as descriptive as any string of adjectives. Here is an example pulled from a story about the last St. Patrick's Day of Pinkie Masters, a famous Savannah, Georgia, tavern owner who was dying of cancer:

> "The doctor gave me this prescription. Cost $200. Can you believe that— $200? Said it would make my hair fall out. It was supposed to make me feel better but I believe it made me feel worse.
>
> "My hair started falling out Monday. Started coming out in big clumps, falling all over the place. It got all over the carpet. You know you can't get that damn stuff up with a vacuum cleaner. I was eating the other day and it started falling down in my soup. . . .
>
> "They cut me around here and up through here," Pinkie says, tracing the route of the scalpel. "I don't know what they found, or what they did. But, thank God, they sewed me back up. . . ."
>
> Pinkie turns again to the pretty Athens law student come by to see him a second St. Paddy's Day and says, "If you asked me to go to bed with you right now, I'd have to say no."
>
> He pats her on the knee again and says, "Come back when I'm stronger."

So we have, in his own cadence, the story of a man struggling bravely against a frightening disease that had made him, for the first time in his life, a weak person.

What we have been speaking of here are verbal pearls. If the quotes you have collected are mere grains of irritating sand, don't use them. A common novice mistake is to tell stories through quotes that could be told far better in the reporter's words without quotes. A pox on you if you ever write a lead that goes anything like this: "We are pleased to report a new partnership between the police bureau and the business community," Chamber of Commerce President Pharr Breeze told newsmen Thursday.

Some of the best stories, in fact, have very few quotes. Since you should know the American language by now, you should be able to use it as well as anyone else to tell a story. Do it.

Final Warnings

Roy Peter Clark, assistant director of the Modern Media Institute in St. Petersburg, Florida, and a respected teacher of newspaper writing, warns his students, "The literary form we use in a story may distort the nature of events, make us the distorters of facts." We convey that warning to you with our agreement. Do not distort facts. Things happened as they happened. A person with a slight limp cannot for your literary purposes become a hopeless cripple. A city of people saddened but generally unalarmed by a recent murder cannot become a city gripped by fear. Write a story as an artist paints, but measure it first as a journalist, as a dispassionate observer with a responsibility for actual, factual reporting.

Note that of all our examples, only one is written in the first person—and that one is an experimental piece. You will almost never get to use *I* in your newspaper stories, unless you are quoting someone else. There are two good reasons for this: (1) use of first person casts doubt on your pursuit of objectivity and on your role as uninvolved observer; and (2) first-person writing invites frivolous and extraneous treatment of stories—as our one example, the strip-joint story, clearly shows. Except when your editor demands something frivolous and extraneous of you, keep yourself out of your stories.

However, there are times when circumstances seem to demand at least an anonymous appearance by a reporter in his or her story. In such instances, the reporter may pop up as *a visitor,* or *the stranger,* or, more honestly, *the reporter.* A case in point is Richard Ben Cramer's story on Johnny Diel and the Son of Sam killing mentioned in Chapter 11. When Diel told Cramer, "You don't understand," Cramer obviously knew he had a quote he wanted to use, but he needed to have Diel saying it to someone. So Cramer as visitor stepped into the story. Some purists condemn such cameo appearances by reporters, but a growing number of mavericks think reporting would be more honest if the writer admitted in the first person that he or she was on the scene. The prevailing attitude among editors seems to be that reporters should stay out of their copy unless they have the proven skill, as Cramer does, to hide themselves behind more significant performers in their stories.

Good writing, it has been said, is rewriting. Be willing to tear down your ill-conceived house and start again at the foundation. Rewriting helps you see the flaws, and in the beginning there will be many. Later, the flaws will be fewer, but no less embarrassing—just easier to recognize and admit.

Listen to your editors. Good editors respect good writers, but nobody likes a hotshot.

Start slowly. The old inverted pyramid will serve you well at the beginning. Test its limits carefully. Even airplanes must taxi along the runway before they soar.

Study the examples we have included in this and the previous chapter. Ultimately, though, you must learn by doing, not by rote.

Now, go forth and amaze the world.

13

Editing

Editing is the process whereby your work is refined by others. Errant spelling and grammar are corrected. Potential libel is eliminated. Clumsy structure is repaired. At least, that is the case if your editors are competent, and usually they are more competent than grumble-prone reporters generally concede. Sometimes a work of art is gutted, but often in the interest of saving the newspaper and the reporter from embarrassment and legal trouble.

Customarily an editor rises to that position only after considerable experience as a reporter. Through experience, he or she has learned what is acceptable and what is not. The editor is more attuned than the novice to the prejudices of the newspaper's management and to the whims of the readers. That is not to say that an editor has some ultimate wisdom you do not possess, but he or she certainly has authority over you, and what your editor says generally reflects policy.

In the business, you will find that there are many editors, so let us attempt to outline who does what.

On many major newspapers, for instance, *the* editor is not really involved in the daily mechanics of the newsroom. The *editor* (or *editor-in-chief*) often as not is the person in command of the editorial page, charged with setting the opinion policy of your newspaper and responsible for writing an editorial column and supervising the writing of staff editorials.

The person lording over your professional life in the newsroom is usually called the *managing editor*. That person is responsible for the day-to-day operation of the news, feature, and sports sections of the newspaper, or for everything but the editorial page and the advertisements. However, the managing editor is primarily an administrator without direct supervision of reporters' duties. The managing editor deals with the newspaper's financial budgets, with hiring and firing practices, and with the overall scheme of the "product."

Under the managing editor in most organizational lineups are two or three people with whom you will have most of your dealings. One is the *news editor* (or in some instances there are both an executive news editor and a news editor), who supervises the placement of your stories in the newspaper and dictates the typography or "layout" of the pages. However, the news editor often is a distant figure in your daily work concerns. Most of your dealings will be with the *city editor* (called *metro editor* on some newspapers). The city editor selects your daily assignments, determines to a large degree who does what, and controls any number of assistants who carry out directions. The city editor usually is the authority figure whom you, as a reporter, are most responsible to. However, his or her assistants generally carry much authority in editing your stories. Especially on big projects—series and such—the city editor usually assumes direct command in doing the planning and resolving confusions.

Organizational structures, of course, vary from one newspaper to the next. Some of the largest papers have *national editors,* in control of a *national desk*—a collection of reporters and assistant editors charged with covering the nation. Some newspapers also have a *state desk* responsible for state news coverage. Also, there are special feature sections with *special editors*—feature editors, lifestyle editors, people editors, fashion editors, women's editors (a position of growing obsolescence in feminist times), special assignment editors, ad infinitum. In the sports department, the *sports editor* usually is very much like *the* editor in that he or she is charged primarily with opinion making. The overseer of the daily sports news flow is the *executive sports editor,* who is to the sports department what the city editor is to the news operation.

Unless you move into a specialized area, you usually will be assigned to the *city desk* and will be controlled by the city editor. "City editor" on most newspapers actually is a euphemism of sorts, since the person carrying that title often has responsibility for state and national coverage as well. Such papers may also have a national and state editor, but often as not their function is strictly that of reviewing *wire copy,* which comes from various national news agencies, for placement in the newspaper.

Once you have carried out an assignment, having conducted the interview, taken all the necessary notes and written the story, you encounter the classic editing process.

On smaller, less technologically advanced newspapers, editors may use the old pencil technique, drawing lines on your copy through stuff they do not like, and inserting by pencil stuff they want added.

More likely, you will relate to your editor through some sort of computer network. At most dailies, you will have written your story by either of two means: (1) on scanner ready paper, or (2) directly into a Video Display Terminal (VDT), tied to a computer that remembers your story and holds it ready for transmission to the newspaper. The scanner ready copy is typed on an electric typewriter using various codes that can be read by an optical scanner that records the story on computer tape. Increasingly, the scanner is becoming an unnecessary step, with reporters being trained to write their stories directly *into* the computer via the VDT. What is seen on the VDT is what is being fed into the all-important computer. The computer is capable of setting the material in type ready to be pasted into a page that then can be photographed and transferred to a plate that can be put on the presses for printing.

Often as not, the editor who checks a story uses the same kind of VDT the reporter uses to write the story. However, ancient rules and techniques apply to editing, regardless of the method used. The editor basically looks for two things: (1) Does the story make sense? and (2) What mistakes has the reporter made? Then, your version is either altered or accepted as is.

More than likely, as a novice reporter, you will not have to concern yourself with the finer points of editing, but it does help to know what the editor is doing. In fact, it helps to be an editor of your own copy. The more problems you eliminate, the more impressed the editors are by your skills. Review everything you write, and insert or delete that which appears necessary to insert or delete. To help you be able to do that, let us offer a few hints as to what the editor is doing and looking for:

- Does the story really make sense? First, the editor reads through the whole story. If he or she is confused, the logical assumption is that the reader will be confused. Sometimes, the editor will try to fix the story; other times, you may get it back for repair.

- Is all the pertinent information high up in the story? If not, the editor may move buried details toward the top. More likely, it will be handed back to you with such put-downs as "lacks focus" or "get to the point" or "I think your lead is in the 13th graph."

- Do you have a working knowledge of English grammar? For every sentence you write, there are rules that some editor has memorized. Split modifiers, mixed metaphors, and just plain poor syntax are hazards of deadline pressure. A merciful editor will patch these up with nary a word. A wise teacher will draw them to your attention—if time permits—and tell you never to do that again.

- Can you spell? F. Scott Fitzgerald had a problem with spelling. Unless you have a novel such as *The Great Gatsby* to your credit, learn to spell. Newspaper editors expect you to know how to spell and are apt to ridicule your slightest lapse, especially if you misspell the name of somebody important. An otherwise excellent reporter we know once spelled a recent Georgia governor's last name "Busby." Unfortunately, his name was Busbee.

• Is the story too long? Ever more frequently, newspapers are faced with space shortages—the so-called "shrinking news hole"—because of newsprint-paper shortages and increasing cost. In addition, readership surveys tell editors that people really don't like to read long stories. If the story is, say, 18 inches long, and the editor thinks it would be fine if it were 12 inches long, he or she may *cut* it, which is the editor's prerogative. Hardly anyone is immune from being cut. Even Ralph McGill, the Pulitzer Prize–winning editor and publisher of the *Atlanta Constitution,* used to complain that his front-page columns were cut.

• What can be eliminated? To cut a story, the editor may whack out (or blip off the VDT screen) whole paragraphs deemed superfluous. In the enthusiasm for detail, some reporters are inclined to repeat certain facts and ideas. To an editor, these repetitions are readily obvious and easily cut out. After that, the process becomes more tedious and arbitrary. After lopping off paragraphs, the editor may begin cutting sentences within paragraphs, with the constant question: "Do we really need that?" Then, the individual words are scrutinized. Could a shorter, perhaps simpler word do better? (*Obfuscate* might be changed to *confuse.*) Is the wording as accurate as possible? (A "gutted" house may replace one the reporter has "burned to the ground except for the walls.") Is the reporter relying too heavily on the words of the interviewee? (Rules that have been "promulgated" may become merely "made public.") Some nonessential words often can be eliminated at first glance. ("The mayor related to the press that he is of the opinion that ice cream tastes quite good" can be written simply as, "The mayor says he likes ice cream.")

Editors, of course, have their quirks that can cause a reporter misery. Some editors, for instance, think that *said* is the very best word you can use when somebody had said something. Others like variety: "he declared" or "she commented" or "he related" or even "she opined." (However, do not confuse merely *saying* and *commenting* with words that lend slightly different meaning to the qualifier, such as "he guessed" or "he implied" or "she hinted" or "she gurgled.") Some editors like to draw fine lines of distinction. Slay or kill, they argue, is not the same as murder, which is a criminal act of homicide. (Homicide, in fact, may or may not be a murder.) But chances are pretty good that a slain person who died under suspicious circumstances has been *murdered* as well. Some editors also insist that *who* rather than *that* should be the pronoun of choice in modifying a reference to a person. (The man *who*, rather than the man *that*.) Other editors prefer *that* for almost everything, arguing correctly that *that* is a "neutral" pronoun. The safest way to walk across such deep waters is to find out what your editors like and try to do it their way.

There are definite regional quirks that are not the editors' fault. In the South, particularly, there seems to be a grander tolerance of colloquialisms, slang, and, most definitely, dialect. Because of the South's rich and disparate dialects, you find editors letting pass such quotes as "I heered the shots, then I seen 'im runnin' " or "How 'bout them dogs" or "I be settin' here." And "y'all" of course is almost as common in Southern newspapers as "you." But again, an editor's quirks can take precedence. Some editors forbid dialect, arguing that it can be viewed as an act of condescension. Others argue just as forcefully that newspapers are too stuffy already and that dialect often adds a touch of color and genuineness.

In the editing process, each newspaper has its set of rules that generally are strictly enforced. These are contained in something called a *stylebook*. At some smaller newspapers, this may be no more than a mimeographed sheet of paper. At larger newspapers, the stylebook may consist of up to two hundred pages and resemble a dictionary in format. Most commonly, newspapers rely on the stylebooks adopted by the Associated Press and United Press International, which vary slightly. Top editors also add their personal idiosyncrasies. In Atlanta, for instance, Atlanta Hartsfield International Airport abruptly became just Hartsfield Airport. There was a brief move on one newspaper to use no middle initials in identifying people in stories. This presented a problem when Robert E. Brown ran against Robert H. Brown in a municipal election. Middle initials quickly were reinstated.

The chief keepers of the stylebook rules are the newspaper's *copy editors*. The *copy desk* is something of a court of last resort in the newsroom, providing a final check to the balancing act of the city desk. In the modern newsroom, copy editing is done via the VDT. Once a city-desk editor has finished reviewing a story on the VDT, he or she presses a few magic buttons, and the story blips from the screen into the computer's memory bank, from which the copy editor can summon it onto his or her VDT screen by pushing another set of magic buttons. It is this last reading by the copy editor, with rare exceptions, that renders the story ready for putting on the presses in the form that readers will see in that day's newspaper.

By the time a story reaches the copy desk at most dailies, the basic wording of the story is considered approved and will be tampered with only sparingly. The copy editors function much as quality controllers in an auto plant. The reporter and the city desk have built the car. The copy editors make sure nobody has left a screwdriver stuck in the fan belt. They look primarily for errors that jump out at them: any glaring grammatical stupidity, misspelled words, or inaccurate street addresses. Copy-desk veterans often are old-timers who know the city and thus know that at a certain point Peachtree Street becomes Peachtree Road. Names are given particular scrutiny, since printing a misspelled name is a cardinal sin.

The copy editor handling a particular story also usually is the one to write a headline for it. That is not an easy job. Countless periodicals thrive on reprinting the worst *faux pas* of headline writers, and headline ridiculing is a favorite pastime of reporters. An example of an amusing and misleading headline was: MURDERER SENTENCED TO LIFE IN WASHINGTON, D.C.

Such misplaced modification occurs because it is very difficult to summarize an entire story in a few words, and occasionally headline writers goof. The *Columbia Journalism Review*'s editors contend that their most popular feature is the reprinting of hilarious flubs and bloopers. Gloria Cooper, the *Review*'s managing editor, compiled some of the best examples in a book, *Squad Helps Dog Bite Victim and other flubs from the nation's press* (Garden City, N.Y.: Dolphin Books, 1980). Dedicated with the words "to err is human," the book documents the unwitting humanity of editors with such examples as: FARMER BILL DIES IN HOUSE, WAR DIMS HOPES FOR PEACE, FOOD IS BASIC TO STUDENT DIET, and TUNA BITING OFF WASHINGTON COAST.

The reporters themselves often get criticized unfairly by readers for "that dumb title you put on the story." At major dailies, reporters have absolutely nothing to do with what headline appears over their stories. One reporter we know was chastised by a reader for a headline mentioning ham radio operators over a story about citizens-band-radio operators. The reporter had made no reference to ham operators, but the headline writer erroneously assumed that the terms were synonymous. (Ham operators, who must undergo a battery of tests before getting a Federal Communications Commission license for long-range broadcasting, consider CB operators rank amateurs who merely toy with their short-range equipment.)

The headline writer is like the football lineman who gets attention only when he misses a tackle. However, filling the big hole above the story with something that will draw a reader's attention to it takes a special skill. Writing headlines is not simply a matter of attaching a "title" to the story. For one thing, the headline must fit. Only so many letters can be stuffed into the space reserved for the headline without having them fall off the page or extend past the column. The headline count, as it is called, varies according to the size of type and how many columns the headline is to cover. Newspapers also have various other rules that make headline writing even more trying—such as requiring that a preposition and its object be on the same line. The headline is expected to capture in five or six words the essence of a story that may run thirty or forty inches long. This is another reason for the inverted pyramid in that it helps the copy editor who is pressed for time sum up the essence of the story.

Puns are fun for copy editors and sometimes catch the mood of a story. Over a sports story about the Atlanta Braves baseball team losing a third straight game to the Cincinnati Reds, one copy editor wrote: BRAVES BLUE AFTER REDS, 3–0. Sometimes, however, puns can be misleading. Over a story about the new popularity of row housing in the city, a feature section copy editor wrote: A "ROW" OVER HOUSING. Actually, there was no "row" in the sense of an argument; the copy editor thought the pun could be used by putting the word in quotes, but he misled some readers into thinking there was something along the line of a zoning dispute. Double meanings and bad taste have to be guarded against. For instance, editors rejected this headline about a shooting that left five persons wounded at a Chinese restaurant: WITH SIX YOU GET EGG ROLL.

The story and headline are parts of a puzzle the copy editor helps put together for the news editor and assistant news editors, who control the page layout, or makeup. These editors call themselves *line drawers,* and they basically are that. They draw lines on a *dummy*—a blank, miniature page that serves as a guide for printers who will compose the plate for actual printing. What the news editors, or layout editors, do is measure the length of a story (by counting characters) and then draw in the appropriate space on the dummy along with the desired space for a headline. Space also is mapped out for photographs, charts, logos, and anything else that is to greet the reader in the first edition. (On some newspapers, the news editors decide only priority play for stories, with separate makeup editors designing the layout accordingly.) The space allotted for a particular headline usually includes a code to tell the copy editor what size type to specify and what the letter count will be. At this point, stories also are sometimes cut, usually from the bottom of the story (which is another argument for the old invert- ed pyramid), in order to fit the space.

Headline writing and type sizing are handled by computers at most large modern dailies. Into the VDT is sent the typed story and headline with all the necessary codes to help it pop out magically ready for paste-up in the composing room, or *backshop,* as it often is called in the trade. From typewriter-size letters on the VDT may come a two-inch-high banner headline.

Problems do not end in the backshop. Therefore, the news desk nor- mally has a representative in the composing room to stomp on any news bugs. The makeup editor has to make hasty and sometimes arbitrary deci- sions. A story that was supposed to fit often doesn't. The bottom is sliced again. The headline comes out with a 72-point error: "Mr. Dinnan" has been made into "Mr. Drinnan." Editors scream. The makeup editor calls for hurried changes to save embarrassment before the presses roll.

Finally, the clock says the presses must roll no matter what, and they do.

14

The First Edition
and the Follow-up

What all the writing, editing, and line drawing produce is an honest-to-goodness newspaper that you as a reporter get to look at before the rest of the world sees it in the form of the first edition. Most large dailies have at least two editions, sometimes several. At the *Atlanta Journal*, for instance, there are five editions: the metro, the final home, the final home replate, the blue streak, and the state. Usually only the front page and the fronts of each section (such as news, features, local news, sports) change to any noticeable degree from one edition to the next as the day progresses and new developments occur in various stories. LEGISLATOR ARRESTED in the first edition actually became LEGISLATOR INDICTED by the final edition, since the grand jury had had time to convene in the intervening hours.

Deadlines are needed to make sure the editions can be delivered on schedule. The more editions there are, the tighter the deadlines. At the *Atlanta Journal*, the first *copy* (story) deadline is 7:30 A.M., meaning that all stories have to be given to the city desk by then. That allows copy editors time to give the stories a once-over before shipping them to the composing room to be prepared for the press run. The first edition is printed and on the streets by 10 A.M. Such early production of an evening newspaper is necessary to meet the ever-growing problems of transportation. Competition from television's evening news also has forced newspapers to attempt to reach the readers before they settle down in front of the set. The *Journal*'s early edition is delivered primarily to the far reaches of north Georgia a hundred miles away. By the time the trucks are loaded and have fought through Atlanta's traffic to get the newspapers to delivery route people in the various towns, it is mid- to late afternoon.

The later the edition, the closer to the heart of Atlanta the newspaper is delivered. The blue streak, in fact, is primarily a *street edition,* placed in boxes in the city and its outskirts to catch the attention of commuters headed home.

However, the first edition provides the foundation upon which the subsequent editions are built, containing most of the syndicated features and stories that are unlikely to change during the day, along with the early versions of developing stories that will change. It is this edition that most of the previous day's planning goes into, and a significant portion of the previous day's work. In the case of evening newspapers, a skeleton crew of reporters and editors may work all night toward development of the first edition. On morning papers, editors and reporters arrive in the early morning to begin putting it together. Early-arriving staff on the evening paper and late-arriving staff on the morning paper catch the late-breaking stories, often the ones that will share space on the front page with the major features.

Although it is the foundation paper, the first edition is also something of a test paper. It gives editors and reporters a chance to see what they have wrought and how they can undo it if it is wrong. If anything, the pace becomes faster with the arrival of the first edition. Editors huddle in meetings, and reporters tear through the pages to find their stories to see what peculiar things their editors have done to them. Although the copy editors already have proofread all the pages, the finished product tends to make more evident whatever they might have missed, since dozens of pairs of critical eyes are by then helping them look. "Hey, this guy's name is Dinnan, not Drinnan," may be the cry of some reporter who has interviewed the fellow before and finds the name glaringly misspelled in 72-point headline type. After everybody denies making the mistake, someone is directed to hurry a correction to the composing room, just as another reporter or editor is discovering that the man's name has been misspelled throughout the story. After more denials, some editor rips the whole offending page from his copy of the paper and begins making circles around all the "Drinnans" with proofreading notes in the margin to make them "Dinnans." The page is hurried to the composing room as a guide to the poor soul in the backshop who will have to cut out all the "Drinnans" and replace them with "Dinnans."

Meanwhile, the person in charge, the managing editor, begins exerting his or her considerable authority. Summoning the various underlings, the managing editor points out what he or she does not like about the first edition. A front-page story on a Republican senatorial candidate is adjudged to have the appearance of supporting the man by its large display. It is relegated to the Metro (second) Section front with fewer pictures. The managing editor likes a story on a family-feud shootout in Gainesville. The managing editor orders it moved from the second front to the front page.

By then, the news editor has some idea of what is developing in the outside world by way of dispatches arriving from various wire services. The news editor also has reports from editors about what reporters might have in hand. There follows a discussion of what should be included in the next edition. A missing child may have just turned up. The president's brother may have just issued a public denial of a first-edition report that he is a foreign agent. The layout editors are already redrawing the lines by this time, altering the look of some pages and preparing a place for more urgent stories.

Even before the first edition is put on the presses, editors and reporters already are working on subsequent editions. While the editors peruse the wire-service copy constantly flowing in, the city-desk editors are talking with reporters on various beats in the newsroom. The first edition may have had a story about a child found murdered. An editor probably will have a reporter try to get in touch with the family for background that could not be obtained earlier, while the police reporter is checking with detectives to see if there are any new leads. Bodies may start turning up in an airplane crash halfway around the world to add to earlier reports that mentioned only that the plane had gone down. As the day progresses, tragedies seem to grow worse in the newspaper business. In the historic Winecoff Hotel fire in 1946, for instance, the *Journal*'s first edition had the death toll at forty. By afternoon, it was learned that 109 people had died.

As new developments occur, stories are given new leads, meaning that the latest news is put on top of earlier information that then begins to take the form of background. Sometimes new leads serve to correct information that was incomplete or erroneous. Reporters, after all, are only as certain as their news sources, who sometimes will lead them astray. In covering legislative and court proceedings, reporters will learn quickly that sources are inclined to paint situations in their favorite colors. A reporter may go into the first edition with a story quoting the governor's legislative floor leader as saying that a particular bill is certain to pass, only to find out minutes later that the vote has gone the other way. BILL TO PASS in the first edition becomes BILL DIES in the second.

The bigger the story, the more likely it will grow in following editions. Sidebars and photographs that were not available earlier may be added. A gas storage tank fire that kills two people may start out as a substantial story on page one, being covered by two reporters, then develop into an overwhelming one covered by a half dozen staffers, interviewing the firemen fighting the blaze, talking with neighbors and friends of the victims, and gathering details from investigators on what caused the explosion and how a recurrence can be prevented.

As the reporters dictate the various stories by telephone, editors may be reassembling the stories back at the office, sticking one item in the main story and another in a sidebar and using the other for a new lead on a separate sidebar altogether. Meanwhile, the line drawers—the news editors—are restructuring the pages for optimum play, often shortening other, less important stories or eliminating them.

There are, of course, both slow days and crazy days. Usually events change slowly enough for editors and reporters to handle them routinely. But sometimes all hell seems to break loose: an axe murder here, a hijacking there, a shootout on Main Street over yonder, and a bomb scare in the newspaper building. With ranks thinned, the city editor may have to ignore lesser events in order to give priority to the big events. A famous story is told of an ambitious reporter who had labored weeks to uncover a story about gangster activities in his city. He called his newsroom full of pride one morning to announce that the story was finished and that he was ready for it to run. Sorry, said the city editor, there wouldn't be room—Pearl Harbor had just been bombed.

Although newspapers thrive on immediacy and timeliness, tomorrow is another day and what escapes today may be recovered the next.

Some stories can be researched, written, and forgotten. Others you have to live with for awhile. New developments, continued interest on the part of your readers or your editors, or simply the realization of unfinished business may demand follow-ups. Oftentimes, the follow-up is a carry-over of an ongoing story. A legislator has just been indicted; now what happens? The follow-up may include a next-day story giving previously unavailable details of the legislator's alleged crimes. It might include a lengthy denial on his part. It could be a profile on just who the indicted legislator is. Or, it could be a *backgrounder* on what the indictment means to the legislator's standing in the legislature, what his absence would mean, what his continued service under a cloud of suspicion would mean, and so on.

There are occasions when the follow-up story may amount to a *second day* story about an event that already has been covered by other news agencies. In such instances, the reporter is expected to find something that nobody else has. That usually is not as hard as it may seem, since all the questions rarely have been asked or all the people interviewed. The best thing to do in those situations is to review the other reports and determine what they don't answer that you would like to know. You may be scooped on news of a sudden independent trucker's strike, but why did it happen and what are the truckers saying? The strike itself may no longer be news, but Joe Trucker's complaint that his family is starving because he isn't allowed by law to haul a big enough load of oranges to Minnesota may be. The lead, in that case, would not be the strike, but Joe Trucker's grumbling.

Breaking stories, those wherein a significant event has just occurred, are the ones most likely to require follow-up. A bus wreck in a small town may be detailed in one day's coverage, but the story usually will cry out for some sort of perspective in the next day's paper. How did the brakes fail? How does this affect the life of the bus driver? What are state school officials going to do to ensure that such accidents don't happen again? What impact did the tragedy have on the local community?

Some stories amount to ongoing sagas. This is especially true of trials, crimes, or civil disturbances. Then, the follow-up simply is a recording of the latest developments. In a trial, a witness may have accused state psychiatrists of ignoring the severe retardation of a young man accused of rape. What do the state psychiatrists say about that? In such cases, you often have to just wait and see. When they testify, you can lead with their explanations—balanced against what has been testified to previously in way of background. In crime stories, you look for the next clue revealed by investigators. Three children have been murdered. Are the cases related? If so, how? What is the public reaction? In the case of civil disorders, you look for the next move. What do officials say? What do the protest leaders say? Was anybody hurt during the night? How long is the unrest likely to continue?

When the events are happening quickly, the follow-up becomes automatic. After you have written stories for one day's papers, the editor usually will come back to you and say simply, "Give me a follow-up for tomorrow." Usually, the editor will offer some suggestions. Sometimes, the editor will expect you to know what to do next.

The follow-up should have a fresh angle, not merely be a rehash of what already has been written, although that may be included in way of background. What if there isn't a fresh angle? There are always fresh angles. The follow-up story, in fact, is a great opportunity to prove you have imagination. You may have written the umpteenth story on racial unrest in Wrightsville, Georgia, but you're still down there and are expected to do new stories. Now what? History is one fallback. What is Wrightsville's history in race relations? Profiles are another possibility. Who are the principals in this conflict? Peripheral viewpoints are yet another possibility. How are the businesspeople affected? How do the good citizens feel about the black eye their community is getting?

There are times when follow-up follows weeks later. Sometimes, the follow-up may be handled by a reporter who was not at all involved in the initial story.

In the case of a story that Ron Taylor did detailing the heat-related death of an inmate at Middle Georgia Correctional Institute, another reporter picked up on the dismissal of some of the involved prison personnel while Taylor was on vacation. Since that reporter had established an interest in the developments, he was also the one who got the information that the prison employees had been subsequently indicted. Taylor's original report served as a source of background for the follow-up stories.

Sometimes follow-up duty will shift from a general assignment reporter to a beat reporter responsible for the arena where the next development is likely to surface. A story that a general assignment reporter covered about a tractor-trailer accident that killed a woman and injured several other people, for instance, became the responsibility of our state government reporter. He learned from the state Public Service Commission that the truck's owner had no permit to operate the truck and had been cited numerous times by the commission for assorted violations. It was that reporter, also, who did follow-up stories on action taken by the commission to punish the truck company owners for the incident. When the driver went to court, however, it became a matter for our county government reporter, who covers trials, to handle.

Follow-up stories, in fact, may require considerable assistance. An ambassador's statement in Atlanta may invite responses from various city and state officials, acquired by beat reporters covering those people, as well as responses from the president, Congress, and various Cabinet officers, all obtained by Washington correspondents.

Editors usually are the ones to decide which stories require follow-up, but there are times when reporters take a particular interest in an issue and watch for any occurrences that might suggest additional coverage for them. A case in point is one of the first stories Ron Taylor did on the "J.L. and J.R." case with the health and science writer about a federal court decision ordering new procedures to ensure the rights of children committed to mental institutions. One of the two key plaintiffs in the case was a twelve-year-old boy who had spent six years at Central State Hospital, Georgia's largest and most controversial institution for the mentally ill. One day, the boy turned up dead. Taylor set about trying to find out what had happened and learned that the boy had been released to his adoptive father and that he had committed suicide. After writing a story about that, Taylor put the matter out of his mind until he learned that the adoptive father had been charged with child abuse in the case. With a renewed interest in the case, Taylor decided that the paper should cover the trial. His editors, however, decided not to bother. But Taylor made occasional calls to the city where the trial was to be held, and when he found out the trial date, decided to go. Once he began calling in stories about the boy's tragic life, gleaned from testimony, the editors decided to put the story on the front page and congratulated themselves for sending Taylor there. Eventually, the case led to a series of articles he did on the plight of neglected and abused children, which included an installment on the Joey Lister case excerpted in Chapter 12.

Usually, follow-up situations are far more routine than that. Something so conventional as the opening of a new airport terminal may lead to a host of follow-up stories. The news may be followed by coverage of the dedication ceremonies, which will lead to coverage of the closing of the old terminal and the first plane into the new. After that will come follow-up stories on how the new terminal is operating. Is the equipment working? Are the planes landing on time? Anybody lost?

Some follow-up takes the form of sudden history chronicled in the traditional *anniversary story*. Such stories usually start when the editor comes to you and wonders aloud, "What ever happened to . . .?" Or, "Do you realize it has been five years since mass murderer Paul John Knowles came through here?" These are important stories, actually, since a common complaint from readers is that they don't always get to find out how things were resolved. They may have followed a particular set of developments for weeks only to have the newspaper apparently lose interest. A grisly murder may be covered and the suspect's arrest noted, but the suspect's trial may be ignored. Is the guy still running loose? Readers worry. Usually editors try to keep up with such cases, but there may be so many important trials during a particular period that not every one of them can be covered. Other times, editors are conscious of the need for follow-up to a fault. One such case was an airplane crash in New Hope, Georgia, that killed 70 people. Every few weeks, it seemed, editors were sending somebody to interview the survivors and the townfolk of New Hope.

Such repetition of coverage, however, has its value. Some historian a century from now may want to know everything there was to know about the New Hope crash, or some other significant event, and he or she may very well be sitting at a microfilm screen—or whatever its 21st-century equivalent—and be reading through your stories for some enlightening nugget. Your name may never make the history books, but there is always a good chance that the facts you collect will. In such modest ways, we contribute to posterity.

15

Upward and Onward

Shortly after the strange case of the violets in the snow, I left the
newspaper game and drifted into the magazine game. And now,
in closing, I wish to leave with my little readers, both boys and
girls, this parting bit of advice. Stay out of the magazine game.

James Thurber, "Memoirs of a Drudge"

Now that you have read the preceding chapters, we assume
that you know something about this peculiar world of journalism in which
you apparently have some interest. You should know by now what you're
up against if you choose to make the newspaper business your career, and
you may even have gotten enough hints to be able to do the job with a
degree of competence at the outset. But once you have wowed your editors
and dazzled your readers, you may begin to wonder what comes next. As in
any business, you can go as far in journalism as your abilities and desires
will take you. There are reporters we know who are adamantly devoted to
covering axe murders and other grotesqueries of our time. Others tire quickly of reporting and look for other opportunities. So, what then?

The blessing of journalism is that it is an information business, and
information has always been a growth industry. We have so much information today, in fact, that we have had to invent smaller and smaller computers that store more and more data—and there is always more. For many
people, newspaper reporting is but a beginning in the information field,
whereas for others it is the preferred position of honor. The experienced
journalist always has career options because his or her skills are at once very
specialized and very general. The journalist uses the special methods of

assembling and conveying information, without being confined to a specific area of information. Journalism has served both the technician and the artist. Through the newspaper profession have passed some of our most famous writers: Charles Dickens, Stephen Crane, Ernest Hemingway, John Steinbeck, O. Henry, Mark Twain, Margaret Mitchell, Carl Sandburg, Erskine Caldwell, James Thurber, Winston Churchill, Robert Frost, William Manchester, H. L. Mencken.

Newspaper reporting can be either a respected end or a reliable means to something else. So let us, in this final chapter, discuss the career options of journalism inside and outside the business.

Staying Inside

Staying a reporter the rest of your working life is no dishonor. After all, you get to go places and see things that most people cannot even get invited to. Some reporters we know have turned down opportunities to move into management because they could not abide the potential isolation from interesting people and events.

Beat reporters tend to get bored more quickly than general assignment reporters, but some beat reporters develop such pleasant ties within their bailiwick that each day's work is much like visiting with old friends. A police reporter we know has been in that position for more than twenty years and has become something of an honorary cop, able to tread where unknown reporters are never allowed to go. General assignment reporters can be seduced by the regular variety and surprise of their assignments. Covering a watermelon-seed-spitting contest isn't bad if the next assignment might put you at a free luncheon for the governor or on the sidelines at the president's inaugural ball.

Some reporters, bored with the routine of beat reporting or the confusion and uncertainty of general assignment reporting, are able to find a niche in specialized reporting. Usually, experienced reporters are hired as specialists because of proven expertise in some important informational area. Medical and science writers, for instance, often are people who have studied that discipline in college and are able to combine an instinct for writing with that knowledge. Movie reviewers usually are specialists who at least have an obsession for attending movies and often have studied movie making and theater. Television writers sometimes are people who worked as broadcast journalists before deciding they preferred the analytical nature of newspapers.

Although editors are inclined to select as specialists those who have established credentials, it is possible for a reporter to, more or less, sneak into specialization. The reporter who shows an undeniable flair for handling series writing or particular kinds of feature stories may be treated as a specialist in those areas without ever having to discuss the possibility. Good editors usually pick up on certain talents (although they may be blind to others), and the reporter can capitalize on the attention. Some writers, for example, show intrinsic ability to write humor, and such writers can, through persistence, set themselves up as the staff specialists in *brites,* or funny stories.

The restless and proud writer is more inclined to grow bored with standard reporting than are those unconcerned that they may go through life unrecognized. Such "real" writers, as they usually call themselves, generally want to be columnists. The column is one definite, but difficult, outlet. The columnist, more than any other reporter-writer on a newspaper, is likely to become something of a star, if for no other reason than that his or her ramblings and musings are displayed prominently and consistently. Usually, the columnist's picture runs with his or her writings, and people therefore recognize the columnist at parties and public places. The columnist may even be invited to appear on television, the medium of celebrity, or to speak at society benefit functions. Getting a column, however, is as much a matter of politics as talent. Newspaper publishers and editors like columnists who do not embarrass them. When the managers anoint one of their employees to undertake a column, they realize they are granting power that may become very hard to take back, so the decisions are made judiciously. Celebrity for a columnist, of course, does not come without a tax. The columnist is expected to write something approaching quality at least three times a week; some newspapers have columnists who write six times a week. The columnist who discovers that he or she no longer has anything to say can fall into an anxious state resembling paranoia. Some merely sink into banality.

But those few who survive the mental blocks and political potshots to write something that passes for literature are rewarded with the possibility of immortality. Newspaper columnists, as much as novelists perhaps, are the social commentators we quote and debate and remember, even after they are dead.

The newspaper columnist who shows a skill for attracting large audiences may be able to broaden his or her horizons through syndication. Newspaper syndicates take writings from various sources and dispense them to several different newspapers. Lewis Grizzard of the *Atlanta Constitution,* for instance, picks up a paycheck from the *Constitution,* but he is also paid by a syndicate that places his columns in other newspapers. Grizzard became a syndicated columnist by first establishing a broad following in Atlanta. Then, an editor submitted examples of his work to a newspaper syndicate, which liked them enough to try to sell them to its client newspapers. That all means more money and more notoriety.

Columnists, as we have mentioned, fall into two major types: General—or featured—columnists and editorial columnists. The general columnist basically is a glorified reporter given the privilege of breaking with traditional journalistic writing by being allowed to use the first person and to experiment within the bounds of newspaper policy. The editorial columnist essentially is an opinion writer with the same privileges as the general columnist but the added benefit of being allowed to sound off on serious issues. Newspapers, however, are not likely to grant opinion privileges to someone whose opinions differ markedly with those of the publishers.

Columnists are not the only ones who have an opportunity for syndication. Some newspapers encourage feature writers to have special articles syndicated. Some newspapers have their own syndication services, which makes the process easier. When the newspaper does not have its own service, editors may submit the writer's work to a syndicate on the condition that the newspaper, as well as the writer, be credited for the work.

Some writers, thus established, break with their employers to become full-time syndicate writers. Jack Anderson, who inherited his column from Drew Pearson, is an example of a columnist who established a freelance enterprise through syndication.

Some reporters find alternative outlets within the company they work for. Most large dailies have Sunday magazines that provide opportunities for newspaper staff writers. However, this is not an automatic market. Such magazine editors like to make a show of requiring in-house writers to follow the channels of all contributors, meaning that they are expected to submit their articles for acceptance or rejection. They may even be expected to send a query letter beforehand, although they may work only one floor below. But, generally, they get paid as an outside contributor is. Such in-house submissions can also lead to your being considered when openings develop on the magazine staff. If it is magazine writing you prefer, in-house freelancing could facilitate a move in that direction.

Some reporters actually do what all reporters seem to talk about doing. They write books. One advantage of being a reporter is that the job puts you in a position to short-cut the most onerous task of non-fiction book writing: doing research. As an employed journalist, you have automatic access to a newspaper library often bulging with background materials—and linked into a nationwide computer research system. You are also the beneficiary of countless story ideas floating around the newsroom that could make wonderful books. Often, a single assignment will produce reams of material that simply will not begin to fit into a newspaper hole but cry for the space of a book.

Until recently, journalism tended to limit the writing experimentation that is helpful to fiction writing, but the journalist routinely has been placed among the people and circumstances of which novels are made. Hemingway's works are laced with images and tales pulled directly from his newspaper and magazine writings. John Steinbeck was researching a magazine piece about migrant workers when he decided instead to make it into a novel called *The Grapes of Wrath*. Two Chicago reporters, Ben Hecht and Charles McArthur, got together on a whim to write a play about their newspaper experiences. The result was *The Front Page*, the satiric classic. The Chicago columnist Mike Royko has stayed in the business despite successes with books based on his newspaper research and writings.

There are journalists who finally admit that they really don't like to write at all. They may become editors. Some reporters enter the field with that as a goal. Others fall into it by accident. For the journalist who wants to stay in the field very long, becoming an editor tends to be the preferred path to success. Editors generally are paid better than reporters. They also have more influence over how things are done in the profession, since they are as much managers as arbiters of writing. Good writers are sometimes drawn to the position with the notion that it is better to lead than to follow. Some bad writers also wind up as editors after admitting that they can't write very well. Some of them make amazingly good editors. Reporters never move directly to positions of publisher or president at major newspapers, but editors sometimes do. Those who get to the top with a sense of mission have had profound influences upon the way we do things.

Outside the Profession

Other journalists decide that the best path is the one that leads out. And the skills they take with them are always in demand.

For the persistent writer, the route leads most directly to freelancing. But keep in mind the standard joke among newspaper people that *freelancer* is an euphemism for "out-of-work journalist." The freelance road can be a rutted one with missing bridges. The journalist who quits the newspaper in a huff to find freedom and dignity may wind up writing government pamphlets for a pittance in order to survive.

The freelancer about whom movies are made usually is the one who has paved the road before leaving the newspaper world by establishing contacts and a reputation for quality work. Some writers, in fact, use the newspaper experience as a springboard to successful freelancing. Gay Talese jumped into the book world with *The Kingdom and the Power*, a gossipy opus on the *New York Times*, his former employer. Kurt Luedtke turned his experience as a reporter and editor into a script for the popular, though controversial, movie *Absence of Malice*.

Perhaps the most common destination for former journalists is public relations. It is an ironic transition, since hardened journalists consider public relations writers to be representatives of special interests. But it is a logical transition, in a way, since reporters spend much time trying to out-guess public relations people. The transformed reporter, therefore, knows best what does and doesn't work when a client is trying to sell a newspaper on a particular idea. The journalist-turned-public-relations-person also has the contacts back at the newspaper that a business or government agency needs to persuade on a particular point of view. Public relations, of course, is a form of communications, and the former journalist is a practiced communicator.

Public relations may, in fact, be the fastest-growing segment of the growth industry of information. More and more businesses and government agencies are hiring spokespersons as buffers between them and the press. Increasingly, the first call a reporter makes to an institution or business is to the office of public relations, variously called *office of public affairs, office of public information, office of press relations,* or *office of communications.* No candidate for major office would dare run today without a press aide; no mayor or governor would be without a press secretary. Even small-town police departments now have press relations people. Consequently, journalism school enrollments have ballooned with public relations majors obviously not planning to try the newspaper business first. That could be a mistake, since the better firms and agencies still raid newspapers for their top talent.

The public relations person who doesn't understand the newspaper business can quickly get into trouble. The newspaper reporter always is on the offensive, and the loyal public relations person is the defender of his or her employer. If the reporter breaks through and sullies the employer's reputation, the public relations person probably will be held responsible. Appreciating the needs of the press can score points for your employer. So attuned to image-building possibilities were leftist guerrillas in El Salvador that they had a public relations man who kept a list of American network and newspaper deadlines to ensure that they were met with some juicy tidbit favorable to the guerrilla movement.

Like the newspaper reporter, the public relations person must be a writer. When his or her employer takes the offensive, it usually is in the form of *press releases,* which glorify some good deed the employer has done. P.J. Corkery, a journalist who tried public relations, described the profession thusly in *Harper's* magazine, "Basically . . . it is still a matter of manufacturing press kits, and I didn't like it."

We can say only that some of our best friends are public relations people, partly because we knew them in the newspaper business.

Some of our other friends are trying to write books. Book contracts tend to persuade reporters that there does exist a lucrative, creative side to writing. At that point, the reporter usually must decide whether to continue writing books from the security of the newspaper office or to take the full literary plunge. Normally, the demands of the more profitable book trade are such that the journalist must let go.

Others, like Luedtke, go for the megabucks of Hollywood by writing screenplays.

As a constant student of the human condition, the journalist may at some point decide to become a teacher. Picking up extra college degrees helps in any profession and is especially advantageous to the journalist, who is expected to know at least a little about everything. And if the fascination with journalism starts to wane, the degrees can lead to teaching jobs. The journalist usually is a student of his own profession, and many journalism schools value the experience and perspective of the former practitioner. Some journalists weave in and out of the profession, practicing for a while and teaching for a while. Roy Peter Clark taught English at Auburn University before he went to the *St. Petersburg Times* as a writing coach. He liked the profession so much that he asked to become a reporter. He eventually carried that experience and his teaching background to the Modern Media Institute in St. Petersburg, where he has become an acknowledged authority on journalistic writing. Other journalists have used the blend of credentials as trained observers and academicians to become respected teachers of history, economics, English, and just about every other discipline you could imagine.

Striking the Happy Medium

The media are plural. The journalist who tires of newspapers may be drawn to the camera or the microphone or to other conveyances of the printed word. It is perhaps a measure of the newspaper medium's earned respect that other media seem to prize acquisition of its former devotees.

Walter Cronkite, TV's retired Uncle Anchor, used to cover wars for United Press before the International News Service merged with it and added the *I* to UPI. When he joined CBS, television was but a flicker on what resembled a radio with a tiny screen. Walter and TV have come far since then. Douglas Kiker was an *Atlanta Journal* reporter trying to become a novelist when NBC called. Experience gained in print journalism evidently transfers to electronic media.

Television has become the moving emblem of modern America, while radio, that first electronic wonder, has evolved as the symbol of all media's survivability. Radio was grasping for air when it bounced back with our rocking and rolling music. Most recently radio has started providing continuous news to a public with its eye on the road. TV did not kill radio; entertainment banality has not killed TV; and people do still read. We are all in this together, this business of informing.

Bicker as we must, journalists have found pleasant homes bouncing about the media. A former Kansas City newspaper reporter we know was drawn by the glamor of TV and became an executive before chucking it to return to newspapers, where he wrote criticisms of television. TV and radio stations frequently try to lure away newspaper reporters because of their abilities to interpret the news and write copy for the microphone personalities.

Although magazines belong to the print family, newspaper reporters often regard them as separate opportunities, choosing to exchange the immediacy and publication certainty of newspapers for the space and gamble of magazines. Magazine staffs are full of former newspaper people, and the newspaper writer usually holds an edge in the tricky magazine freelance market.

Journalists sometimes reverse their routes or take several at the same time. Richard Reeves built his reputation as a columnist for *Esquire* magazine, then became a syndicated newspaper columnist. Cleveland Amory became a radio personality after writing reviews for *TV Guide*. George Will, the *Washington Post*'s Pulitzer Prize–winning resident conservative, writes a regular column for *Newsweek* magazine and pops up often on ABC's "Nightline," which also features Brit Hume, the former chief researcher for Jack Anderson, for whom he occasionally wrote.

One of modern newspaper's heroes, Watergate reporter Carl Bernstein of the *Washington Post* turned his fame from *All the President's Men,* the book and the movie, into a lucrative contract with ABC.

James Thurber once said that falling back on journalism is like falling back into an open case of carpentry tools, but with a little care, the tools that journalism provides will help you hammer your way into a solid profession.

Index

Academic courses, 2
Action words, 115
Adjectives, 99, 133
Advocacy journalism, 107–8
Agee, James, 108
Allegations, 103
American Council on Education for Journalism, 2, 19
Amory, Cleveland, 188
Anderson, Jack, 184, 188
Anniversary stories, 180
Assignments, 45–46, 49
Assistantships, 4, 5
Associated Press (AP), 117, 120, 171
Atlanta Constitution, 111
Atlanta Journal, 34, 35, 40, 46, 72–79, 82, 83, 110, 136–37, 174
Attributions, 98, 103, 121

Backshop, 172
Bar graphs, 81
Baum, Laurie, 137
Beat reporters, 26, 34–39, 182
Beebe, George, 20–21
Benton, Joe, 72, 74
Berger, Meyer, 138
Bernstein, Carl, 12, 102, 188
Bloopers, 172
Board of education, 62–64
Brande, Dorothea, 17
Bray, Cheryl, 72, 73
Breaking stories, 177
Bribes, 105–6
Budget system, 46–48
Bugging, 93
Bureaucracy, 63, 64, 66
Bylines, 14

Caldwell, Erskine, 182
Capote, Truman, 154
Carafe form, 136–37
Carter, Jimmy, 16, 78–79, 90
Celebrities, 15–16
Charts, 81, 82–83
Christensen, Mike, 146, 154
Christian Science Monitor, 56
Churchill, Winston, 182
City editors, 168
City government, 61–63
City hall, 61
Clark, George, 76
Clark, Roy Peter, 165, 187
Clemens, Samuel, 14
College training, 1–5
Color stories, 87
Columnists, 130, 183–84
Community newspapers, 2–3
Computer systems, 7–8, 91, 169, 173
Confidential sources, 52, 53
Congress, members of, 67–68
Conjunctions, 118
Conjunctive adverbs, 118
Constitution of the United States, 12
Cooke, Janet, 109
Cooper, Gloria, 172
Copy editors, 171–73
Corkery, P.J., 186
Council, 61–62
County commission, 63
County government, 63–64
Courts, 61, 65–67
Crain, Michael, 71
Cramer, Richard Ben, 140–42, 144–45, 148, 154, 165
Crane, Stephen, 182

Credit unions, 20, 21
Criticisms, 131
Cronkite, Walter, 112, 187
Cross-checking, 102, 104
Cunningham, Hugh, 3

Deadlines, 2, 23–24, 174
Declarative sentences, 134
Dependent clauses, 134
Dialect, 163–64, 171
Diamond form, 135, 139–40
Dickens, Charles, 17, 108, 182
Drawings, 70, 80–81
Duffy, Mike, 27–28

Editing stipend, 4–5
Editorial board, 130
Editorial columns, 130, 184
Editorials, 129–30
Editors, 96, 99, 167–73, 185
Electronic communications, 14–15
Emotion, 149–54
Empathy, 99
Ethics, 95–112
    advocacy journalism, 107–8
    bribes, 105–6
    decision to publish, 111–12
    fact versus truth, 100
    fairness, 97–100
    invasion of privacy, 107
    jokes, 110
    libel, 100–105
    lies, 109
    objectivity versus subjectivity, 96–97
    obscenity, 110–11
    sensationalism, 106
    sources, 108–9
Evasion, 89
Evening Star, Montgomery County, 39, 40
Evers, Medgar, 138–39
Exclusive stories, 41–44
Executive branch, 60
Experimentation, 160–62

Fact versus truth, 100
Fairness, 97–100
Fair trial versus free press controversy, 65
Faulkner, William, 114
Favorite, Louie, 76, 79
Feature columns, 130, 184
Feature stories, 127–28
Federal government, 66–68
Fiction writing, 17–18, 184–87
Financial assistance, 4–6
Fire departments, 61, 63
First edition, 174–76
First impressions, 7
First person, 165
Fitzgerald, F. Scott, 169
Follow-up stories, 48, 177–80
Fort Lauderdale News, 34
Fowler, Gene, 120
Freebies, 105–6
Freedom of Information Act, 17
Freedom of the press, 12, 65

Freelancing, 185
Frost, Robert, 182
Fuller, Chet, Jr., 2, 162
Futures file, 59–60

Gag rules, 65
Gannon, James P., 139, 156
General assignment reporters, 26, 27–33, 182
Gifts, 105–6
Goolrick, Chester, 79
Goose egg form, 140–42
Government reporting, 34, 58–68
    city government, 61–63
    county government, 63–64
    federal government, 66–68
    state government, 64–66
    tools, 59–60
Governor's office, 64
Grammar, 118, 133, 134, 169
Graphics, 70, 81–83
Graphs, 70, 81–82
Grizzard, Lewis, 183

Hard news, 127
Harris, Karen, 155–56
Harvey, Paul, 139
Headline writing, 9, 172–73
Hecht, Ben, 185
Hemingway, Ernest, 2, 17, 53, 99, 114, 127, 182, 184–85
Henry, O., 182
Hiatt, Fred, 34–35
Howard, John, 81
Hullinger, Edwin Ware, 14
Human interest stories, 127
Hume, Brit, 188

Iceberg effect, 53, 55
Ideas, 45–49
Instinct, 88
Internship, 4, 5–10
Interpretive stories, 128–29
Interviewing, 84–90
    note taking, 90–94
Invasion of privacy, 107
Inverted pyramid form, 116–17, 135–37, 166, 172
Investigative stories, 129

Jefferson, Thomas, 12
Johnson, Bob, 15
Jokes, 110
Judicial branch, 60

Kennedy, John F., 18
Kiker, Douglas, 187
King, Martin Luther, Jr., 16
Kirkhorn, Michael J., 21
Klein, David G., 81

Language, 124–27, 163–65
Leads, 115, 117, 119–24
Legal records, 104
Legislative branch, 60
Libel, 3, 91, 100–105

Library, 53, 54, 104
Lies, 109
Line drawers, 172
Line graphs, 81–82
Linn, Minla, 77–78
Listening, 88, 89
Logo, 83
Logs, 22
Luedtke, Kurt, 13, 185, 187

Macaulay, Thomas Babington, 12
MacAvoy, Paul W., 81
Magazine writing, 184, 188
Mailer, Norman, 88
Malicious libel, 101
Managing editors, 167–68
Manchester, William, 182
Mangiafico, Nancy, 74, 75
Maps, 70, 83
Marvin, Lee, 55
Marvin, Michelle Triola, 55
Mayor's office, 62
McArthur, Charles, 185
McClendon, Jerome, 73, 78–79
McDowell, Charles, 113, 124, 138, 163
McGill, Ralph, 131, 132, 170
Mencher, Melvin, 19
Mencken, H.L., 182
Miller, Gene, 9, 16
Minneapolis Tribune, 138
Mistakes, 3, 10, 96
Mitchell, Margaret, 182
Mitchelson, Marvin, 55–56
Montgomery, Bill, 27, 145–46
Moore, William, 16
Murphy, Reg, 67

Name/phone file, 52, 59
Names and addresses, 102–3
National editors, 168
National security, 111
Naughton, Jim, 110, 140, 153, 157
New Journalism, 97, 108
News briefs, 117
News editors, 168
News features, 127
Newspaper Fund, The, 19, 20
Newspaper Guild, The, 19
Newspaper internship, 4, 5–10
Newsroom, 15
News scoops, 41–44
News stories, 115–16, 118–19, 127
New York Times, 12, 18, 55, 56, 81, 82, 111, 185
New York Times Index, 54
Notebooks, 59, 91–93
Note taking, 90–94
Novelists, 17–18, 184–87
Nut graph, 139, 140

Obituaries, 121–22
Objectivity, 96–97
Obscenity, 110–11
Off-the-record interviews, 94
Orr, Lillian, 56

Orr, William B., 55, 56
Overtime, 20

Paragraphs, 114–15
Pearson, Drew, 184
Pentagon Papers, 12, 111
People magazine, 55, 56
People news, 128
Personal opinions, 98–99
Photocopy, 54
Photography, 69–80
Police departments, 61, 63
Political power, 16–17
Portfolio, 6
Potts, Jack, 79
Power of the press, 12–14
Presumption, 100
Prison reporting, 35–39, 86
Privacy, invasion of, 107
Privacy Act, 17
Provable truth, 101
Public relations, 21, 185–86
Pugh, Charles, 15
Puns, 172

Question lead, 120

Radio, 187–88
Raises, 19
Readers's Guide to Periodical Literature, 54
Reeves, Richard, 188
References, 6
Reporters:
    beat, 26, 34–39, 182
    general assignment, 26, 27–33, 182
    special assignment, 26, 39–44
Research, 53–57, 184
Reston, James, 131
Retractions, 102, 105
Reviews, 131
Rewriting, 165
Rossi, Frank, 148–49
Rossini, Gioacchino, 81
Royko, Mike, 185

Salaries, 18–21
Sandburg, Carl, 182
Sasower, Doris, 55
Scene setting, 154–56
Scholarships, 4, 5
Schwartz, Mike, 34–35
Screenplays, 185, 187
Seabrook, Charlie, 2
Sears, Edward, 51–52
Secrecy, 17
Senators, 68
Sensationalism, 13–14, 106
Sentences, 134
Separation of powers, 60
Serrin, William, 148, 154
Sheriff's department, 63
Shifts, 21–22
Sidebar, 138
Sig, 83
Significance graph, 139, 140

Simplification, 156–58
Skepticism, 50, 52
Sketch artists, 70, 81
Skinner, Bud, 86
Slander, 100
Slug, 46
Soft news, 127
Sources, 50–57, 108–9
Space shortages, 170
Special assignment reporters, 26, 39–44
Special editors, 168
Specialization, 182–83
Speed writing, 91
Spenkelink, John, 27–33
Sports editors, 168
Sports writing, 131
Spot news, 127
Staff editorial, 130
State editors, 168
State government, 64–66
State police, 64
Steinbeck, John, 182, 185
Straight narrative, 137–39
Student newspapers, 2–5
Stylebook, 171
Stylistic Journalism, 108, 132–66
Subjectivity, 96–97
Summary lead, 120
Suspended interest lead, 120
Syndicated columns, 130, 183–84

Talese, Gay, 185
Tape recorders, 91, 92–93
Taylor, Ron, 86, 87, 90, 104–6, 122, 145, 147,
    149–51, 154–55, 157, 159–62, 178, 179
Teaching, 21, 187
Teel, Leonard Ray, 86, 151–52
Television, 21, 124–25, 187–88
Terrell, Angela B., 3
Thurber, James, 11, 15, 181, 182, 188
Tight writing, 114–15, 125–26, 158–59
Timeliness, 116
Truth versus fact, 100
Twain, Mark, 14, 182
Typing, 3–4

United Press International (UPI), 171
U.S. Attorney, 67
U.S. Court of Appeals, 67

U.S. District Court, 67
U.S. Magistrate's Court, 66–67

Valley Independent, 19
Van Smith, Howard, 16
Veterans' hospitals scandals, 50–51

Wall Street Journal, 55, 135, 139–40
Washington Post, 12, 35, 102, 109
Watergate, 12, 17, 111
White, Arnold Henry, 14
Wicker, Tom, 15
Will, George, 188
Williams, Katherine, 15
Williams, Wayne, 137
Wilson, Sir Angus, 77–78
Wire copy, 168
Wolfe, Tom, 131
Woodward, Bob, 12, 102
Working day, 21–25
Writing, 113–66
    carafe form, 136–37
    diamond form, 135, 139–40
    editorials, 129–30
    emotion in, 149–54
    experimentation, 160–62
    feature columns, 130, 184
    feature stories, 127–28
    goose egg form, 140–42
    headlines, 9, 172–73
    interpretive stories, 128–29
    inverted pyramid form, 116–17, 135–37, 166,
        172
    investigative stories, 129
    language, 124–27, 163–65
    leads, 115, 117, 119–24
    news stories, 115–16, 118–19, 127
    reviews and criticisms, 131
    rewriting, 165
    scene setting, 154–56
    simplification, 156–58
    sports, 131
    straight narrative, 137–39
    Stylistic Journalism, 108, 132–66
    tight, 114–15, 125–26, 158–59
Written proof, 102

Zachariah, Poozikala Chako, 35